YOUNG MEN WHO HAVE SEXUALLY ABUSED

THE NSPCC/WILEY SERIES
in
PROTECTING CHILDREN
The multi-professional approach

Series Editors: Christopher Cloke,
NSPCC. 42 Curtain Road,
London EC2A 3NX

Jan Horwath,
Department of Sociological Studies,
University of Sheffield,
Sheffield S10 2TU

Peter Sidebotham,
Warwick Medical School,
University of Warwick,
Coventry CV4 7AL

This NSPCC / Wiley series explores current issues relating to the prevention of child abuse and the protection of children. The series aims to publish titles that focus on professional practice and policy, and the practical application of research. The books are leading edge and innovative and reflect a multi-disciplinary and inter-agency approach to the prevention of child abuse and the protection of children.

All books have a policy or practice orientation with referenced information from theory and research. The series is essential reading for all professionals and researchers concerned with the prevention of child abuse and the protection of children.

YOUNG MEN WHO HAVE SEXUALLY ABUSED

A Case Study Guide

Andrew Durham

John Wiley & Sons, Ltd

Other Wiley Editorial Offices

John Wiley & Sons Inc., 111 River Street, Hoboken, NJ 07030, USA

Jossey-Bass, 989 Market Street, San Francisco, CA 94103-1741, USA

Wiley-VCH Verlag GmbH, Boschstr. 12, D-69469 Weinheim, Germany

John Wiley & Sons Australia Ltd, 42 McDougall Street, Milton, Queensland 4064, Australia

John Wiley & Sons (Asia) Pte Ltd, 2 Clementi Loop #02-01, Jin Xing Distripark, Singapore
129809

John Wiley & Sons Canada Ltd, 22 Worcester Road, Etobicoke, Ontario, Canada M9W 1L1

Wiley also publishes its books in a variety of electronic formats. Some content that appears in
print may not be available in electronic books.

Library of Congress Cataloging-in-Publication Data

Durham, Andrew.
    Young men who have sexually abused: a case study guide / Andrew Durham.
        p.   cm.
    Includes bibliographical references and index.
    ISBN-13: 978-0-470-02238-2 (ppc)   978-0-470-02239-9 (pbk)
    ISBN-10: 0-470-02238-8 (ppc)   0-470-02239-6 (pbk)
        1. Teenage sex offenders – Psychology.   2. Teenage sex offenders – Great Britain –
    Case studies.   3. Teenage child molesters – Great Britain – Case studies.   4. Teenage boys
    – Great Britain – Sexual behavior – Case studies.   5. Teenage sex offenders –
    Rehabilitation.   6. Adolescent psychotherapy.   I. Title.

    HV9067.S48D87 2005
    616.85'836–dc22   2005026190

British Library Cataloguing in Publication Data

A catalogue record for this book is available from the British Library

ISBN-13 978-0-470-02238-2 (ppc)   978-0-470-02239-9 (pbk)
ISBN-10 0-470-02238-8 (ppc)   0-470-02239-6 (pbk)

Typeset in 10/12pt Palatino by SNP Best-set Typesetter Ltd., Hong Kong
Printed and bound in Great Britain by TJ International Ltd, Padstow, Cornwall, UK
This book is printed on acid-free paper responsibly manufactured from sustainable forestry
in which at least two trees are planted for each one used for paper production.

CONTENTS

ABOUT THE AUTHOR

Andrew Durham has the Advanced Award in Social Work (AASW), and a Ph.D. in Applied Social Studies, from the University of Warwick, which researched into the impact of child sexual abuse. He has over 20 years' experience of providing therapeutic services to children and young people, and is a specialist in post-abuse counselling and interventions for children and young people with sexual behaviour difficulties.

He is currently a consultant practitioner and manages the Sexualised Inappropriate Behaviours Service (SIBS) in Warwickshire. He is a visiting lecturer at the University of Warwick. He also occasionally works as an independent child care consultant, undertaking therapeutic work with children and young people, consultancy, lecturing and training. He is registered with the Law Society as an expert witness, and has been an adviser to the BBC.

He is the author of *Young Men Surviving Child Sexual Abuse – Research Stories and Lessons for Therapeutic Practice* published by John Wiley in 2003. He has also published a range of other papers and chapters on the subject of child sexual abuse.

FOREWORD

One of the most contentious and difficult issues to confront child welfare and criminal justice over recent years has been when and how to work with children and young people with sexual behaviour difficulties or involved in sexual offending, the majority of whom are young men. The complexity and the contentious nature of the issues raised stem from a number of factors that may have seriously impeded the development of practice interventions in this field.

A principal barrier lies in longer-standing and inherent difficulties in recognising and responding appropriately to child sexual abuse. Sexual offending challenges so much of what is taken for granted about the nature of relationships between men, women and children and takes place against a societal context which has mirrored and reinforced the denial and minimisation of offences that is the objective of offenders themselves. This has contributed to an enduring wall of silence that has proved difficult to breach, bringing serious implications for young people affected.

If, despite incontrovertible knowledge about the scale and impact of child sexual abuse, it has proved difficult to break this wall of silence, how much more challenging are the issues posed when those involved in inappropriate or harmful behaviour are themselves young? Where children and young people are concerned, disbelief has been even greater as the harmful or abusive behaviour concerned departs so far from our ideas and images of what childhood and young adulthood should be. This is compounded by the general state of knowledge about, and approaches to, sexual development and behaviour. Historically, professionals involved with children in educational and other settings, as well as parents themselves, have not been confident in understanding and responding to children and young people's developing sexuality. This has resulted in profound uncertainties about how to distinguish or define what is sexually inappropriate or harmful and confused and contradictory approaches to children and young people's sexual development.

There have, as well, been a number of different theoretical approaches attempting to account for sexualised or sexually abusive behaviour, prominent among which are those approaches that aim to identify 'high-risk' individuals. Different theoretical approaches direct the practitioner to what may appear a bewildering array of practice interventions. Again, practitioners in hard-pressed agencies may feel that the ability to evaluate critically such divergent theoretical perspectives and practices lies only with those who are specialists in this field.

Work in any setting with sexual behaviour or sexual offending is challenging. A combination of the factors described above generates particular challenges for practitioners trying to work in a holistic and sensitive way with children and young people, without disregarding the seriousness of the behaviours they have been involved in or overlooking the impact of abuse on their victims. These hurdles are not only being faced by those working in specialist teams established to work with children and young people with inappropriate or harmful sexual behaviours; a detailed understanding is also relevant to residential workers, workers in children and families' teams, family placement workers and, indeed, foster carers, all of whom have a role in contributing to therapeutic work.

This book offers a significant way forward for social work practitioners and others involved in working with, or caring for, boys and young men who have been involved in sexually inappropriate or harmful behaviour and sexual offending. A particular strength is the balance offered between knowledge, research and practice considerations, and the ways in which the interrelationships between these are maintained throughout the book. The approach taken is grounded in a theoretical base that takes full account of the significance and nature of the social context, and the nature of the connections between gender, power and sexuality. This demonstrates how work with young people displaying sexually inappropriate or harmful behaviours can be conceptualised as work with children and young people in need, without minimising the seriousness or harmful nature of sexually inappropriate behaviours. A robust base is established for exploring therapeutic interventions informed by the author's considerable practice and research experiences and illustrated with case study materials.

The issues discussed in this book are not going to go away: as the broader social context shifts and changes, then so does the nature of the issues that have to be confronted. The advent and rapid development of new information and communication technologies mean that the ease with which sexually abusive and demeaning images can be accessed is thought to have contributed to an escalation in sexual offending. Reports from the UK and elsewhere indicate that young men, in particular, form a significant proportion of offenders. Concerns have also arisen about the general desensitising effect of new technologies and how young people's attitudes about sexuality and relationships are likely to be affected by them. That such changes are anticipated by this book emphasises its timeliness and value as a child protection resource aimed at ensuring that children and young men who have been involved in sexually harmful or abusive behaviour receive appropriate help and therapeutic intervention.

Christine Harrison
Senior Lecturer
Applied Social Studies
University of Warwick

1

INTRODUCTION

The prevalence of children and young people with sexual behaviour difficulties is becoming widely known in the literature. Home Office criminal statistics for England and Wales in 1996 show that 35 per cent (700/2,000) of
people cautioned for sexual offences were between the ages of 10 and 17. Of
6,500 people who were cautioned or found guilty of sexual offences, 23 per
cent were aged between 10 and 20 (Home Office, 1997). The vast majority of
these young people were male (Masson & Morrison, 1999). Children and
young people are generally being exposed to increasing amounts of sexual
information at an increasingly earlier age (Gil & Johnson, 1993) and are often
confronted by complex sexual and social dilemmas before they have the
intellectual and emotional maturity to cope (Moore & Rosenthal, 1993; Gil,
1996). It is therefore no surprise that many children and young people are
showing increasingly sexualised behaviours and demonstrating, much
earlier in their lives, an awareness of sexual matters.

The wide social availability of sexual information serves to emphasise the
importance of talking to children and young people about sexual matters, as
part of the responsibilities carried by parents and other adults entrusted with
their emotional well-being and development (Moore & Rosenthal, 1993;
Johnson, 1999). There is also evidence that it is beneficial for children and
young people to be encouraged to talk to each other in a more formalised
manner, through the use of structured peer support, particularly where there
has been sexual abuse (Alaggia & Michalski, 1999). Without this support,
children and young people are left to cope with the many confusing and
prejudiced messages propagated by the media, popular culture and the
fashion industry.

Throughout society, there is a powerful and oppressive social policing and
shaping of sexuality and sexual desire (Steinberg, Epstein & Johnson, 1997;
Durham, 2003). In particular, young people receive very powerful messages
that emphasise the compulsory nature of heterosexism, which in turn leads
to circumstances where young people are pressured to demonstrate their
heterosexual competencies. This is particularly pertinent for adolescent boys,

where homophobia, characterised by homophobic name-calling and other bullying, becomes a significant feature of day-to-day peer group interaction (Nayak & Kehily, 1997; Durham, 2003). The consequences of being left to cope with these messages, as a predominant – and often the only – source of sexual information, is that children and young people become prey to oppressive images and stereotypes of 'acceptable' sexual behaviour. These create anxieties and self-doubt, and oppressively internalised misunderstandings about personal attributes and sexual and social competencies (Jubber, 1991; Bremner & Hillin, 1993). This leads to circumstances where many young people overestimate the sexual knowledge, understanding and competencies of their peers (Moore & Rosenthal, 1993). For some this leads to personal anxieties, retreat and sometimes solitude and depression; adolescence becomes a period of uncertainty and high anxiety. For others, these beliefs can significantly influence decisions to engage in abusive sexual behaviours.

In working with children and young people, Social Work, Health and Education services, and other related professions are charged with the responsibility of challenging these myths and stereotypes, countering them with more thoughtful and appropriate information and providing opportunities for the development of greater insight into how misunderstandings are generated. Working in this way allows children and young people to understand how myths and stereotypes enslave them in self-doubt, create personal anxieties that prevent them from reaching their potential and, for some, contribute to individual decisions to sexually abuse others.

This book will explore critically many of the current theoretical and practice issues involved in working therapeutically with children and young people who have instigated inappropriate or harmful sexual behaviours and will present extensive details of programmes of holistic therapeutic intervention. These programmes have been drawn from my practice and research experience of working as a specialist consultant, in a Social Services Department, dealing with over 500 cases, over the past 10 years. The book will emphasise the importance of approaching this area of practice with a clear understanding of why sexual abuse is widespread in our society, arguing that accurate theorising and effective therapeutic intervention will be based upon recognition of how socially embedded the problem of child sexual abuse is, and that it is in the main perpetrated by men or boys. Alongside these theoretical and practice issues, the book will also explore in detail seven case studies of young men who have committed varying acts of inappropriate or harmful sexual behaviours, analysing the therapeutic intervention that was provided for them, drawing out lessons for sensitive yet challenging practice. The case studies will highlight diversities in the paths that led the young men into committing acts of inappropriate or harmful sexual behaviour, and will identify the need for therapeutic intervention to be holistic and reach beyond purely offence-specific work, to address the wider needs in the young men's lives, and to be linked to the provision of family support. Whilst each account presents a unique story, the study will identify aspects of commonality, both within the young people's experiences, and in the therapeutic responses they received. To this end, an ecological practice framework will be identified, through which to make sense and gain better understanding of children and young people's experiences, and on which to base future therapeutic practice. This framework will allow us to examine the wider social and cultural influences on children and young people's decisions to behave in a particular way. By looking at the wider social messages a young person receives about how he or she should feel and behave, we can find clues about how a wide range of factors may have intersected and accumulated to precipitate the circumstances, thoughts, feelings, beliefs and power relationships behind the inappropriate or harmful sexual behaviour.

TERMINOLOGY

Throughout the book children and young people will be referred to as 'children and young people'. There will be no references to 'young abusers' or 'young perpetrators', instead the preferred phrase will be 'children and young people who have sexually harmed', or 'children and young people who have committed harmful or inappropriate sexual behaviours'. The extended phrases are considered to be more respectful and convey a reminder that first and foremost we are dealing with children and young people, alongside a positive aspiration that there is hope that they can change and move away from the problematic behaviours in question. A similar approach was taken in my previous study of young men who have been sexually abused (Durham, 2003). In referring to the sexual behaviours, rather than seeking to identify an all-encompassing phrase, the book will use the terms 'harmful', 'inappropriate', 'abusive' and 'aggressive' as appropriate to the context of the circumstances under discussion. Where possible, the book will use the past tense, 'young men who have sexually harmed', rather than the present tense, 'young men who sexually harm'. Throughout most of the text, masculine terminology will be used. However, whilst the book is about 'young men who have sexually harmed', reference to 'children' or 'young people' will be made when the content is applicable to all children or young people, and not just to boys and young men. Indeed, many of the issues to be discussed will be helpful to practitioners involved in working with girls and young women, especially the practice framework presented in Chapter 2, which can be used equally to analyse both the concepts of 'masculinity' and 'femininity'.

ORIGINS OF THE CASE STUDIES

At this stage it is important to note that all of the case studies in this volume are composite studies developed from practice experiences, all the names used are pseudonyms, and the circumstances described bear no direct resemblance to people in real life. Each case study will present an initial synopsis of the circumstances of the young man, and details of the inappropriate or harmful sexual behaviour he has committed. Following this, there will be an initial analysis of the main issues involved in the case, before presenting a 'case plan' that will give the details of therapeutic work undertaken with the young man and members of his family, including details of support provided to carers. Finally, there will be a discussion of the outcome of the work, and the continuing circumstances of the young man. The case studies will, by way of cross-reference, refer to specific intervention issues that will be analysed in the individual chapters of the book. The case studies and intervention issues discussed throughout the book are grounded in the experiences and accounts of the young men in the case studies, and many other children and young people referred to me during the course of my work and research as a specialist consultant working across a shire county, and from additional private practice. By using composites, the identity of the original cases are completely obscured, but behavioural details are real, and should therefore be considered to be the equivalent of qualitative field research, in the sense and spirit of the grounded theory approach (Glaser & Strauss, 1967; Durham, 2003).

HOW TO USE THIS BOOK

Part One of the book provides a theoretical context and discusses initial practice issues. Part Two provides extensive detail of a complete therapeutic intervention programme for young men who have instigated inappropriate or harmful sexual behaviours, containing detailed case studies of its application. The case studies demonstrate that the programme has been applied with significant variation, in accordance with each young person's needs, although having common core components that must be included. By reading the book from cover to cover, the reader will be able to understand the overall links that have been made between research knowledge and theory, and grounded therapeutic practice. Having read through the book, it can be subsequently used as a practice reference manual. The individual case studies will provide additional details and insights for this purpose, and can also be used for training purposes, with students, practitioners or perhaps foster carers being given a copy of the initial synopsis, alongside key questions relating to the training purpose – for example, what are the therapeutic needs of the young person; what are the support needs of the family; what are the implications of having the young person placed with you in foster care?

STRUCTURE OF THE BOOK

Part One   Theoretical Context and Initial Practice Issues

Chapter 2   A Practice Framework for Holistic Therapeutic Intervention

There are many theoretical explanations of how or why children and young people commit harmful or inappropriate sexual behaviours – developmental theories, trauma adaptation theories, preconditions theories, sexual abuse cycles, social learning theories, sociological theories. This chapter will briefly explore some of these explanations and will present an analytical practice framework that is able to accommodate many of their aspects, but with a particular emphasis on the importance and relevance of the social context of young people's experiences as being pivotal to our understanding of their behaviours. The framework emphasises the importance of anti-oppressive and child-centred approaches to the work, overtly modelling an appropriate use of adult power and specifically challenging oppression based on age, 'race', class, gender, ability and sexuality. The chapter will also provide a brief outline of the holistic therapeutic intervention schedule that will be discussed more fully throughout the course book. The chapter will conclude by using the framework to draw together a matrix of the potential influences on a young person's harmful sexual behaviours. Readers will see that many of these influences will be borne out in the case studies that are presented throughout the book.

Chapter 3   Assessing Sexual Behaviour

In working with young people's harmful or inappropriate sexual behaviours, it is important to be very clear about what these behaviours are, and which behaviours are to be considered appropriate and not harmful. It is also important to recognise that there is wide variance of opinion, standards and values within the community and across cultures and religions, about which behaviours are considered to be acceptable. Acceptability of sexual behaviours also has a historical dimension. It has long been recognised in the literature that the context of children and young people's overall development, including not least their sexual development, is constantly changing (Gil & Johnson, 1993). The changing social context and the wide variation of personal standards and values make it difficult to establish a baseline of acceptable or appropriate sexual behaviours. However, by being clear about what we mean by sexual abuse, it is possible to define those sexual behaviours that are harmful. This chapter will seek to address some of these problems of assessing sexual behaviour by initially setting out a flexible and widely encompassing definition of child sexual abuse and inappropriate and harmful sexual behaviour, followed by materials that will be helpful to practitioners and carers in assessing the appropriateness of sexual behaviours.

Chapter 4 Family Assessment

The responses of parents or carers to their child's inappropriate sexual behaviours may greatly influence the success of any intervention, or alternatively contribute to maintaining those behaviours. Parents and carers have an important role to play in supporting a child or young person to be motivated towards taking responsibility for his behaviours, and attending programmes of therapeutic intervention. They will have an important role in continuing to supervise and monitor the behaviours of their child or young person. Practitioners should therefore make every attempt to work with parents, explain the work being undertaken and to emphasise the positive benefits of their support. This chapter will outline the rationale, process and content of a comprehensive and specialist family assessment, concluding with a discussion of the key issues involved in providing ongoing family support.

Chapter 5 Foster Care

When foster carers provide placements for children or young people who have sexually harmed or who have shown inappropriate sexual behaviours, they are faced with a range of very difficult and challenging tasks. In managing these placements successfully, foster carers are required to deploy a high level of skill and patience, and will require a significant degree of professional support. This chapter will explore many of the difficulties faced by foster carers in these circumstances, and will discuss the necessary arrangements that need to be in place to support them, and to minimise the risk of the young person committing further harmful or inappropriate sexual behaviour. In particular the chapter will provide a template for a written agreement between foster carers and other professionals, which clearly identifies the nature and precise details of the young person's harmful or inappropriate sexual behaviour and specifies the necessary supervision and support arrangements to prevent their recurrence. Finally, the chapter will draw attention briefly to many of the issues highlighted for foster care having relevance for placements in residential care.

Part Two   Therapeutic Intervention with Young Men Who Have Sexually Abused

Chapter 6   Assessment and Initial Engagement

In assessing children or young people who have committed harmful or inappropriate sexual behaviours, there is a need to establish their account of what has taken place, and to consider the extent to which this has congruence with what others have reported. In collecting this information, practitioners will from the outset need to simultaneously look for clues about the young person's abilities and competencies, and his willingness to avoid such behaviours in the future. A holistic assessment will consider the whole person, his life and his relationships with others, and it will search for strengths within the young person on which to build upon his commitment and willingness not to harm others. The assessment will importantly need to keep at the forefront the immediate risks presented to others by the young person – setting in place adequate support and supervision arrangements for all parties involved. This chapter will explore some of the key issues in carrying out these assessments, looking at the difference between static and dynamic risk assessment factors, and the importance of balancing risks against strengths. The chapter will then derive a guide to the essential components of an initial assessment, and will conclude with a detailed examination of the process of initial engagement, highlighting the need for a sensitive and transparent approach that will empower the young person in a manner which allows him to consider his mistakes and make important steps towards an improved way of managing his life, without hurting others. The chapter will discuss how to manage an assessment if the child or young person has himself been sexually abused. It will include a suggested initial written agreement, and will discuss methods of motivational interviewing.

Case Study – Neil (15)

Neil is a 15-year-old white British boy, and lives with his mother Jan and his younger brother Ricky who is 11, and his sister Becky who is six. Until recently, Jan's partner Ian, who is 25 and the father of Becky, also lived with the family. Following concerns being raised by a family doctor around the origin of a medical complaint, the police and Social Services, following Child Protection procedures, interviewed Neil. Neil was tearful and disclosed that Ian had sexually abused him on many occasions, but that he thought it was mainly his own fault, because he feels that he could have stopped it. The sexual abuse was extensive and was sustained over a period of two years. Ian admitted abusing Neil and received a six-year prison sentence. There were also reports that Neil had sexually touched other boys on a school trip. Jan has expressed concerns that Neil had on several occasions exposed himself to his younger brother Ricky, and that these incidents were often accompanied by inappropriate sexual remarks. No police charges were brought against Neil, but he agreed to receive therapeutic support.

Chapter 7   Exploring Patterns of Behaviour

Many researchers and therapeutic practitioners in the field of sexual offending are in agreement that cognitive behavioural methods from the field of behavioural psychology are an appropriate component of an intervention programme for people who have sexual behaviour problems (Salter, 1988; Marshall, Laws & Barbaree, 1990; Ryan & Lane, 1991; Araji, 1997; Calder, Hanks & Epps, 1997; Hackett, 2004). These methods explore the connections between thoughts, feelings, physiological responses and behaviour, how behaviours are reinforced and what purpose or function they serve, or what need they meet in the individual. Therapeutic intervention, using these methods, seeks to assist the individual in understanding and developing a ready awareness of the interconnections between these processes, looking at thoughts, feelings and physiological responses before, during and after the behaviour being considered. By presenting a range of useful practice materials, this chapter will specifically explore how the patterns of harmful or inappropriate sexual behaviour can be broken down into their component parts, and how doing this provides many opportunities for behavioural change – the 'Four Steps and Four Stops' is a child- or young-person-centred representation of Finkelhor's (1984) four preconditions of sexual abuse and 'Steps to Offending' is a further development of this; 'STFA – Situation, Thought, Feeling and Action' is a simplified behavioural chain; 'Patterns and Cycles' will explore some of the principles of sexual offence cycles, and will present a simplified offence pattern diagram that can be completed by children and young people, followed by a brief discussion of 'Thinking Errors'. Finally, 'Changing Sexual Fantasies' will discuss the values and principles involved in helping young people develop appropriate sexual fantasies.

Case Study – Tony (14)

Tony, a white British boy, was 14 when his six-year-old sister Helen reported indirectly to her teacher that he had sexually assaulted her. At a subsequent police and Social Services interview Helen explained in detail that this had happened on five occasions over the past 12 months, and that she had told her parents and that her father had punished Tony by punching him and taking his computer off him. Tony was interviewed and admitted the offences, and reported a catalogue of emotional and physical abuse committed by his father. Tony was 'accommodated' by the Social Services Department and placed in foster care. He received a Final Warning from the police, on the basis that he agreed to undertake a programme of specialist therapeutic work. Tony never returned to live with his family.

Chapter 8   Victim Empathy

This chapter will explore critically the concept of empathy, placing the issue alongside wider considerations of adolescent development and social oppression. Empathy is an important issue in sexual abuse, in that those who abuse often fail to consider adequately the impact of their behaviour on the victim. This can often be a distressing part of the work for the child or young person who has abused, as it is a time when he has to fully consider the impact of his behaviour. The young person is encouraged and supported into thinking about what he has done and experiencing feelings about the harm he has caused, and if appropriate to find ways to put this into action, for example by writing or stating an apology to the victim, and by making commitments to behave in a more positive manner in the future. There will also be an exploration of how this aspect of the work may precipitate disclosures of experiences of being sexually abused. The chapter will present a wide range of practice materials and techniques aimed at enhancing a young person's empathy and general understanding of other people's perspectives.

Case Study – Alan (15)

At the age of 14 Alan, a white British boy, was convicted for sexually assaulting Paul aged five and Stuart aged seven – the two sons of his father's new partner. Alan's mother is addicted to heroin, and had not lived with him for the past six years. Alan's father is often away from home and, as a result, Alan has lived with several different family members. Alan has also had difficulties at school, he finds it hard to concentrate, and is often taunted, called names and sometimes bullied by his peers. After committing these sexual offences, Alan moved to live with his Aunt Alice. Alan received a police Final Warning and agreed to undertake a programme of therapeutic support aimed at addressing his sexual behaviours and helping him to resolve his family problems. He continued to receive therapeutic support for 18 months. He eventually returned home to live with his father's new family, after a 'family safety plan' was set up.

Chapter 9   Sex and Relationships Education

Sex and relationships education is a lifelong learning process of discovering and acquiring information, developing knowledge and skills and forming attitudes about gender, sex, sexuality, relationships and feelings. Most young people will explore their sexuality with or without adult approval; it is helpful if they are encouraged to feel comfortable with their growing sexuality, so that they can develop their self-esteem and have a positive self-image, and feel comfortable about making their own decisions. To do this, all children and young people need to have access to age-appropriate sex and relationships information and advice. If a child or young person has been exhibiting inappropriate or harmful sexual behaviour, then it is particularly important that he receives an assessment of his sexual history, and, based on this assessment, some formal sex and relationships education as part of a wider programme of addressing these behaviours, and helping him to develop the knowledge and skills to meet his future needs appropriately. This chapter will discuss the components of a comprehensive programme of sex and relationships education, exploring some of the values involved, which will vary between different cultural and religious perspectives. It will also explore issues relating to informed consent and peer pressure, sexuality, and sexual oppression, including homophobia and pornography. The chapter will also signpost the reader towards a range of sex and relationships education resources, including information about contraception and sexually transmitted diseases.

Case Study – Luke (15) and Jon (15)

Luke and Jon are 15-year-old black Afro-Caribbean non-identical twin brothers. Luke and Jon are very close friends with their neighbour and school friend Colin, who is a white British boy, also 15; they have known each other all their lives and their parents are also close friends. The boys would regularly sleep over in each other's houses for most weekends. On one particular occasion when Colin had been staying over, he had woken up to find Jon and Luke in one bed, engaging in sexual activity. On another night Jon was up late and Luke was asleep. He woke up Colin and asked him if he would like to get into his bed. He felt quite pressurised and agreed to do this for a short while. Jon's mother Marcia heard a disturbance and entered their bedroom, to find Jon and Colin in bed together. Luke and Jon's parents approached the local Social Services Department for help, which led to all three boys being questioned by social workers about what had happened. It was established that Jon had instigated the behaviours, and had used a degree of pressure to get Luke to cooperate. A programme of therapeutic work was planned for Luke and Jon, following a police decision at a planning meeting to take no further action.

Chapter 10   Self-esteem

Children and young people who commit inappropriate or harmful sexual behaviours often have multiple difficulties in their lives, and quite complex needs. Holistic approaches to therapeutic work recognise the importance of addressing these wider needs and will seek to build upon children and young people's strengths, competences and self-esteem, so that they become more able to meet their needs appropriately, and live positive lives without harming others. If a child or young person does not value himself, he is not likely to value others and is therefore more likely to treat others badly, either intentionally or unintentionally. This chapter will explore issues relating to self-esteem and will discuss and signpost some practical ways of addressing the wider needs of children and young people who have sexual behaviour difficulties – raising self-esteem, developing positive friendships, improving family attachments, developing positive problem solving, managing peer conflicts and achieving positive life experiences.

Case Study – Mark (9)

Mark is a nine-year-old white British boy and is very intelligent, although he does not achieve well at school, and finds it hard to concentrate. Mark has had a disrupted life; his parents separated when he was four. At this time he lived for 15 months with his father in a one-bedroom flat, sleeping on a sofa-bed. For the past three years, Mark's father has settled into a new family, he has remarried and has two stepchildren, Stephen aged six and Jill aged four. Mark has considerable conflict with his stepmother, the outcome of which is that he can only stay with the family for limited periods of time. During this period, Mark has lived partly with his mother, and partly with his paternal grandmother. Mark's mother has bouts of severe depression and has an alcohol problem. For 18 months she lived with a man who was physically and sexually violent towards her. On many occasions this man was physically violent towards Mark, often blaming him as being the cause of his problems. Mark witnessed a great deal of this violence. Eventually Mark moved to live permanently with his grandmother. It was reported to Social Services that, at school, Mark had put his hand down another boy's trousers and touched his penis. Two weeks later, there was a police and Social Services investigation into reports that Mark had sucked the penis of his six-year-old stepbrother, and forced him to do the same to him. It was also reported that he forced Stephen to lie on top of Jill, both without clothes on. An extensive programme of therapeutic work was undertaken with Mark, and with members of his family, including providing extensive support for his grandmother.

Chapter 11   Relapse Prevention

As a young person approaches the end of a programme of work, it is important that he or she has developed ways to apply what they have learnt to their day-to-day lives, and to be able to manage their risks appropriately. There will be many circumstances where he will be faced with decisions, the outcome of which will take him either towards or away from further harmful or inappropriate sexual behaviours. This stage of the work is often referred to as 'relapse prevention'. This chapter will outline briefly the main principles of relapse prevention, and will discuss a range of practical techniques for helping a child or young person avoid committing further harmful or inappropriate sexual behaviours. It is important for these techniques to be realistic and achievable, and tailored to the specific needs of the individual child or young person in a manner that addresses his unique pathway into committing the sexual behaviours in question. It is also important for relapse prevention work to be conducted in a context of building and developing children and young people's strengths, competencies and abilities to be able to live a positive life and meet their needs appropriately.

Case Study – Stephen (9) and Graham (14)

Stephen is a nine-year-old white British boy who has lived in foster care with Kevin and Alison Hunter for the past two years. Graham, a 14-year-old white British boy with moderate learning difficulties, had also lived in the placement for the past three years. It had been reported that on three occasions, Stephen had sexually touched two girls in his class at school. He has also been heard using sexualised language in the playground. Mr and Mrs Hunter have also reported that Stephen often uses inappropriate sexual language at home and always tries to watch adult television programmes. The Hunters reported that one night in the foster home, Stephen went into Graham's bedroom and took his clothes off and woke Graham up asking him to show him his penis. Mrs Hunter was disturbed from her sleep by the landing light going on and went into Graham's bedroom and interrupted the situation. Stephen became distraught and blamed Graham for what had happened. Graham convinced Mrs Hunter that he was fast asleep before Stephen entered his room. Despite reassurance, Graham told his social worker that he no longer feels happy sharing his placement with Stephen, as he feels that he is going to be accused of doing something else. It was later established that Graham had been sexually abusing Stephen over the past three months and that he had threatened Stephen to keep quiet and encouraged him to come into his room at night time to play sexual 'games'. Prior to this incident it was not known that Graham had been sexually abused when he was five years old, prior to coming into care. Both Stephen and Graham received individual therapeutic support.

Chapter 12   Evaluation

In conducting programmes of therapeutic work with children and young people who have committed harmful or inappropriate sexual behaviours, it is essential to have a continuous and ongoing evaluation of the work being undertaken. The initial evaluation will be at the stage of an initial assessment report, where early important decisions about the child or young person's life will be made. These decisions will centre on the immediate needs for risk management in terms of securing and maximising the safety of all parties deemed to be at risk. As the work progresses into its interim stages, further evaluations may lead to additional assessments, changes in therapeutic direction, changes in supervision arrangements, placement changes, returns home and so on. A final evaluation will assess the overall effectiveness of a therapeutic programme, reporting positive changes or unresolved issues, and will conclude with a statement about the nature and level of ongoing risk presented by the child or young person, and the projected future role of others involved in his life, in terms of maintaining the changes made, by providing support and guidance. This chapter will consider a range of issues in carrying out these various stages of evaluation. It will initially identify the purpose of an evaluation, exploring in detail its essential content, recognising the importance of looking at risk and strength factors. The chapter will also consider statistical factors associated with a positive outcome, and will discuss some of the possible prediction errors, and will set out a checklist of essential evaluation factors, followed by guidance on the nature and content of a final assessment report.

Case Study – Carl (14)

Carl is a 14-year-old white British boy who lives with his mother June and stepfather David, and his brother Ian who is 17. Carl is of average intelligence, but has a range of physical and intellectual disabilities. Carl attends mainstream school, and receives special needs support. His range of disabilities have been formally diagnosed as being dyspraxia, but the diagnosis also recognised that this may overlap with aspects of Asperger's syndrome. From the age of six Carl began to repeatedly fondle his genitals, both at home and in public. He would always respond immediately to gentle correction, allowing his attention to be diverted. However, this would not stop him from repeating the behaviour, which became more and more problematic, particularly as he progressed through puberty. When Carl was 12, he began to masturbate, and would need to be reminded constantly by his parents and his brothers that this was a private activity that should not take place in the presence or in the sight of others in the family household. At school, when he was approaching the age of 11, Carl began to expose his penis to other pupils and made attempts to touch girls on their breasts and genitals. From around the age of 12, Carl's behaviours became much more frequent, and started to become much more overtly sexual, to the point that other pupils and some staff began to feel threatened by them. Carl's ability to respond to correction and diversion were hindered by his disabilities. Carl was referred for a programme of therapeutic work to address his inappropriate sexual behaviours, in the wider context of his disabilities.

Chapter 13   Conclusions

This chapter will draw together the main themes and conclusions of the book, again highlighting the importance of a holistic approach to therapeutic intervention with children and young people who have committed harmful or inappropriate sexual behaviours.

Part One

Theoretical Context and Initial Practice Issues

A PRACTICE FRAMEWORK FOR HOLISTIC THERAPEUTIC INTERVENTION

INTRODUCTION

There are many theoretical explanations of how or why children and young people commit harmful or inappropriate sexual behaviours – developmental theories, trauma adaptation theories, preconditions theories, sexual abuse cycles, social learning theories, sociological theories. This chapter will briefly explore some of these explanations and will present an analytical practice framework that is able to accommodate many of their aspects, but with a particular emphasis on the importance and relevance of the social context of young people's experiences as being pivotal to our understanding of their behaviours. The framework emphasises the importance of anti-oppressive and child-centred approaches to the work, modelling overtly an appropriate use of adult power and specifically challenging oppression based on age, 'race', class, gender, ability and sexuality. The chapter will also provide a brief outline of the holistic therapeutic intervention schedule that will be discussed more fully throughout the course book. The chapter will conclude by using the framework to draw together a matrix of the potential influences on a young person's harmful sexual behaviours. Readers will see that many of these influences will be borne out in the case studies that are presented throughout the book.

THEORISING CHILDREN AND YOUNG PEOPLE'S HARMFUL SEXUAL BEHAVIOURS

Many theories and explanations have been put forward and are well documented in the literature (Finkelhor, 1984; Ryan & Lane, 1991; Araji, 1997;

Hackett, 2004) as explanations as to how or why some children and young people engage in harmful or inappropriate sexual behaviours. These theories, often overlapping, include the following.

Developmental Theories

These are explanations based on understandings of what is widely considered to be normal psychosexual development, and the achievement of developmental milestones, and the development of social and familial values and standards. These explanations focus on what happens when this process is disrupted, particularly if it involves a disruption of a child or young person's attachments.

Attachment and Intimacy

There is a growing acknowledgement that knowledge of childhood attachment and intimacy can be an important factor in understanding subsequent sexual behaviour and relationships (Finkelhor et al., 1986; Araji, 1997; Santry & McCarthy, 1999). Through childhood attachments – a sense of being wanted by and wanting to be with another person, usually a parent or parents as the primary caregiver(s) – a person develops a capacity for intimacy that becomes important in relationships in later life. Intimacy is emotional warmth and closeness in relationships with others, which, as it develops, comes to involve vulnerability, a risk of being rejected brought on by the state of wishing to be, and accepting the need to be, wanted by another. During adolescence, the desire for intimacy and physical closeness with others transfers from parental relationships to peer relationships. Parental relationships remain important, but, over time, become secondary. Adolescent desire for intimacy runs alongside and intertwines with biological development and the need and wish for greater physical closeness and sexual experience. Adolescent intimacy involves greater mutuality and commitment, whereas childhood intimacy was more based on a need and dependency that was hopefully met by caregivers.

It has been argued that a disruption in the childhood processes of developing attachment and intimacy can impact on relationships and sexual behaviours in later life and for some people leads to sexual offending (Finkelhor, 1984; Friedrich, 1995; Araji, 1997). Failing to secure attachments in early life deprives the child of the opportunities to learn and develop the skills needed to achieve intimacy with others. This can lead to isolation and emotional loneliness. Subsequent relationships may be shallow or superficial and therefore unfulfilling, leaving a person without a sense of belonging, or being wanted. These are characteristics that are often identified in the histories of people who have committed sexual offences (Araji, 1997; Calder et al., 1997). It could be phrased that for some people, these characteristics produce a 'risk-state' of sexual offending. This has certainly been the case for some of the young men whose case histories are discussed in this book. However, it is important to note that not everybody who experiences insecure, disrupted or non-existent attachments in childhood goes on to commit sexual offences. Neither does it explain why this is more likely to happen for boys than girls. An attachment and intimacy deficit is a factor that will likely contribute to the life processes that lead to sexual offending, but it is often embedded in a whole range of other related factors.

Trauma/Adaptation

These are explanations based on behavioural responses to traumatic experiences, usually sexual abuse – but also taking in other aspects such as physical and emotional abuse – traumagenic dynamics including traumatic sexualisation (Finkelhor et al., 1986) and internalised representations of sexual abuse or other experiences of aggression and victimisation that are subsequently re-enacted (Ryan, 1989). Many of these explanations make reference to aspects of *post-traumatic stress disorder* (PTSD), whereby the child or young person experiences recurrent and intrusive traumatic memories, often following contact with stimuli associated with the initial event, and often characterised by parallel processes of memory constriction or blocking and flooding of memory – flashbacks, etc. (Herman, 1992).

Four Preconditions of Abuse

Finkelhor's (1984) four 'preconditions' model – developed further by Finkelhor et al. (1986) – is a multi-factor model, linking theories about why some people sexually abuse with disinhibitors, triggers (1 and 2) and environmental factors (3 and 4), and has been widely used as a framework for therapeutic intervention. Briefly, the four preconditions are:

1. *Motivation to sexually abuse* – a combination of not being able to meet sexual needs through contact with adults or alternative sources, and an emotional congruence and pattern of sexual arousal through which sexual contact with children is seen as desirable.
2. *Overcoming internal inhibitors* – not all, but most people have inhibitions about having sexual contact with children. This precondition explores a

variety of ways these inhibitions are broken down to allow the individual to justify his actions to himself.

3. *Overcoming external inhibitors* – most people who abuse know that others will not approve of their actions and will need to seek opportunities for unsupervised contact with a child, or at least contact that is not supervised by those who would disapprove.

4. *Overcoming the victim's resistance* – many children are able to avoid abuse, some less so; there is evidence that abusers will seek out the most vulnerable children and young people and go to great lengths not only to set up opportunities to abuse (3), but to 'groom' and persuade children and young people to cooperate with being sexually abused, and not tell others. This will be done through a variety of combined methods ranging from the provision of treats, special attention, convincing the child that they themselves are looking for the sexual contact, etc., to the use of threats of violence, threats of negative family consequences and the use of overt force (Durham, 2003).

Sexual Abuse Cycle

This is a cognitive behavioural chain that looks at thoughts and feelings before, during and after sexually harmful behaviour, linking aspects of power and control to sexual arousal, sometimes related to addictive aspects. In basic terms, the cycle goes through the following stages: circumstances and thoughts – fantasy – planning – setting up – abuse – guilt/fear – rationalisation – cycle repeats (Salter, 1988; Kahn, 1990; O'Callaghan & Print, 1994; Morrison & Print, 1995; Cunningham & MacFarlane, 1996; Araji, 1997). It is important to note, however, that with children and young people there may not be an extensively developed cycle, and the term 'pattern of behaviour' may therefore be more accurate. Alongside the cycle there are other related *cognitive theories* based on cognitive deficits such as empathic dysfunction, distorted thinking and relapse processes. Again, analysis is based on linkages between situation, thoughts, feelings and action.

Spiral of Sexual Abuse

This is an adaptation by Sullivan (2002) that combines the four preconditions of abuse with the sexual abuse cycle, to allow a more flexible and open-ended approach that allows repetition of the different stages, and demonstrates the evolutionary and escalating nature of sexual abuse. The spiral identifies eight stages: motivation to sexually abuse, fantasy, guilt/fear of consequences, role of cognitive distortions, fantasy/masturbation, refining cognitive distortions, preparation/grooming, abuse. This framework allows for combinations of different types of abuse, and emphasises flexibility and a movement away from typologies of offenders and is therefore quite consistent with the approach of this book.

Social Learning and Modelling

These are behavioural explanations based on children and young people learning their behaviour in various ways from seeing or experiencing it and imitating it. They are often linked to the concept of paired associate learning whereby aggression is paired with pleasurable feelings, including sexual feelings, but also possibly feelings of being powerful and of being noticed, etc. Through this pairing harmful sexual behaviour can be reinforced and therefore become more likely to recur (Ryan, 1989).

Sociological Theories

These explanations are based on arguments that socially and politically constructed gender roles in a context of hierarchy and social oppression generate dominant themes of masculinity and femininity that shape and organise people's lives. These theories are sometimes considered to be controversial and have been met with resistance, but are really the only theories that adequately account for why the majority of sexual abuse is committed by males (Durham, 2003). These theories also highlight the impact on children of an eroticised culture and the sexualised media portrayal of children and young people.

Media and Culture

At a personal and peer level, and from an increasingly early age, children and young people are subjected to a random bombardment of sexual information from a variety of sources – television, internet, sex education lessons, campaigns about 'safe sex' and sexually transmitted diseases, parental advice, abuse prevention programmes, music and fashion industry, the sex industry and not least from their peers, though not always truthful and perhaps often exaggerated. Children and young people often report that they have learnt about sex mainly from their peers. This is in many ways an indictment of the current state of sex and relationships education available for young people, although many young people are more comfortable in gaining knowledge from their peers rather than from adults. This highlights

the benefits of the use of structured peer education in providing sex and relationships education to young people (Alaggia & Michalski, 1999). It is also
important to acknowledge that sex and relationships education is a lifelong
learning process of acquiring information, developing skills and forming
attitudes and beliefs about sex, sexuality, relationships and feelings.

Aspects of these theories will be discussed more fully as they arise throughout the various chapters and case studies of this book. Some of them are more
rigorous than others and get closer to explaining why some children and
young people commit harmful sexual behaviours, whilst others focus on how
the behaviours are committed and are in some ways more geared towards
shaping practice interventions. Gray and Pithers (1993) refer to a 'balanced
approach' as being a theory for developing a holistic intervention programme
rather than a theory aimed at explaining sexually aggressive behaviours.
The practice framework presented in this chapter seeks to extend this by
signposting an approach that is on the one hand eclectic and holistic –
accommodating many of the theories discussed above – and on the other hand
allowing practitioners to progress with a clear understanding as to why we
have sexual abuse in our society and why it is mainly committed by males.
The framework also allows for the uniqueness of each child or young person's
involvement in these behaviours, whilst at the same time drawing out their
commonalities. Following the practice framework, the chapter will present
a brief outline of a holistic and flexible practice intervention schedule for
children and young people who display harmful sexual behaviours.

ANALYTICAL PRACTICE FRAMEWORK

In approaching therapeutic interventions with children and young people
who have sexual behaviour difficulties, this framework seeks to ensure that
practice proceeds with a clear understanding of why we have sexual abuse
in our society and why it is mainly committed by men and boys, a fact
widely recognised in the sexual abuse literature (Durham, 2003). The framework was initially developed through my doctoral research into the impact
of sexual abuse on the lives of young men (Durham, 1999, 2003). This
research study was essentially post-structural in its method and analysis,
having an emphasis on language and discourse. Jackson (1992) identifies
three main themes of post-structuralism. First, language is seen as constructing, rather than transmitting, meaning and subjectivity is constituted
through language. Second, there is a denial of the existence of an essential
self outside culture and language. Third, there is no possibility of an objective scientific truth, and knowledges are seen as 'discursive constructs' (p.
26) produced from particular positions. From the outset, my research placed

an emphasis on diversity and the uniqueness of individual experiences. In particular, the research established that gender, power and sexuality were significant issues in sexual abuse and that it was important to understand how these factors play out in their social context. However, as the research unfolded, the young men were found to have had experiences, beliefs and feelings that they held in common. Uncovering such facets did not deny or compromise the uniqueness of each young man's experience, but rather served to highlight common struggles, concerns and fears.

In developing the framework, I was aware that whilst post-structuralism presents a challenge to the essentialist nature of structural theory, arguing that it homogenises groups of people and launders out diversity, it has also been noted that it has the danger of unseating some of the classic analytical concepts, for example, woman, class, 'race'. In this respect it has been criticised for breaking down and fragmenting the solidarity of oppressed groups, allowing space for traditional or classic oppressive relationships to establish increased potency, through being hidden within the tapestry of difference (Barrett & Phillips, 1992). Furthermore, the statements from the young men who took part in my research presented a challenge to the post-structural notion of reality being mediated by language. The extent to which this occurs is related to the social context in which the language is used. In an oppressive social context of patriarchal relations, the use of particular types of language can invoke and carry forward social oppression and thereby significantly influence interpersonal power relationships. Individual words and phrases have the potential to invoke wider social understandings. In this sense, language potentially becomes a tool of oppression. Simple statements or even words could embody significant meanings, which directly relate to widespread and socially embedded oppression. It was shown, for example, that the use of the word 'queer' in the context of adolescent peer group relations has a particularly powerful impact. It can make some people significantly more powerful and others significantly less powerful. The use of this word was shown to be capable of invoking multiple oppressive discourses about personal identity, and social misconceptions about the nature and impact of child sexual abuse. Equally, carefully chosen language can invoke positive discourses, such as citizenship, children's rights, or positive personal identities.

In seeking a rapprochement that allows us in some way to reconcile these theoretical inconsistencies (essentially the contradiction between post-structural and structural approaches), and hold on to both common and unique experiences at the same time, a new approach for therapeutic practice and research is implied. This approach seeks to allow diverse interpersonal language and individual experiences to be considered in a context of social oppression. This approach utilises Cooper's (1995) concept of 'organising principles', to allow for multiple dimensions of inequality and social oppression: 'Rather than basing analysis on axes of oppression, gender, class and race can be conceived as "organizing frameworks" or less systematically "principles" that over-determine each other in their operation and effects' (Cooper, 1995, p. 11).

Racism, for example, is considered as it interacts with other structures of social oppression, such as age, gender or sexuality. No single aspect of social oppression is seen as an absolute determinant of social power. It therefore becomes easier to account for the complexities of interpersonal relationships, for example, between a white woman and a black man, or between a white child and a black woman. The white woman may have less power by virtue of being a woman, but may have more power through being white. Similarly, a white child may have more social power than a black adult or, in certain circumstances, than a gay man. The location and social context of these power relationships can also be highly significant in determining their outcome.

I have drawn some of these theoretical considerations together to form the analytical framework, represented in Figure 2.1. The framework allows a study of power relationships at different but interrelated levels of social interaction, in the context of widespread oppressive social and political influences. At the centre of the framework, the individual is an agent of choice and action, with wishes, desires and beliefs. Individual experience, however, is subject to, and created by, interactions with others. Each level of interaction constitutes a site of learning and influence. Each individual is a member of each level and so not only receives its influence, but also contributes to its influence on others. This may, for example, be at a peer group level or at the level of the wider political and social context, where processes of hegemony and consensus involve each individual in receiving beliefs, carrying them forward within themselves, passing them on to others and so forth. The extent of the influence will vary according to many factors, some of which may relate to class, 'race', gender, sexuality, age or ability. The influence of each level is interdependent, and will vary according to the individual's circumstances, age and development.

The most immediate level of interaction is family and kinship. In most circumstances, for a young child this is the site of initial interactions, relationships and learning, and continues to have a varying influence over time. The next level of interaction is the social network of extra-familial relationships and interactions. Within this network is located the peer group and access to other close and intimate relationships, experienced through schools and possibly pre-school networks, social and leisure contacts and work or college. The three levels – individual, family and peer group – are located in the wider social and political context, which again influences and interacts with each level, and also contributes to the determination of interactions between the different levels. The framework explicates the apparatus of

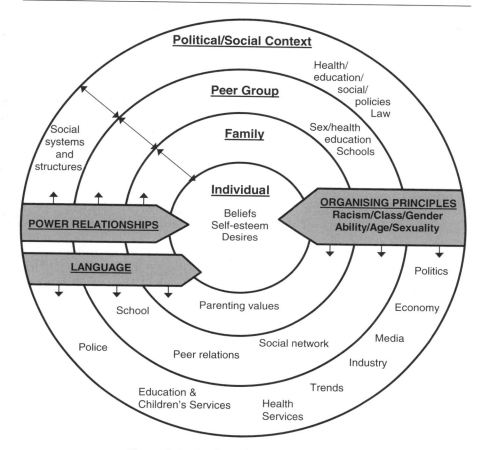

Figure 2.1 Analytical practice framework

oppression and social disadvantage, as a context in which to understand diverse individual experiences. It allows an analysis of interpersonal power relationships and highlights the significance of language in mediating and carrying forward oppression, alongside recognition of the importance of power and sexuality. The framework has usefulness for a wide range of therapeutic practice, and in particular the arena of sexual abuse where issues of power, gender and sexuality are pertinent.

In working with young people with sexual behaviour difficulties, the framework allows us to examine the wider social and cultural influences on their decisions to behave in a particular way. By looking at the wider social messages a young person receives about how he or she should feel and behave, we can find clues about how a diverse range of factors may have intersected and accumulated to precipitate the circumstances, thoughts, feelings and beliefs behind an abusive or inappropriate act. The framework also allows us to explore the power relationship between a person initiating inappropriate or harmful sexual behaviour and the victim. The 'organising principle' of gender is a particularly significant aspect of the framework, and considering that over 90 per cent of child sexual abuse is committed by men or boys (Morrison, Erooga & Beckett, 1994; Home Office, 1997), it is helpful to explore the concept of 'masculinity', so as to understand why. Before doing so, it is important to acknowledge that there are incidences of children and young people being sexually abused by girls and women. It has been argued that there is widespread social and professional denial of female child sexual abuse, which has contributed to its under-reporting (Elliot, 1993; Saradjian, 1998) – denial of the act of abuse taking place or denial of the responsibility of the woman committing such an act. Sexual abuse committed by males or females is likely to entail an abuse of power and responsibility and leave a child feeling hurt and guilty for what has happened. Many of the approaches to working with boys and men who have sexually abused will apply to girls and women, particularly the cognitive behavioural aspects of the work, and the sex and relationships education and issues around sex and the law and informed consent and the misuse of power. Clearly there will be different emphases, for example, the differences in social and psychological development and changes at puberty.

MASCULINITIES

The concept of 'hegemony' has been used to describe dominant forms of masculinity (Carrigan, Connell & Lee, 1987; Connell, 1987). Hegemony was a term used by Gramsci in his development of work by Lenin (Joll, 1977). In literal terms it means ascendancy, domination or leadership. Gramsci (1971) extended the concept to use it as an explanation of how one group in society dominates and subordinates another group. This is not dependent on economic and physical power alone, but has ideological dimensions, whereby large numbers of a subordinate group are led into accepting the values of the dominant group. Hegemonic masculinities are characterised by an essential control of the self, the environment and others, namely women, children and other men. Connell theorises a hierarchy of masculinities amongst men, 'hegemonic, conservative and subordinated' (1987, p. 110), located within structures of power. He emphasises the importance of examining power relationships between men in order to understand men's relationships with women and children and, in particular, men's violence. Taking such a perspective forward, it is possible to conceptualise a more dynamic multiplicity of contested masculinities, interacting with other social oppressions. Masculinities are varied, shifting and changing across different historical, situational, cultural, temporal and spatial contexts (Cornwall & Lindisfarne, 1994). Individual men or boys will present differing masculinities at different times and in different places and circumstances (Pringle, 1995; Hearn, 1996). Hearn suggests that the term 'men's practices' (1996, p. 214) more accurately represents an understanding of the diversity of what men do, where, when, how and why.

There are tensions here. On the one hand, there is an attempt to conceptualise a multiplicity of masculinities, which moves towards questioning the term 'masculinity' itself. On the other hand, it is recognised that there are dominant forms of masculinity that render other forms subordinate; dominant and subordinated discourses are produced mutually (in addition, where there is subordination, there will be resistance). However, there is no simple question of choice about which 'masculinity' to present where. There are particular forms of masculinity that are dominant in most circumstances and become the socially accepted norm. The negotiation of individual masculinities takes place in an oppressive social context in which heterosexism and homophobia are the norm (Sedgwick, 1990; Nayak & Kehily, 1997; Wolfe, Wekerle & Scott, 1997).

Warner (1993) argues that most social theory takes a heterosexist perspective, in which heterosexuality is normalised and seen as functional to the social order, never requiring explanation, and that themes of homophobia and heterosexism pervade almost every document in our culture. As a consequence, other sexualities are marginalised, problematised and excluded. He further argues that a non-oppressive gender order can only come about through a radical change in the theorising and conceptualising of sexuality, with shifting styles of identity politics and the generation and valuing of new cultures. In following through some of the arguments put forward by Warner, it could be argued that in many ways the debate is predominantly about heterosexism. Particularly in adolescent peer cultures, notions of acceptable masculinities would appear to be at least a significant vehicle for, if not a fundamental constituent of, homophobia. In this context, heterosexuality would appear to be a defining line in power relationships. In most circumstances, heterosexual forms of masculinity are more powerful than others.

MASCULINITIES AND SEXUAL ABUSE

Within patriarchal relations, dominant or hegemonic masculinities are oppressively defined in terms of a restrictive range of acceptable behaviours (Durham, 1999). The intertwining or conflation of biological sex and gender potentially creates confusion and doubts for the individual. For the male, masculinities, defined in terms of strength and power and natural domination, are not biological realities, and require constant nurturing, affirmation and repression of unacceptable 'feminine' behaviours – passivity, vulnerability, 'weakness', sensitivity, intimacy, etc. (Kaufman, 1987; Connell, 1989; Frosh, 1993). In patriarchal relations, power bestows benefits; one way (the prescribed way) to exercise power is to subordinate someone else – the greater the need to emphasise or affirm masculinities, the greater the need to subordinate someone else. Furthermore, the greater the extent to which this subordination is done, the greater the power, and hence the benefits, but also the greater the deception, and, ultimately, the greater the harm done to all. Sex, violence, power and gender are combined to construct dominant forms of masculinities that are invested in and expressed through the body, and are central to self-esteem and identity.

For many men, the everyday experience of patriarchal relations is sufficient to provide the necessary benefits and nurture for being male, although this is not to deny the need for constant masculinising affirmations and access to 'legitimate and acceptable' closeness to other males. For other men, these benefits are not felt. Other circumstances and negative experiences accentuate self-doubts and repressed emotions and call into play the need for affirmation through the use of a more overt force. Sometimes physical violence may suffice, but for some the doubt is so great that affirmation has to be experienced through the body, as physical and/or sexual violence and domination. There is an illusion of, and subsequent disappointment with, power in these circumstances, which after a short passage of time thwarts the affirmation. This goes some way to explain the repetition and escalation of men's sexual violence (Kelly, 1988). It has been argued that masculinities are particularly fragile during adolescence:

> In adolescence the pain and fear involved in repressing 'femininity' and passivity start to become evident. For most of us, the response to this inner pain is to reinforce the bulwarks of masculinity. The emotional pain created by obsessive masculinity is stifled by reinforcing masculinity itself. (Kaufman, 1987, p. 12)

These factors help us understand why men or boys commit the majority of sexual abuse (Durham, 2003). The scale and prevalence of child sexual abuse cut across all boundaries: class, gender, age, 'race' and disability (Kelly, 1988; Herman, 1990; MacLeod & Saraga, 1991). The use of the framework (see Figure 2.1) allows us to explore with a boy his received beliefs about his 'masculinity' – for example, how he may have been encouraged to avoid or deny his weaknesses and vulnerabilities by not crying, or by avoiding intimacy, or simply not being encouraged to develop intimacy skills – and how they have influenced his thoughts and feelings about being a boy or a man and how this has all been processed and translated into action and behaviour. It also allows us to consider closely, in a wide variety of ways, the meanings, textures and dynamics of his interpersonal power relationships.

At this stage it is important to note again that whilst most young people who sexually abuse are men or boys, there are women and girls who also sexually abuse, or who have inappropriate sexual behaviours. The practice framework has an equally important application to therapeutic work with girls. In a similar way to that in which boys receive oppressive messages and beliefs about their 'masculinity', girls receive oppressive messages and beliefs about their 'femininity'. The patriarchal construction of 'masculinity' is mirrored by an oppressive construction of 'femininity' that emphasises weakness, passivity and subordination to masculinity. Girls receive mixed and confusing messages about their identities and their sexual behaviours, and are often pressured into subordination (Steinberg et al., 1997; Kaufman, 1987; Carrigan et al., 1987). Again, as with boys, the framework allows us to understand and explore with a girl her received beliefs about her 'femininity', the influences on her thoughts and beliefs and how they are translated into day-to-day interactions.

THERAPEUTIC INTERVENTION

This section presents a brief outline of the holistic therapeutic intervention schedule, for children and young people with sexual behaviour difficulties. The various aspects of the schedule are discussed more fully throughout the remaining chapters of the book.

Many writers have noted that children and young people who display sexual behaviour difficulties are themselves vulnerable, many having experienced a multiple range of family problems and various forms of abuse, but not necessarily (and not isolated) sexual abuse (Ryan & Lane, 1991; Morrison et al., 1994; Morrison & Print, 1995; Cunningham & MacFarlane, 1996; Araji, 1997). If this is the case, the appropriate intervention is one that challenges the inappropriate or harmful sexual behaviours, but also provides a high level of support and guidance. This enables young people to begin to address the many problems in their lives and to develop a positive lifestyle, moving away from inappropriate sexualised behaviours.

Initially, the specific circumstances of the abusing behaviour need to be addressed and arrangements made for adequate supervision and the protection of others. During this assessment phase, a child or young person is taken through a process of being engaged in an agreement to undertake therapeutic work, which explores explicitly his harmful sexual behaviours. At this stage, the work moves on to explore the circumstances of the abusing, comparing the young person's description of his behaviour to the descriptions and statements which may have been made by the victim(s). It may be possible to map out a behavioural cycle or pattern that can be used to help the young person understand and interrupt their immediate abusive behaviour. This stage also involves an exploration of the young person's sexual history. At a later stage, this work is extended into a full exploration of the young person's predisposing thoughts, thinking errors and abuse-related sexual fantasies. Once an understanding of these circumstances has been established, it is important to take the young person through a detailed consideration of the impact of his behaviour on the victim (sometimes known as victim empathy or perspective-taking work). In addition, it is important to address any deficits in the child or young person's age-appropriate understanding of sexual behaviour and sexuality and related issues, such as sexual oppression, sexism, homophobia, etc. It is likely that an intervention will need to address the young person's own victim experiences, whatever they are, and to address the wider issues in the young person's life, which are likely to have contributed to the decision to sexually abuse. These may involve permutations of personal, peer and family-related issues. The work concludes with a comprehensive relapse prevention plan.

Full theoretical considerations and details of interventions with young people with sexual behaviour difficulties, incorporating many aspects of this schedule, have been documented elsewhere (Salter, 1988; Kahn, 1990; Ryan & Lane, 1991; Morrison & Print, 1995; Araji, 1997; Calder, 1999, 2002). Araji (1997) has reviewed much of the relevant literature and has described a range of intervention programmes. Many of these programmes have a strong emphasis on the cognitive behavioural element, but often fail to take a sufficiently critical approach to gender and sexuality in a manner that adequately addresses a wider conceptualisation of the causes of sexual abuse (Postlethwaite, 1998; Durham, 1999, 2003).

The practice framework allows the practitioner to address his or her power relationship with the child or young person and emphasises the importance of a transparent approach to the work, which explains the process from the outset and maintains a high level of respect, whilst acknowledging that some behaviours are problematic. The framework allows us to examine how young people may have internalised oppressive stereotypes, beliefs and misunderstandings, through which they may have in some ways become able to justify their actions to themselves, or may have generated powerful motivations for committing the abuse. For example, a boy living, for whatever reason, in fear of his self-perceived heterosexual 'inadequacies' may engage in behaviours geared towards heterosexual affirmation. He may have beliefs about his own inadequacies or incompetence through being oppressed as a 'child' (Archard, 1993) within a chaotic family, or a family characterised by sexual aggression and domestic violence. He may have felt more powerful, or more like a 'real man' or 'one of the boys', through committing sexual acts with a weaker, younger or less powerful person. The framework can be used to explore the dynamic power differential between the young person and the person he abused. This may lead to greater insight, with the young person being helped to see where he is located within the multiple influences and discourses which may have shaped his thinking, leading him into a situation where he made the decision to sexually abuse or behave in a sexually inappropriate way. The framework effectively gives the young person a map through which to interpret and negotiate the past, present and future landscape of his sexuality. It can assist him in negotiating positively about the future influences on his behaviour. These applications of the framework are drawn together in Figure 2.2 below.

It is important at this stage to note that an assessment of the child or young person needs to be accompanied by a comprehensive assessment of the family (this will be discussed in detail in Chapter 4). The practice framework highlights that the family is an important mediator of wider social influences, as does the *Framework for the Assessment of Children in Need and their Families* with its emphasis on a dynamic interaction between the child's developmental needs, parenting capacity and family and environmental factors (Department of Health, Department for Education and Employment and Home Office, 2000). In particular, the family assessment has to establish the extent of the parent's or carer's knowledge and acceptance of the reported inappropriate or harmful sexual behaviours and the extent of their motivation and cooperation with the planned assessment and intervention. It also has to assess the family's ability and willingness to adequately supervise the child or young person and to set appropriate boundaries for the safety and protection of all.

CONCLUSIONS

This chapter has considered briefly some of the existing theoretical explanations of why children and young people engage in harmful or inappropriate sexual behaviours, before moving on to present a new analytical practice framework for a holistic approach to therapeutic intervention. It was argued that the framework was able to accommodate many of the existing theoretical approaches, whilst at the same time highlighting the importance and relevance of the social context of children and young people's experiences as being pivotal to understanding how and why these behaviours take place. Importantly, it was argued that the framework more adequately addresses the issue of why we have sexual abuse in our society and why

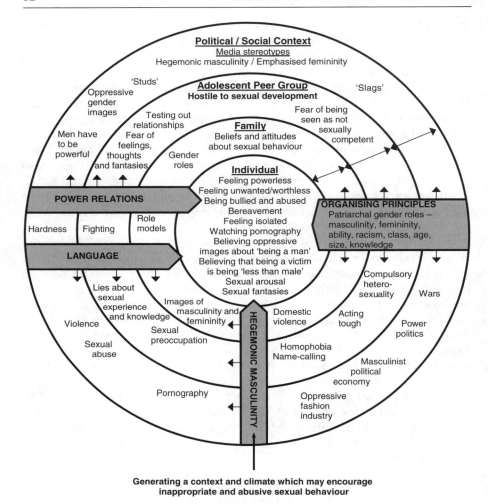

Figure 2.2 The social context of young people's inappropriate and abusive sexual behaviours

mainly men or boys commit it. The anti-oppressive approach of the framework allows a full exploration of abusive power relationships and circumstances of compulsory heterosexuality, homophobia and peer pressure and how they may have influenced a young person's decision to behave in a sexually inappropriate or abusive manner. The framework provides a theoretical underpinning for the practitioner, and provides helpful ideas for working directly with children and young people.

3

ASSESSING SEXUAL BEHAVIOUR

INTRODUCTION

In working with young people's harmful or inappropriate sexual behaviours, it is important to be very clear about what these behaviours are, and which behaviours are to be considered appropriate and not harmful. It is also important to recognise that there is wide variance of opinion, standards and values within the community and across cultures and religions, about which behaviours are considered to be acceptable. Acceptability of sexual behaviours also has a historical dimension. It has long been recognised in the literature that the context of children and young people's overall development, including not least their sexual development, is constantly changing (Gil & Johnson, 1993). To appreciate this one only needs to compare advertisements and television programmes from the 1950s with those of the present day, or compare the Walt Disney cartoon character 'Snow White' with her 1990s counterpart 'Pocahontas', to find increasingly sexualised images. Recently there have been significant changes in the UK law that governs sexual behaviour. Following a reduction in the age of consent for gay male sexual activity, recent changes in UK law – The Sexual Offences Act 2003 – have removed homophobic aspects of previous laws, again reflecting a change of values and standards.

In recent years, the changing context of young people's sexual behaviours has been escalated by developments in information technology, most notably computer technology, digital photography and the internet. These developments have widened significantly the social availability of explicit sexual material, including an area of particular concern, the increased production of images of child sexual abuse (Carr, 2003). Notwithstanding the direct harm this will have caused to the children involved, these images, indirectly, will go on to create further harm and will potentially have an impact on some people's perception of acceptable sexual behaviours, allowing them to attempt to justify sexual abusing to themselves and to others. The images are also likely to be used to skew children's perception of sexual acceptability as part of the process of being sexually abused. Generally the increased availability per se of pornography through the internet will increase the probability of children and young people viewing explicit and exploitative sexual material. These factors underscore the importance of providing comprehensive sex and relationships education for children and young people from an early age.

The changing social context and the wide variation of personal standards and values make it difficult to establish a baseline of acceptable or appropriate sexual behaviours. However, by being clear about what we mean by sexual abuse, it is possible to define those sexual behaviours that are harmful. This chapter will seek to address some of these problems of assessing sexual behaviour by initially setting out a flexible and widely encompassing definition of child sexual abuse and inappropriate and harmful sexual behaviour, followed by materials that will be helpful to practitioners and carers in assessing the appropriateness of sexual behaviours.

DEFINING CHILD SEXUAL ABUSE AND INAPPROPRIATE SEXUAL BEHAVIOUR

The vast range of unique individual experiences of child sexual abuse makes it hard to achieve an encompassing definition. Some prevalence studies have recognised this by asking respondents about ranges of sexual experiences and have then applied differing definitions that show hugely variable outcomes (Kelly, Regan & Burton, 1991; Cawson, Wattam, Brooker & Kelly, 2000). Influenced by these approaches and the work of Finkelhor et al. (1986), Morrison and Print (1995), and the definition in *Working Together to Safeguard Children* (Department of Health, Department for Education and Employment and Home Office, 1999), which draws a distinction between contact and noncontact behaviours, wide and lengthy definitions of both 'child sexual abuse' and 'inappropriate or harmful sexual behaviours' are proposed. These definitions present a range of options and defined behaviours (Durham, 2003, 2004b):

Child Sexual Abuse

1. Forced or coerced sexual behaviour that is imposed on a child (person under 18 years old), and/or
2. Sexual behaviour between a child and a much older person (five years or more age discrepancy), or a person in a caretaking role, or a sibling, and/or

3. Sexual behaviour where the recipient is defined as being unable to give informed consent by virtue of age, understanding or ability.

Inappropriate or Harmful Sexual Behaviour

1. Initiated sexual behaviour which is inappropriate for a child's age and development, and/or
2. Initiated sexual behaviour which is inappropriate in its context. For example, behaviour that is considered acceptable in privacy occurring in non-private circumstances, and/or
3. An initiated sexual act committed:
   (a) against a person's will;
   (b) without informed consent;
   (c) in an aggressive, exploitative or threatening manner.

Contact and Non-contact Behaviours

1. *Contact behaviours* may involve: touching, rubbing, disrobing, sucking and/or penetrating. It may include rape. Penetration may be oral, anal or vaginal and digital, penile or objectile.
2. *Non-contact behaviours* may involve: exhibitionism, peeping or voyeurism, fetishism (such as stealing underwear or masturbating into another's clothes), involving children in looking at or in the production of pornography, and obscene communication (such as obscene phone calls, and verbal and written sexual harassment or defamation).

ASSESSING CHILDREN AND YOUNG PEOPLE'S SEXUAL BEHAVIOURS

Johnson and Feldmeth (1993) identified a continuum of four clinically derived definable clusters of sexual behaviour for pre-adolescents:

1. natural and healthy sex play
2. sexually reactive
3. extensive mutual sexual behaviours
4. children who molest.

The behaviours in group 1 are considered to be developmentally appropriate. The remaining three groups raise varying levels of concern; in group 4 there are clear concerns about the victimisation of others. The behaviours corresponding to each group in Johnson and Feldmeth's model are detailed as follows.

Group 1 – Natural and Healthy Sex Play

- exploratory in nature and characterised by spontaneity and light-heartedness
- intermittent and balanced with curiosity
- similar in age, size and development level
- embarrassed but not with strong feelings of anger, fear or anxiety

Group 2 – Sexually Reactive

- often done in view of adults and may be frequent
- can generally be distracted, but erupt again when scared or anxious
- many of the behaviours are autoerotic or directed towards adults
- no coercion
- not really directed outward towards others
- a partial form of re-enactment of sexual abuse
- shame, guilt, anxiety and fear but not intense anger

Group 3 – Extensive Mutual Sexual Behaviours

- extensive, often habitual and may include the full spectrum of adult sexual behaviours
- persuasion, willing partners, not coercion
- often distrustful, chronically hurt and abandoned by adults
- these children relate best to other children
- little desire to stop
- not an aggressive or retaliatory function

Group 4 – Children Who Molest

- frequent and pervasive
- a growing pattern of sexual behaviour problems is evident in their histories. Intense sexual confusion
- sexuality and aggression are closely linked
- bribery, trickery, manipulation or emotional or physical coercion
- not often physical force, as victims are chosen for their vulnerability
- impulsive, compulsive and aggressive
- problems in all areas of their lives

It is important to remember that children can move across these different groups, or have aspects of different groups at the same time. Being able to locate a child in one of these groups will have implications for the nature and level of intervention needed, and the risks presented to others. It is particularly important to make a distinction between children in groups 2 and 4. Johnson and Feldmeth's categories are a helpful guide that emphasises the importance of assessing each child or young person, going some way to highlight the heterogeneity of children and young people's inappropriate or harmful sexual behaviours. It is important to not lose sight of the uniqueness of the individual circumstances of each child, and to have a framework through which to assess a wide range of circumstances.

Hall, Matthews and Pearce (2002) have analysed the sexual behaviours of a sample of children who have been sexually abused and have identified five empirically based typologies:

1. Developmentally expected sexual behaviour.
2. Unplanned interpersonal sexual behaviour (developmentally problematic).
3. Self-focused sexual behaviour (developmentally problematic).
4. Planned interpersonal sexual behaviour (developmentally problematic).
5. Planned, coercive interpersonal sexual behaviour (developmentally problematic).

These typologies involve the child's response to being sexually victimised, and have included family and parental factors in accounting for the behaviours.

1. Developmentally Expected Sexual Behaviour

- no problematic sexual behaviours
- not actively involved or sexually aroused in their own sexual victimisation
- single perpetrator, usually abused individually without sibling or peer involvement
- non-sadistic abuse
- have experienced generally positive parenting

2. Unplanned Interpersonal Sexual Behaviour (Developmentally Problematic)

- spontaneous and sporadic developmentally problematic interpersonal sexual behaviours
- actively involved in own sexual victimisation, but no arousal

- single perpetrator, usually abused individually without sibling or peer involvement
- non-sadistic abuse
- positive parenting – good supervision, healthy family sexual attitudes

3. Self-focused Sexual Behaviour
(Developmentally Problematic)

- frequent and extensive masturbation and sexual preoccupation
- sexual arousal experienced during sexual victimisation
- single perpetrator (mainly), usually abused individually without sibling or peer involvement
- non-sadistic abuse
- blame themselves for own sexual abuse
- some parenting problems – some parent–child role reversal, some family violence
- some problematic family attitudes regarding sex, but not sexual inter-action
- parental difficulties in setting limits on the child's sexual behaviours

4. Planned Interpersonal Sexual Behaviour
(Developmentally Problematic)

- interpersonal sexual behaviours – extensive adult-type sexual acts
- planned but not coercive sexual behaviours
- high levels of masturbation and sexual preoccupation
- active participation and sexual arousal in their own sexual victimisation
- experienced sadistic abuse, causing discomfort
- often with multiple perpetrators, multiple victim contexts
- poor parental boundaries, role reversal, family dysfunction, poor parental skill
- inadequate parental supervision – therefore potential access to other children
- problematic family sexual attitudes, sometimes patterns of sexualised interaction

5. Planned, Coercive Interpersonal Sexual Behaviour
(Developmentally Problematic)

- extensive and persistent adult-type sexual behaviours – planned and coercive

- high levels of problematic masturbation, sexual preoccupation and sexual gestures
- frequent child-on-child sexual behaviours, siblings taught to act as perpetrators
- own sexual victimisation involved sadism, arousal and a high level of participation
- multiple perpetrators, abused in multiple victim contexts
- children experience pairing of sex and violence from an early age
- poor parental supervision, easy access to other children inside and outside family
- problematic family sexual attitudes, family dysfunction, family violence, criminality
- sexualised family interaction, role reversal, parental maltreatment histories

A SIX-STEP CUMULATIVE FRAMEWORK FOR ASSESSING YOUNG PEOPLE'S SEXUAL BEHAVIOUR

The following criteria can be used to try to determine whether a young person's sexual behaviour is appropriate, inappropriate or harmful (derived from Pithers, Gray, Cunningham & Lane, 1993, and Johnson, 1999). A progression through each level reflects an increasing degree of concern and a stronger indication that the young person has a problem:

1. Sexual activity compared to developmental level.
2. Relative power of children?
3. Use of intimidation, force, trickery or bribes.
4. Secrecy.
5. Compulsive or obsessive.
6. Progression.

I. Sexual Activity Compared to Developmental Level

This initial step, in determining whether a sexual behaviour is a problem or not, involves comparing a child's developmental level with the type of sexual behaviour taking place.

- Is the behaviour beyond the developmental level of that child?
- Is there any knowledge about how the child or young person may have obtained the sexual information?
- Is there a history of sexual abuse?

- Does the child have access to pornography, or has the child witnessed adult sexual behaviour?
- Is the level of interest in sexual behaviour out of balance with other aspects of the child's life and interests?
- Is the child's language more consistent with adult sexual expression?
- Are the sexual behaviours significantly different from those of other same-age children?

2. Relative Power of Children

A sexual behaviour is likely to be a problem if one child participating in it has more power than another. Power differentials may exist by virtue of a child's age, gender, class, race, ability – intellectual and physical – and status amongst peers. The practice framework presented in Chapter 2 is useful in assessing the components of an interpersonal power imbalance and how it may be unfolding in a particular circumstance.

- Does one young person have a habitual leadership role and why?
- Is one of the young people more popular amongst his peers?
- Are the children at different developmental levels?

3. Use of Intimidation, Force, Trickery or Bribes

Developmentally appropriate sexual behaviours involve curiosity and game playing, not intimidation, force, trickery or bribes. It is important to assess whether informed consent has been given.

- To give informed consent, a person has to be:
    - old enough to understand what they are consenting to
    - have enough knowledge and information
    - be in a situation where it is just as easy to say 'no' as it is to say 'yes'
    - they must not feel under any pressure
- Does one of the young people appear unhappy or uncomfortable; do they wish to complain?

4. Secrecy

It is important to make a distinction between privacy, embarrassment and secrecy. Privacy is the right to protection from intrusion, while secrecy implies the avoidance of the consequences of an action that a child knows or senses is wrong or harmful.

- Does the young person deny the activity beyond natural embarrassment at being discovered?
- Are there deliberate attempts to hide the activity?
- Does one young person explain or present excuses more than the other?

5. Compulsive or Obsessive

A compulsive behaviour involves an apparent inability to control that behaviour, whilst an obsessional behaviour is an apparent continual preoccupation with that behaviour. As far as a child's sexual behaviour is concerned, both or either of these may indicate that there is a problem.

- Sexual behaviours which continue in spite of consistent and clear requests to stop.
- Does the young person appear to be unable to stop himself from engaging in sexual activities? The level of concern here will clearly depend upon the age of the young person.
- Sexual behaviours which occur in public or other places where the young person has been told they are not acceptable.
- Is fear, anxiety, deep shame or intense guilt associated with the sexual behaviours?
- Do the sexual behaviours cause physical or emotional pain or discomfort to the young person or to others?

6. Progression

It is important to establish if there is a progressive element to the behaviours, the extent to which there has been an increasing intensity or frequency of behaviour, or whether behaviours have been intensified and developed alongside fantasies.

- Do the sexual behaviours progress in frequency, intensity or intrusiveness over time?
- Does the young person use sex to hurt others?
- Is anger or violence associated with the sexual behaviour?
- Does the young person use distorted thinking to justify his sexual behaviours?

STAGES OF TYPICAL SEXUAL DEVELOPMENT

In considering these behaviours, it is important to consider what would be expected as normal or typical sexual behaviour for children and young people of different ages.

Ages 0–5 Years

At this age children are curious about most things, including their bodies. They may often be happier without any clothes on. At this age and throughout their development, children may find comfort in holding or fondling their genitals. It can act as a self-comforting as well as an exciting behaviour.

At these ages children will also be curious about other people's bodies. This may result in children trying to look at or touch other children's (of a similar age) genitals. This exploratory looking and touching will not be coercive.

Ages 6–10 Years

School-age children continue to be curious about their bodies. At this age their sexual and gender curiosity may be expressed in the games they play. Games such as 'Doctors and Nurses' and 'Mummies and Daddies' may be fairly common. Boys may compare the size of their penises. Children will begin to show an interest in sexual words and rude jokes, though little interest in the opposite sex may be evident. Children may continue to be interested in their own and other people's bodies, especially if they begin to develop their own secondary sexual characteristics; some children may commence masturbation.

Ages 11–12 Years – Pre-adolescence

As children's sexual awareness begins to develop, they may become anxious to establish relationships with their peers. They may begin to derive increasing pleasure and enjoyment from masturbation. By this age most children will have experienced some formal sex education, and may become increasingly curious about sexual knowledge. Some young people may engage in sexual activity, such as kissing and fondling with their peers. They may imitate sexual activity that they have seen or heard about. Most of these behaviours will be with members of the opposite sex, though some people may engage in sexual activities with peers of the same sex.

Ages 13–18 Years – Adolescence

During this stage many young people will have gone through puberty and are likely to have increasing levels of sexual knowledge, interest and feelings, these being related to the extent of their physical development.

At this stage young people may express their developing sexuality through sexual innuendo, flirtations and courtship behaviours. They may have had sexual experiences within a peer relationship. Typical experiences can include consenting non-coital sexual behaviour (e.g. kissing, fondling, mutual consenting masturbation). Adolescence can also be a time when powerful emotions are experienced and expressed. These emotions may coincide with sexual experiences or be separate from them.

Although the age of consent is 16, some young people may have engaged in sexual intercourse before reaching these ages. Other young people may not have engaged in sexual activity with their peers and may have little interest in doing so. Some young people may engage in explicit sexual discussion amongst peers using sexual swear words and telling obscene jokes. They may show interest in erotic material and use it in masturbation.

Some young people may become competitive and proud about their sexual activity, which may in turn create pressures and anxieties for others. It is not uncommon for young people to feel they have to lie about their involvement in sexual activity in response to this competitive peer scenario, which is often reinforced by media images.

Adolescence is a stage when young people may become conscious about developing their own identity in many respects; as a result images and fashion may become an increasing priority. This becomes closely related to the continuing development of a sexual identity. At this stage, peer influences may have a heightened significance. For some young people there may be discrepancies between sexual orientation, sexual experiences and their sexual identity.

Adolescence is also a stage when some young people become more distant from their parents or carers. Sometimes this can be paradoxical as they can be seen to be struggling with areas of their lives where adult guidance might be beneficial. This may be particularly true in relation to the development of sexual identity, and sexual behaviour. Additionally this is an area which many parents and carers find difficult or uncomfortable, particularly if this is an area which has not received open discussion at earlier stages. In these circumstances, young people may find it easier to talk to other adults or their peers.

CONCLUSIONS

This chapter has highlighted the rapidly changing social context of children and young people's sexual behaviours, and the consequent difficulty in establishing a common baseline of appropriate and acceptable sexual behaviour. It was recognised that through changes in technology, children and young people are potentially gaining more access to explicit sexual material, and that quite often some of this is exploitative and harmful. After presenting definitions of 'child sexual abuse' and 'inappropriate or harmful sexual behaviour', the chapter discussed Johnson and Feldmeth's (1993) four groups of children's sexual behaviours, arguing that they were useful, but that it was important not to lose sight of the uniqueness of each child's circumstances, and that the groups were not absolutes and that children cross over between them. It was recognised that the model can be a helpful tool in shaping appropriate therapeutic intervention. The chapter also presented empirical typologies of children's sexual behaviours derived by Hall et al. (2002). These typologies took account of how children had responded to prior experiences of sexual abuse, and recognised the importance of family and parental factors. Finally, the chapter presented a six-step cumulative framework for assessing young people's sexual behaviour, alongside information about typical or 'normal' age-related sexual behaviour. Building on this, the next chapter will highlight the importance of the family context of young people's sexual behaviours.

EXERCISE: DO YOU HAVE CONCERNS ABOUT THESE BEHAVIOURS?

Using the material from this chapter, consider which of the following behaviours you would consider to be unacceptable or concerning, and why?

1. A boy and girl both aged 4 touching each other's genitals.
2. A 6-year-old boy simulating sexual intercourse with a 5-year-old girl.
3. Teenagers aged 17 and 15 engaged in sexual intercourse.
4. Two 15-year-old girls kissing and masturbating each other.
5. Three boys aged 7 looking at and touching each other's penises.
6. A 12-year-old girl playing 'Doctors and Nurses' with a 5-year-old boy.
7. A 12-year-old boy exposing his penis in the park.
8. A group of 11-year-old boys looking at a soft pornographic magazine.
9. A 15-year-old girl having sex with a 29-year-old man.
10. A 10-year-old boy attempting to kiss the genitals of an 8-year-old girl.
11. A 10-year-old girl digitally penetrating the anus of an 8-year-old boy.
12. Two 5-year-olds found in bed together wearing their underwear.

13. Two 13-year-old boys hugging and fondling each other's genitals.
14. An 11-year-old boy and a 12-year-old girl tongue kissing.
15. A 3-year-old masturbating in bed before going to sleep.
16. A 14-year-old girl and boy masturbating each other.
17. A 6-year-old and a 4-year-old exploring each other's bodies.
18. Two 15-year-old boys kissing and masturbating each other.
19. Two 7-year-olds kissing.
20. A 14-year-old boy fondling the genitals of a 12-year-old girl.
21. A 10-year-old girl touching the penis of a 7-year-old boy.
22. A 4-year-old boy touching his genitals in front of his classmates.
23. A 7-year-old girl and boy taking their clothes off together.
24. A 16-year-old girl and a 17-year-old boy, both with mild learning disabilities, engaged in sexual intercourse.
25. An 8-year-old boy tongue kissing with his 7-year-old sister.
26. Two 13-year-old girls hugging and fondling each other's genitals.
27. A 15-year-old boy having sex with a 29-year-old woman.
28. A 3-year-old girl pointing to her father's penis and asking what it is.
29. A 15-year-old watching 'soft-core' pornography on television.
30. A 16-year-old girl and boy watching 'hard-core' pornographic videos.

4

FAMILY ASSESSMENT

INTRODUCTION

The discovery by parent(s) that their child has inappropriate sexual behaviour, or has sexually harmed another person, is most often traumatic. Parents are likely to be aware of the social intolerance of sexual abuse and will have many anxieties and fears about the potential consequences for their family. Parents are often shocked and confused by these behaviours and are likely to have a range of fears and anxieties – why has my child behaved in this way? What will happen if friends, neighbours or others find out? How will I keep my other children safe? Will their friends still be able to come and play? How can I manage my child in the future, so that he does not do it again? What have I done to cause this? Conducting a family assessment in these circumstances is not easy. At a time when parents are feeling vulnerable and possibly responsible for what has happened, they are likely to be subjected to a range of personal and searching questions, as professionals will need to establish very quickly whether or not it is safe for the young person to continue living with the family. From a child protection perspective, professionals will need to know a range of factors including: whether or not there are aspects of the home environment that have significantly contributed to the harmful sexual behaviour; whether or not there are factors that are likely to lead to further incidents; whether there are other children present who could be at risk. Simultaneously, professionals will need to be able to offer support and reassurance, and begin to identify existing parental skills that can be harnessed in securing the safety and protection of all the children or young people in their care.

Existing research (and some of the case studies presented later in this book) recognises a range of family characteristics in the histories of children and young people with harmful or inappropriate sexual behaviours including: discontinuity of care, multiple parent figures, parental experiences of sexual abuse, problematic intra-family relationships, domestic violence, parental mental health, poverty, drug and substance misuse (Hackett, 2004).

Whilst trying to establish relevant links or perhaps direct causal factors, it is important not to pathologise families, and to remember that many families characterised by some of these problems do not have children who have committed inappropriate or harmful sexual behaviours.

Building on our understanding from Chapter 3 of the importance of assessing the immediate context of children and young people's harmful or inappropriate sexual behaviours, this chapter will explore the importance of family assessment and support, identifying the key issues involved and presenting a family assessment schedule, concluding with a discussion of the key issues involved in providing ongoing family support.

FAMILY ASSESSMENT SCHEDULE

When assessing the inappropriate or harmful sexual behaviours of a child or young person, it is important not to lose sight of the family and social context in which the behaviours have taken place. An assessment of the family should therefore be completed alongside the assessment of the young person. The practice framework in Chapter 2 highlighted that the family was an important mediator of wider social influences, as does the *Framework for the Assessment of Children in Need and their Families,* with its emphasis on a dynamic interaction between the child's developmental needs, parenting capacity and family and environmental factors (Department of Health et al., 2000). The responses of parents or carers to their child's inappropriate or harmful sexual behaviours can greatly influence the success of any intervention, or alternatively contribute to maintaining those behaviours. Parents and carers have an important role to play in supporting a child or young person to be motivated towards taking responsibility for their behaviours, and attending programmes of therapeutic intervention. They will have an important role in continuing to supervise and monitor the behaviours of their child or young person. Practitioners should therefore make every attempt to work with parents, explain the work being undertaken and to emphasise the positive benefits of their support.

Expectations about the supervision of the child or young person will need to be stated very clearly, alongside any necessary changes to family routines, such as bedroom sharing, or use of the bathroom. Practitioners should ensure that there are mechanisms or procedures in place to ensure that every family member has access to opportunities to feel safe in reporting anything they feel uncomfortable about. It is best that these arrangements are stated in writing. A detailed example of one of these agreements is provided in Alan's case study. The placement agreement outlined for foster carers in Chapter 5 may also be adapted for birth families.

The family assessment schedule detailed below relates specifically to family issues associated with the supervision and care of a child or young person with inappropriate or harmful sexual behaviour, and will comple-ment, and, indeed, is likely, to draw from and contribute to, other existing assessments – for example to those conducted as part of *Framework for the Assessment of Children in Need and their Families* (Department of Health et al., 2000). It is important for these family and child interventions to take place in an anti-oppressive framework, which respects both the child and adult's rights, whilst encouraging them to be proactive in their responsibilities. Some of the questions that need to be asked may be experienced as being intrusive and may, by some parents, be considered to be unnecessary. This underlines the importance of practitioners taking a transparent and sup-portive approach, giving full information about the relevance and impor-tance of the questions, and laying the foundations for future work that will hopefully be building on existing parental skills. Parent(s) have a critical role and have important and valuable information to share. Essentially a posi-tive strengths-building approach is needed, to establish parents or carers as key members of a team of people committed to assisting the young person to move away from harmful or inappropriate sexual behaviours. To sum-marise, the aims of the assessment would be:

1. To establish the extent of the parent(s) or carer's knowledge and accept-ance of their child's reported harmful or inappropriate sexual behaviours.
2. To engage and support parent(s), and assess the degree of their motiva-tion to cooperate with an assessment and support an intervention for their child or young person.
3. To assess the parent(s) or carer's willingness and immediate ability to set boundaries to reduce situations of risk.
4. Assessment of family dynamics and history, and the extent to which they may have contributed to the young person's harmful or inappropriate sexual behaviours, and the extent to which parent(s) or carer(s) are pre-pared to accept change.
5. Assessment of existing parental skills and aspects of current family dynamics that can be utilised to reduce the risks of further harmful or inappropriate sexual behaviours.
6. To build on existing parental skills and improve their knowledge and understanding of their child's sexual behaviours.
7. To look for ways of providing additional support for parent(s) in man-aging the difficult tasks ahead of them and keeping their children safe.

GUIDELINES FOR COMPLETING A FAMILY ASSESSMENT

The following headings are presented as guidance for the completion of a family assessment report. They should be preceded by details of family composition, the name of the young person and brief details of the harmful or inappropriate sexual behaviour, alongside details of report authorship, etc.

1. The Child or Young Person's Family and Social History

- Details of the child or young person's family relationships, identifying key attachment figures and any history of loss or bereavement.
- Details of sibling relationships and dynamics.
- Details of any key extended family relationships or key extra-familial adult friendships.
- Known details of the child or young person's peer relationships.
- The child or young person's education history and current school progress.
- Brief history of the child or young person's general health and development.

2. Level of Knowledge and Acceptance of the Harmful or Inappropriate Sexual Behaviour(s)

- Parent(s) or carer's understanding and knowledge of the alleged inappropriate sexual behaviours, how they found out and who else knows and how.
- The extent to which it is accepted that the behaviour has happened, and who the parent(s) or carers feel is responsible.
- The parent(s) or carer's attitude and beliefs about the behaviour.

3. Level of Discussion with the Child or Young Person

- The extent to which parent(s) or carer(s) have discussed the inappropriate or harmful sexual behaviours with the child or young person.
- The nature and context of the discussion, whether other children in the family have been talked to, and if not, why not.

4. History of Abuse in the Family

- Known details of physical or sexual abuse which the child or young person has experienced, and whether or not it was reported and what the consequences were.
- How the parents or carers perceive the impact the abuse has had on their child or young person.

- Sexual abuse experiences of other family members.
- Parent(s) or carer's general understanding of the impact of child sexual abuse.
- Other significant life experiences the child or family have experienced, and whether or not there is any perceived connection with the current harmful or inappropriate sexual behaviours.

5. Knowledge of the Child or Young Person's Sexual Behaviours and Development

- Parent(s) or carer's knowledge of the level of the child or young person's sexual development, activities and understanding.
- Parent(s) or carer's knowledge of the child or young person's experiences of intimate or sexual relationships with peers.
- The nature and extent to which sexual matters have been discussed with the child or young person.
- Parent(s) or carer's understanding of the extent of sex education the child or young person (and other children) has received, and where from.
- Parent(s) or carer's knowledge of any other sexual behaviours the child or young person may have been involved with, and whether they are considered appropriate or inappropriate.

6. Other Concerning Behaviours or Difficulties

- Other behaviours the child or young person may have engaged in or difficulties experienced. This could include alcohol or drug misuse, other aggressive behaviours, such as fighting, verbal abuse, bullying, deliberately hurting others, cruelty to animals and other antisocial behaviours.
- The extent to which the child or young person expresses care and concern about others.
- Any other difficulties or problems the child or young person has or has experienced – health and mental health, social skills, peer group or friendship problems, problems with intimate or sexual relationships, education, experiences of oppression such as racism or homophobic name-calling.
- The extent to which parent(s) or carers perceive the child or young person's difficulties as being related to the sexual behaviour problem.

7. The Daily Life of the Child or Young Person

- Parent(s) or carer's knowledge of the child or young person's friendships, including age and gender.

- Whether or not the parent(s) or carers consider these friendships to be age appropriate.
- How and where their child's time is spent with friends, and how much time is spent alone.
- The extent to which the parent(s) or carers are aware of their child or young person's whereabouts.

8. Protection of Other Children

- Details of action taken by parent(s) or carer(s) to protect other children from their child or young person's harmful or inappropriate sexual behaviour, both inside and outside the home.
- The extent to which they feel this protection is necessary.

9. Family Discipline and Control

- Details of house rules, privacy and family discipline, punishments, sanctions and rewards.
- How problems are approached and dealt with, and how conflict is resolved.
- Details of who exercises the most authority in the family and how it is articulated.
- Details of family relationships, whether or not there are any significant divisions or alliances.
- The extent to which difficulty is experienced in exercising discipline and control, boundary setting and so on, and the child or young person's acceptance of it.

10. Household Circumstances

- Details of the physical layout of the house.
- Where parent(s) or carer(s) and children spend their time, who sleeps in which bedroom, and where the bedrooms are located in the house.
- The use of locks and bolts, bathroom rules – whether bathroom and bedroom doors are knocked before rooms are entered.

11. Sexually Explicit Information

- Details of any use of sexually explicit materials at home, books, pornographic pictures, videos and internet, etc.

- The extent to which adult sexual intimacy, behaviour or conversation takes place in the presence or within earshot or sight of children or young people.
- The extent to which children or young people are allowed access to sexually explicit information, including unsupervised use of the internet.

12. Acceptable Sexual Behaviours

- Details of sexual behaviours considered acceptable for children or young people to engage in, and how this is allowed to vary according to age or development and gender.
- Attitudes and beliefs about gay and lesbian sexuality, again in relation to age and development.

13. Commitment to Intervention

- The extent to which the parent(s) or carer(s) are committed to the intervention plan.
- The extent to which they will continue to be involved and how they will support the young person's attendance of sessions.
- Whether or not other members of the family require any form of help or inclusion in the plan, including help for any child or young person who has been victimised.
- Details of any changes the family will make as a result of the discussions which have taken place.

14. Assessment Summary and Family Intervention Plan

- Statement of any risks or concerns identified by the assessment.
- Statement of the family's needs in terms of reducing any risk or concerns which may contribute to circumstances where harmful or inappropriate sexual behaviours may occur.
- Summary of the extent to which the family is willing and able to engage in a programme of work aimed towards preventing their child or young person from committing harmful or inappropriate sexual behaviours in the future.
- Detailed plan of how the family are going to be supported in addressing the gaps or difficulties identified by the family assessment.
- Details of how the family are going to be generally supported in managing and supervising their child or young person.

SUPPORTING FAMILIES OF CHILDREN AND YOUNG PEOPLE WITH SEXUAL BEHAVIOUR DIFFICULTIES

It is essential that an assessment of the family is followed up with a commitment to a plan of providing ongoing support and guidance. The gaps identified by the assessment will provide direction for the support plan, indicating the nature and extent of family intervention required. This is a strengths-based approach that seeks to build upon and enhance parental competences by the provision of relevant information – for example, about the extent and nature of sexual abuse; the particular circumstances of their child or young person's behaviour; how and why young people may seek to minimise or deny their harmful sexual behaviours; issues about young people's sexual development; or perhaps more generalised information about behaviour management and child care – this could include such areas as: promoting growth and stimulation, building positive attachments, information about child development, problem solving, conflict resolution, etc. Taking this encouraging approach conveys to parents a belief in the potential for a positive outcome for themselves and for their children.

It is important, as part of the assessment, for families to be provided with a 'safety plan'. The extent of this plan will depend on the nature of the concerning sexual behaviours, and whether or not there are younger children present in the household (see Alan's case after Chapter 8 for a fully detailed plan). In many circumstances this plan, or aspects of it, will need to be set up immediately, before the assessment is completed. This initial family safety plan can subsequently be modified as necessary, in accordance with information provided by the full assessment. A typical plan would include:

- The minimum requirements for risk management, in terms of house rules and supervision.
- A clear identification of actions that are 'risky', i.e. those behaviours or interests that could lead to further harmful or inappropriate sexual behaviours.
- Details of house rules – bedroom use, bathroom use, etc.
- Agreements about supervision.
- Agreements about meeting as a family to discuss the working of the plan.
- Details about each child or young person's opportunities to speak about the plan in private.
- Details of professional support to be provided to the family in managing the plan.

By involving, where possible, all children in the household, the plan conveys to all children the message that their future safety is being fully considered and taken seriously. Importantly it conveys to the young person who has engaged in the harmful or inappropriate sexual behaviour the message that the children in the family will be supervised and will have continued opportunities to talk in private. It also provides a structure for everybody and carries a message of trust and belief in the young person's ability to change, and that it is possible to manage the situation without anybody having to leave the family. It is helpful to emphasise that the 'family safety plan' is about professional and family partnership in managing a very difficult situation, the long-term aim being that the family become able to manage the plan without ongoing professional support.

CONCLUSIONS

This chapter has explored many of the issues involved in assessing and supporting the families of children and young people who have shown harmful or inappropriate sexual behaviours. It has described an ecological approach, consistent with the practice framework outlined in Chapter 2, emphasising the relatedness of individual, family, peer and wider social contexts. The chapter has cautioned against a pathologising or parental deficit approach and has emphasised the value of a strengths-based methodology, building upon parental competences, without losing sight of the important and essential need to ensure the safety and protection of children and young people. The chapter provided guidelines for the completion of a comprehensive specialist family assessment that complements other more mainstream child and family assessment structures. The assessment allows the practitioner to recognise existing parental strengths alongside an identification of gaps and learning needs. This in turn facilitates the formulation of an ongoing plan of intervention and support for the family, including, if necessary, a 'family safety plan' that provides a structured approach to ongoing risk management. For the child or young person who has committed the harmful or inappropriate sexual behaviour, the family assessment and subsequent support plans convey a belief in his potential ability to change, and develop appropriate sexual behaviours, and give a positive message about the future safety of all children in the family.

5

FOSTER CARE

INTRODUCTION

When foster carers provide placements for children or young people who have sexually harmed or who have shown inappropriate sexual behaviours, they are faced with a range of very difficult and challenging tasks. In managing these placements successfully, foster carers are required to deploy a high level of skill and patience, and will require a significant degree of professional support. Foster carers are having to balance constantly the need to manage the risks to others presented by the young person alongside the young person's need to socially and sexually mature into being able to meet his needs appropriately, without harming others. In these circumstances there are usually no legal restrictions on the young person's liberty. In most cases anyway, the young person is likely to have regular contact with other children and young people through school attendance. In these circumstances contact with others is managed by agreement and negotiation between the young person, the foster carer(s), schools and the placing social worker. It has to be said, however, that there is considerable compulsion on the young person to cooperate with such agreements, as without such cooperation it is likely that child protection procedures, or at worse legal measures to in some way restrict his liberty, will have to be pursued. This is, of course, dependent on the level of risk presented to others or in some circumstances the level of risk or danger faced by the young person himself. In managing these risks, it is clear that there has to be a high degree of liaison and cooperation between a number of people including the young person, parents, foster carer, social workers, teachers, foster care support workers, specialist workers and so on. This chapter will explore many of the difficulties faced by foster carers in these circumstances, and will discuss the necessary arrangements that need to be in place to support them, and to minimise the risk of the young person committing further harmful or inappropriate sexual behaviour. In particular the chapter will provide a template for a written agreement between foster carers and other professionals, which clearly identifies the nature and precise details of the young person's harmful or inappropriate sexual behaviour and specifies the necessary supervision and support arrangements to prevent its recurrence. Finally, the chapter will draw attention briefly to many of the issues highlighted for foster care having relevance for placements in residential care.

MANAGING RISK AND PROVIDING SUPPORT

Foster carers taking on placements of children and young people who have shown harmful or inappropriate sexual behaviours are immediately faced with managing, on a day-to-day basis, the risk of harm to any child they may have contact with: children of relatives, children of friends and neighbours or children not known to them. This places the carer in an important role in terms of gathering information, monitoring patterns of behaviour, reporting incidents, alongside providing support and care. Additionally it is likely that the carer will be central to the management of difficult family relations and contact. Carers are required to set and maintain strict boundaries throughout the placement, and will have a key role in assisting the young person with his relapse prevention plan (see Chapter 11). Carers are likely to feel the burden of responsibility for offence prevention. Skill and sensitivity are required in being able to carry out this important role, without giving the message that the child or young person is worthless or never to be trusted again, whilst at the same time not colluding with the child or young person's attempts to minimise or deny the need for such control. It is important for carers to have knowledge of the nature and scope of the therapeutic work being undertaken with the young person. Therapeutic intervention programmes need to be closely integrated with the life of the child or young person placed. Carers will have to face constantly the aftermath of a child returning home from intervention sessions which may have been difficult and challenging for the young person. The essential role of foster carers in these circumstances is to provide a safe and secure haven for the child or young person, and to build his self-esteem and sense of self-worth, which given his circumstances are likely to be quite low. Helping the child or young person in this way creates an essential foundation to enable him to have renewed faith in himself and his abilities, creating a belief that he can live his life and meet his needs without harming others.

Alongside the difficult and challenging task of balancing day-to-day care and control, carers are faced with the potential anxiety caused by having to be familiar with the harmful incidents which may have already occurred. Carers will require preparation for the potential personal impact such information could have. There may also be reactions from close family or friends with children. There is a potential for some of the carer's personal and social relationships to be disrupted by the practicalities of risk management, in terms of a placed child or young person's contact with other children. The surveillance and supervision required may entail constant dilemmas as tricky circumstances may require immediate decisions and action. Carers have to face the decision of who to inform and how much information is to be shared. This is likely to be a recurring problem as new situations arise.

The complexities of these placements require clear and thorough preparation and coordination. It is helpful for these details to be mapped out into a clear written agreement to be signed at the start of the placement by all parties involved with the placement, including the child or young person. It is important at this stage for information to be clear and systematically exchanged. Opportunity needs to be given for the concerns of all parties to be expressed and addressed. In order to guarantee the success of the placement and the addressing of all relevant issues, it is important for individual therapeutic work to be in place at the start of the placement. The placement agreement specifies the need for ongoing liaison between all parties throughout the placement. Particularly important is the balance that needs to be struck between the confidentiality of an intervention programme and the level of information which has to be shared in the interests of safety and offence prevention. The following specialist foster care placement agreement was designed by myself and has been used by the Sexualised Inappropriate Behaviours Service (SIBS) in Warwickshire for over 10 years.

PLACEMENT AGREEMENT

This is a partnership agreement between the foster carer(s), the social worker, the specialist therapeutic worker, the child or young person and other parties deemed relevant or appropriate, such as the parent(s) or possibly the link worker, or a member of the Youth Offending Team (YOT). All parties are considered to be part of an intervention team, with the child or young person at the centre. Together this team is working to minimise the risks the child or young person presents to others and to him- or herself. The written agreement will provide the following information to all parties concerned.

Details of Harmful or Inappropriate Sexual Behaviour(s)

1. Number of incidents.
2. Age, relationship and gender of victim(s).

3. Nature (detail) of incident(s).
4. Details of the situation in which the behaviour(s) occurred.

Legal Consequences

1. Details of police, court and YOT involvement.
2. Details of any criminal justice disposals made in respect of the young person.

Details of Supervision within Placement

1. Specified details of required supervision arrangements within placement.
2. Household rules about use of bedrooms and bathroom.
3. Specified arrangements as regards contact with family members, child relatives, other children and the extent to which this has to be supervised.

Other People Who Need to Know

Details of other people who (usually for child protection purposes) need to know about the child or young person's past harmful or inappropriate sexual behaviours, and potential future risks.

Intervention Details

Details of therapeutic intervention to be provided for the child or young person – frequency, location, name of practitioner and contact details. An agreement must be in place with the child or person, to undertake therapeutic work to address his or her sexual behaviour difficulties, unless this work has already been satisfactorily completed in the past.

Any Other Relevant Information

1. Details of support to be provided to the carers – nature and frequency, and who by.
2. Details of liaison between the specialist practitioner and the foster carer(s).
3. Details of any family contact arrangements, liaison with parents, etc.
4. Details of key contact person in school.

Signatures

The agreement is to be discussed, agreed and signed by all parties involved directly with the placement, including the child or young person.

PRE-PLACEMENT PREPARATION

Prior to the completion of the placement agreement, and setting up the placement, preparatory work must be undertaken with the child or young person. This work must make it clear that details of the child or young person's sexual behaviour difficulties will be fully shared with the proposed foster carer(s). It is helpful to frame this in terms of there being a foster carer(s) who, in knowing the full details of the young person's harmful or inappropriate sexual behaviours, is prepared to provide a placement to support him and help him to avoid repeating the behaviours in the future.

Similarly, prior to the completion of the placement agreement, and setting up the placement, preparatory work must be undertaken with the foster carer(s). This work must make it clear that the child or young person is aware that details of his or her sexual behaviour difficulties have been fully shared with the foster carer(s). At this stage foster carers must be told the full details of the risks presented by the child or young person, and the required level of supervision and monitoring. It is important to ensure that the foster carer(s) have received appropriate training, and have a good working knowledge and understanding of age-appropriate sexual behaviours, and are able to identify sexual behaviours which are harmful or inappropriate, and have awareness of some of the thoughts and processes which may take place alongside. It is also important to be satisfied that despite the full and challenging knowledge of a child or young person's harmful or inappropriate sexual behaviours, the foster carer(s) is able to accept him or her as a person, without judgement. It must be established that the foster carer(s) understands the importance of making immediate contact with the child or young person's social worker if they observe or have reported to them possible evidence of further harmful or inappropriate sexual behaviours.

Throughout the placement, it is important that foster carers will be able to continue to support and encourage the child or young person's attendance and cooperation with the programme of therapeutic work. If possible at this stage, the specialist worker may identify any specific tasks or defined aspects of support which will reinforce the work being undertaken, and contribute to the minimisation of risks. It is also important to ensure as appropriate that the child or young person's parents are kept fully informed of progress and, where necessary, involved in the intervention process.

SUPPORTING CARERS

It is important for there to be an agreement that throughout the placement, the child or young person's social worker will provide ongoing support for the foster carer(s), providing information about the progress of the thera-peutic intervention, and responding to any questions or concerns raised by the carer(s). The child or young person's specialist therapeutic worker must in turn provide the child or young person's social worker with sufficient information to allow the provision of effective support to the carer(s). Where appropriate, the specialist worker may wish to liaise on particular issues directly with the foster carer(s). It is also helpful for carers to receive inde-pendent support in their own right from a link worker from their own foster care support service, particularly at times when specific difficulties or per-sonal problems have arisen. It is helpful for all these separate workers to have regular liaison, and to meet as necessary together with the foster carer(s), to discuss and review the progress of the placement.

RESIDENTIAL PLACEMENTS

Many of these information and support issues apply equally to circum-stances where a child or young person with harmful or inappropriate sexual behaviours is placed in residential care. There need to be clearly stated poli-cies about the management of these behaviours and the supervision and pro-tection needs of other vulnerable children and young people. Professional residential carers will need to receive an appropriate level of training, and will require ongoing support. It is of equal importance in residential care for there to be a close liaison and sharing of information between day-to-day caring practitioners and the young person's specialist therapeutic practi-tioner(s). Again it is helpful, at the start of the residential placement, for all these factors to be detailed in a specialist written agreement, similar to the foster care agreement.

CONCLUSIONS

This chapter has explored the complexities of providing foster care place-ments for children and young people who have harmful or inappropriate sexual behaviours. It was recognised that foster carer(s) are faced with a dif-ficult and challenging task and have significant support needs in managing the personal impact of the work. It was recognised that it was important for these foster carers to receive appropriate training, and to be considered as essential members of a team of professionals working to help the child or young person make important and positive changes in his life. It was recognised that particularly at the early stages of a placement, and at the early stages of a therapeutic intervention, there are likely to be significant potential risks to other children and young people, and that it is important for a clear and explicit exchange of information between professionals, with the management of the placement and the progress of the child or young person's therapeutic work being closely integrated. To this end, the chapter provided details of a specialist written foster care placement agreement, to be completed and signed by all parties involved, including the child or young person. Finally, the chapter noted that many of these issues were equally relevant for residential or institutional placements.

Part Two

Therapeutic Intervention with Young Men Who Have Sexually Abused

6

ASSESSMENT AND INITIAL ENGAGEMENT

INTRODUCTION

In assessing children or young people who have committed harmful or inappropriate sexual behaviours, there is a need to establish their account of what has taken place, and to consider the extent to which this has congruence with what others have reported. In collecting this information, practitioners will from the outset need to simultaneously look for clues about the child or young person's abilities and competencies, and his willingness to avoid such behaviours in the future. A holistic assessment will consider the whole person, his life and his relationships with others, and will search for strengths within the child or young person on which to build upon his commitment and willingness not to harm others. The assessment will importantly need to keep at the forefront the immediate risks presented to others by the child or young person – setting in place adequate support and supervision arrangements for all parties involved. There is an obvious tension here, because on the one hand the practitioner is seeking to engage a child or young person in a therapeutic process that requires his agreement and cooperation, and on the other hand is potentially setting limits on his liberties and freedom, for the sake of protecting others. Clearly the extent of this tension will depend upon the level of harm caused by the behaviours, and the extent to which the child or young person acknowledges that they have taken place, and the extent he is prepared to take responsibility for what he has done. These are some of the essential tasks of an initial assessment of a child or young person who has committed harmful or inappropriate sexual behaviour. This chapter will explore some of the key issues in carrying out such assessments, looking at the difference between static and dynamic risk assessment factors, and the importance of balancing risks against strengths. Following this, the chapter will examine the process of initially engaging a child or young person in a process of therapeutic work, and derive a guide to the essential components of an initial assessment.

ASSESSMENT FACTORS

Static and Dynamic Factors

More simply, these are unchanging and changing factors. Static factors are the unchanging features of a child or young person's history, for example, an experience of being physically or sexually abused, past criminal offences, a previous history of sexual offending, its nature and when it started, etc. Dynamic factors are changing factors and include factors such as a person's lifestyle, his ability to make friends, his attitude towards his behaviours, or towards others, his self-esteem, social skills, etc. Static factors can be assessed on the basis of research knowledge about their statistical association with recidivism, and dynamic factors are more likely to be assessed by clinical prediction or therapeutic assessment. Ideally an assessment will consider both static and dynamic factors (see Hackett, 2004).

Predisposing, Precipitating and Perpetuating Factors

Predisposing risk factors include prior sexual victimisation, past abuse, family problems, poor social skills and low self-esteem. Precipitating factors include poor emotional management, thinking errors, poor impulse control, poor conflict management and fantasies about sexual abuse. Perpetuating factors include a lack of supervision, gratification from emotional or sexual releases, poor information about positive sexuality and gender shame. These can be more simply considered in terms of before, during and after – predisposing factors being historical, precipitating factors being quite imme-diate to the inappropriate or harmful sexual behaviour, and perpetuating factors being predictive into the future. Linked to these factors are four possible responses that determine the likelihood of sexual abuse being committed – self-managed responses, trauma-induced responses, com-pensatory responses and external supervision. These responses interact to determine the nature and degree of risk presented by a child or young person (Gray & Pithers, 1993; Araji, 1997).

Balancing Risks and Strengths

These approaches seek to arrive at a determination of risk by balancing a child or young person's risks against his strengths or assets. This approach has been taken by Gilgun's (1999) Clinical Assessment Package for Client Risks and Strengths (CASPARS), which is ecological in its scope, and identifies five domains which are essential to child and family well-being: emotional expressiveness, sexuality, peer relationships, family relationships, family embeddedness in the community. A child or young person's resilience – his ability to cope with and adapt to adversity and his ability to mobilise personal and social resources – will moderate his risk factors. Sometimes risks may override assets, and at other times assets may moderate risks. This explains the wide variation of outcomes in relation to single known variables, such as a prior experience of child sexual abuse. Gilgun identified four classifications by risks and assets – Type 1: High Assets/Low Risks; Type 2: High Risks/High Assets; Type 3: Low Assets/Low Risks; Type 4: Low Assets/Low Strengths. The aim of therapeutic intervention is to move children and young people into Type 1.

INITIAL THERAPEUTIC ENGAGEMENT

It is important to remember that even though a child or young person may have committed an extremely harmful act towards another child, he is still a child or young person himself. The practice framework in Chapter 2 allows us to understand aspects of the adult–child or adult–young person power relationship and translate it into meaningful action that will reassure him. It is also important to remember that the child or young person is likely to have suffered some form of abuse, loss or disruption in his own life, which may include sexual abuse. It is therefore imperative to adhere to the principles of anti-oppressive child or young person-centred practice from the outset. Approaches to practice need to incorporate a critique of dominant social constructions of childhood that emphasise innocence and powerlessness and move towards alternative discourses of empowerment, based on children and young people's competencies (Butler & Williamson, 1994; Butler & Shaw, 1996).

In attending a therapeutic session about having committed a sexually abusive act, or behaving in a sexually inappropriate manner, a child or young person may be anxious, embarrassed or possibly afraid of the process. The practitioner's awareness of this is best stated and addressed as soon as possible. Equally, a child or young person may deny all knowledge of his alleged behaviours, or may be attending under duress, perhaps as part of a legal disposal or criminal conviction, or at the insistence of his parents. In gaining a child or young person's trust, a transparent approach is essential. The child or young person needs to know quite quickly how the practitioner is going to approach working with him, and what the ground rules are. He needs to be told that the intervention is about him and that an attempt will be made to explore fully the circumstances that have led to his reported difficulties and behaviours. The child or young person also needs to know that he will be supported through the difficult stages of the work and that the approach is not about punishment, but is about empowering the child or young person in a manner which allows him to consider his mistakes and make important steps towards an improved way of managing his life, without hurting others.

It is helpful at this stage to have a written agreement outlining the nature and purpose of the work to be undertaken. This agreement should inform the child or young person that he will be undertaking a programme of work in relation to specified sexual behaviours, and that he will be asked to talk in detail about his sexual knowledge, thoughts and fantasies. The agreement should also address the rules of confidentiality, stating that, where possible, an appropriate level of confidentiality will be maintained. This is a crucial factor that will have a potentially significant influence on the extent to which the child or young person will feel able to take part fully in a therapeutic process, which will require him to discuss some deeply personal issues. In discussing confidentiality, the agreement should explain clearly that information relating to the actual or potential harm of the child or young person or another person may have to be shared with others in sufficient detail to ensure safety and protection. It is important to give clear examples about the type of information that would have to be shared; for example, if the child or young person discloses that a further child has been sexually abused, or that the nature of the sexual abuse he has committed is significantly different from what has been uncovered by the investigation. This may have both legal and therapeutic implications; it is very important to have prior multi-agency agreement about the nature and type of information that would have to be passed on for further investigation. It is also important to give examples of the type of information that will not have to be shared; for example, personal feelings and thoughts about sexuality, expression of feelings about other family members or issues that the child or young person specifically states that he would not wish to be shared. In these circumstances, if it appears that sharing such information would be helpful to him, then it will be necessary to explain why and negotiate the child or young person's permission to share it. In giving examples about confidentiality to the child or young person, it is helpful to discuss a range of varied examples from his day-to-day life. The written agreement with the child or young person should also clarify the legal age of sexual consent.

The practice framework reminds us that careful and thoughtful use of language is important. Carefully chosen language can be empowering and pave the way for a child or young person to begin to think in a more positive manner. Careless use of language can be oppressive and move the child or young person in the opposite direction of negative thinking and resistance to change. For example, it is unhelpful to use the phrase 'young abuser'. I often wonder about the damaging impact on the child or young person of walking into the premises of services that adopt this phrase or use 'adolescent sex offender' in their project title and on their paperwork. I recently read a report about a young person that had 'Adolescent Sex Offender Worker' under the practitioner's signature. We need to move forward on this and be more thoughtful and less oppressive in the way in which services are described. The framework allows us to see how language can invoke powerful discourses; these can be positive or negative. The phrase 'sex offender' or 'paedophile' carries considerable currency, and for a child or young person such phrases can potentially drain their confidence and belief in their own competence to move forward into an offence- or abuse-free lifestyle. The phrase 'young person who has sexually abused' is more helpful and less deterministic, as it immediately conveys a message of hope by separating the young person and the behaviour, whilst, importantly, not denying that the behaviour has been carried out by the young person.

There are many tensions at the early stages of this type of work. On the one hand, the practitioner will be attempting to remain child- or young person-centred, addressing the adult–child power dimension. On the other hand, the child or young person may be resisting engagement and denying difficult and abusive behaviours that the practitioner knows have taken place. The practitioner has to simultaneously engage the child or young person and assert an authority that states, in no uncertain terms, that his inappropriate or abusive actions have to be addressed. It is not really possible to confront a child or young person about his behaviours, in a meaningful sense, until some form of therapeutic relationship has been established. The child or young person has to be supported in being able to withstand the confrontation, otherwise he is likely to close down and only engage at a shallow level, if at all. The practitioner needs to convey a respect towards the child or young person, alongside a belief that he can move forward from his behaviours and be different. The rationale behind the practitioner's actions and statements needs to be fully explained at each stage. There may well be resistance, disagreements or blatant denial. The principles of motivational interviewing (Miller & Rollnick, 1991) are very helpful in managing this.

The goal of motivational interviewing is for the child or young person, and not the practitioner, to be facilitated to express concerns about the problem behaviour and to express arguments for change. The child or young person is encouraged to express both sides of his ambivalence and the arguments for change. The basic principles of this approach are that denial is a functional behaviour, and not a personality trait, and that motivation occurs in an interpersonal context between the practitioner and the child or young person. Accurate empathy on behalf of the practitioner is important; the style of the practitioner is a significant determinant of the outcome. Labelling and direct confrontation are considered to be unhelpful. The type of confrontation is more about confronting the client with himself; arguments are avoided, and resistance is diffused. In achieving this, it is helpful to express empathic concern about some of the immediate discomfort the child or young person may be experiencing, either about himself, what he has done or about other aspects of his life – for example, the impact of being moved away from home, or perhaps about family loss, or being bullied at school. The child or young person can then begin to understand and feel that the work to be undertaken is not about hurting or punishing him, but about helping him to make improvements in his life. The engagement process is the foundation of all work to follow.

GUIDELINES FOR COMPLETING AN INITIAL ASSESSMENT OF A CHILD OR YOUNG PERSON WHO HAS COMMITTED HARMFUL OR INAPPROPRIATE SEXUAL BEHAVIOUR

These guidelines have been derived from Gray and Pithers (1993), Araji (1997), Gilgun (1999), Calder et al. (2001) and Hackett (2004), and from my own practice experience. They are detailed under the following eight categories:

1. The alleged harmful or inappropriate sexual behaviour
2. Sexual history
3. Developmental history
4. Social history
5. Health
6. Educational history
7. Personality, emotional regulation and self-esteem
8. Summaries, risk assessment and therapeutic proposals

1. The Alleged Harmful or Inappropriate Sexual Behaviour

In coming to this work, the child or young person will be well aware that information is known about his inappropriate or harmful sexual behaviours, and is likely to be anxious about being asked to discuss them. Given that this is his likely anticipation and continued anxiety, it is best to alleviate some of this tension by discussing the alleged behaviours as soon as possible – the extent to which this will be possible will vary between individual cases. It is helpful to communicate that you are aware of what has happened, and that the work is about finding solutions and making improvements in the child or young person's life. These questions will also provide important information about the ongoing level of risk, and the child or young person's need for supervision, protection, reassurance and so on.

- What is the child or young person's explanation of the alleged harmful or inappropriate sexual behaviour? How does this match the investigation reports?
- To what extent does the child or young person acknowledge that he has committed harmful or inappropriate sexual behaviour?
- To what extent does the child or young person accept responsibility for the behaviour? Does he in any way attempt to shift any proportion of the responsibility on to the victim, or on to any other person?
- Does the child or young person attempt to deny or minimise the behaviour in any way?
- Does the young person have any explanation of why he committed the behaviour? To what extent did he derive sexual pleasure from it?
- What are the child or young person's perceptions of his parents' reaction and response to his behaviours? Do others know – what was their response? Do any of his friends or neighbours know about it?
- Was the behaviour preceded by masturbatory or other sexual fantasies? What were the child or young person's thoughts, feelings and actions before, during and after the inappropriate or harmful sexual behaviours?
- If the behaviour was repeated, how did the child or young person rationalise and justify it to himself?
- Did the child or young person say anything to himself in order to overcome knowing that what he was doing was wrong? How did he justify and minimise the behaviours in his own mind?
- Did the child or young person purposefully seek to harm his victim?
- What was the power relationship between the child or young person and the victim?
- What does the child or young person say about how and why he chose his victim? How did he get his victim to go along with the behaviour? Was there force involved? Was the victim 'groomed' into cooperation?
- What was significant about the time and place where the behaviour occurred – for example, to avoid detection?
- Are there times and places when the child or young person was alone with the victim and the behaviour did not occur, and, if so, how does he explain this?
- Are there times when the child or young person thought about committing harmful or inappropriate sexual behaviour but chose not to?
- What did the child or young person say to the victim in order to try to prevent him or her from telling about the abuse? Did he make any threats?

- What does the child or young person understand about the impact of his harmful sexual behaviour on the victim? Does he express any remorse? Is he able to express empathy towards the victim?
- Is the child or young person motivated towards changing his sexual behaviours by undertaking a programme of therapeutic work? Does he have the ability to change? How well has he engaged in the process so far?

2. Sexual History

Assessing a child or young person's sexual history will provide important clues as to how or why he has engaged in inappropriate or harmful sexual behaviour. Assessing sexual history will enable the practitioner to identify the extent of the child or young person's sexual development and understanding, alongside information concerning his sexual experiences, habits and patterns of arousal. It will provide information about the young person's sexual attitudes, the attitudes of his family and his sexual orientation, sexual preferences, etc. It will provide an opportunity for discussion about experiences of unwanted sexual contact, or exposure to sexual behaviour between others, or exposure to pornography. It will provide an initial opportunity for the practitioner to establish a dialogue about sexual matters with the young person. In doing so, it is important from the outset to establish a common understanding of the language to be used, acknowledging that people often find it uncomfortable or embarrassing to talk about sexual matters, explaining why this is currently necessary because of the young person's inappropriate or harmful sexual behaviours.

- What is the history of the child or young person's understanding of sexual behaviour – how and where did he learn about it?
- What is the child or young person's current level of sexual knowledge, and is it appropriate for his age?
- What are the child or young person's sexual experiences – masturbation, intercourse, etc. – and at what age were they experienced? Is the young person currently sexually active? What is the pattern and extent of his sexual arousal?
- Does the child or young person have sexual fantasies, and are they appropriate for his age?
- Has the child or young person ever watched or read pornography – magazines; video/DVD; internet? Does he use any of them for masturbation purposes? Does he use any of these materials now, and why? What is the young person's general attitude towards pornography?

- Has the child or young person ever experienced any unwanted sexual contact? (By embedding this question, phrased in this manner, with general questions about the young person's sexual history, it may be less threatening than a direct question about sexual abuse. It is a matter of therapeutic judgement whether or not at this stage to follow this up with more direct questioning.)
- Is the young person able to distinguish between familial love, caring and affection and sexual attraction and desire?
- What is the young person's sexual orientation? How does he describe his own sexuality? Has he had any homosexual experiences, and how does he feel about them?
- Has the child or young person ever experienced name-calling, bullying or any other form of oppression based on his actual or perceived sexuality?
- What is the child or young person's attitude to men, women and children? How does he perceive his own masculinity – what is important to him about being a man or boy, and why?
- Does the child or young person associate friendship, relationships, attachment and intimacy with sexual behaviour?
- What is the young person's understanding of informed consent in sexual relationships?

3. Developmental History

It is very important to have a good understanding of the child or young person's emotional and physical development, as a context for building an understanding of his pathway into committing harmful or inappropriate sexual behaviours. Depending on the nature and circumstances of the child or young person, and the behaviours in question, it may be necessary to have specialist medical assessments, for example, if there are suspected mental health issues, learning difficulties, speech and language difficulties, physical health issues and so on. It is important for these issues to be checked out with other key professionals during the early planning meetings that should have taken place as an initial response to the child or young person's behaviours. In a more generalised sense, these questions will build upon the existing knowledge of the child or young person's emotional, physical and psychological development.

- What are the child or young person's key developmental experiences?
- Does the child or young person's social and psychological development match his chronological age?
- Does the child or young person have any key attachments with adults in his immediate family or key attachments with adults outside the immediate family?

- Does the child or young person have attachments with his siblings or with other young people – relatives, peers, etc.?
- Has the child or young person experienced any disruption to his key attachments?
- What are the child or young person's most significant life events?
- Who does the child or young person consider to be the most important person or people in his life?
- Has the child or young person experienced any abuse – sexual, physical, emotional, social oppression, racism – inside or outside the family, including at school or in the neighbourhood?

4. Social History

As with developmental history, there may be existing knowledge about the child or young person's social history. These questions will give important information about how the child or young person currently functions in terms of friendships, social relationships, interests, leisure pursuits, attitudes and so on, and will provide clues about how he needs to be helped in meeting his future needs appropriately.

- Does the child or young person have any key friendships?
- Does the child or young person have any leisure interests or hobbies? How does he spend his time?
- Does the child or young person have any difficulties with his social relationships? Has he ever been bullied? Has he ever bullied others?
- Has the child or young person committed any criminal offences, particularly sexual offences or offences of violence against the person?
- Does the child or young person drink alcohol or misuse substances or take drugs? Why does he do this, and what impact does it have on his life?

5. Health

There may be some health issues that are directly relevant to the nature of the child or young person's inappropriate or harmful sexual behaviours. The presence of ongoing health difficulties will in most cases be likely to have an impact on the child or young person's day-to-day feelings about himself, his life and his social relationships.

- Has the child or young person ever had any significant health difficulties? Is he generally well at the moment?

- Does the child or young person take any medication, or currently receive treatment from a doctor?
- Has the child or young person ever had any mental health issues, including autism?

6. Educational History

In terms of the child or young person's abilities and understanding, these questions will provide important information about the level and pace at which the therapeutic work should be conducted. The child or young person's level of educational achievement will also have a significant impact on his current and future life.

- What is the child or young person's history of schooling?
- Does the child or young person currently attend school, and what is his current progress? Does he like school?
- Does the child or young person have any difficulties with his learning? Does he have any special educational needs?
- Does the child or young person have any particular difficulties at school – with his peers, or with particular teachers?
- Is the child or young person motivated to achieve well at school?
- Does the child or young person have positive aspirations for when he leaves school?

7. Personality, Emotional Regulation and Self-esteem

The child or young person's attitudes and personality will have a significant bearing on how he is likely to receive the work, and how he is likely to view the prospect of making positive improvements for the future – making positive personal and social relationships, attitude towards others and towards the victim, etc.

- How does the child or young person generally present in terms of his personality? Does he engage well? Is he generally friendly? Does the child or young person have a positive outlook on life?
- How does the child or young person view himself? Does he have positive expectations of others?
- Does the child or young person feel generally in control of his life and his actions? Does he feel he is allowed to make his own decisions? Does he feel able to do so?

- How does the child or young person feel about himself? Is he positive? Does he describe himself as being happy?
- Does the child or young person experience guilt and shame? Does he get angry? How does he manage his anger? Does he have a history of aggression or violence?
- Does the child or young person consider readily the needs and feelings of others, and how does this affect his actions and behaviours?

8. Summaries, Risk Assessment and Therapeutic Proposals

These questions draw together the overall conclusions of the initial assessment and set the future therapeutic agenda for the child or young person.

- What are the key or essential findings of each section of the report?
- What bearings do these findings have on the reported inappropriate or harmful sexual behaviour? How do they interact to precipitate elements of risk?
- What is the nature and extent of future sexual risk presented by the child or young person?
- What immediate measures need to be taken to manage, contain and reduce the risks presented by the child or young person?
- In response to these findings, what are the key proposals for future therapeutic work?

These are the key questions that will need to be established during the initial assessment. It is important for this assessment to be conducted in parallel with a specialist family assessment, as detailed in Chapter 4. The length of time taken to complete the assessment will often vary in accordance with the extent and nature of problems and difficulties uncovered, and with the child or young person's response in terms of openness and cooperation. Whilst this assessment schedule is structured and prescriptive, it is important to keep to an approach that recognises the uniqueness of the child or young person's life, circumstances, history and personality, as being the essential context of the assessment.

These assessments are complex, and practitioners should not be expecting to find single causes for children or young people's harmful or inappropriate sexual behaviours. The causes often amount to an intersection of many events and circumstances in a child or young person's life, creating a unique pathway to the behaviours in question. The assessment is about uncovering that pathway by exposing the connections between the different experiences, and explaining how they acted together to precipitate the sexual behaviours. If the child or young person has been sexually abused, it will be necessary to address the impact of this as part of the work. At an early stage, a decision will have to be made about when this should be done. If a child or young person is highly traumatised by his abuse, then this may have to be addressed almost straightaway. Whichever aspect of the work is being addressed, the other aspects will have to be kept in sight. It is helpful and important to inform the child or young person that most people who have been sexually abused do not go on to sexually abuse others, and that it is necessary to explore how the child or young person's experiences may have influenced his subsequent behaviours and beliefs. It is important to understand that a prior experience of sexual abuse is neither necessary nor sufficient in explaining the cause of sexually abusive behaviours (Grubin, 1998; Durham, 2003).

CONCLUSIONS

This chapter has explored many of the key issues involved in conducting an initial assessment of children and young people who have committed harmful or inappropriate sexual behaviours. Distinctions were drawn between static or unchanging and dynamic or changing risk factors. This was followed by an examination of Gray and Pithers's (1993) conceptualisation of predisposing, precipitating and perpetuating risk factors, and Gilgun's (1999) strengths-based practice that took into account children and young people's resilience as a potential mediator to risk. The chapter then presented some guidelines for completing an initial assessment. It was emphasised that it was important to keep to an approach that recognises the uniqueness of the child or young person's life, circumstances, history and personality as being the essential context of the assessment. Practitioners were also reminded not to be expecting to find single causes for young people's harmful or inappropriate sexual behaviours. Causes often amount to an intersection of many events and circumstances in a child or young person's life, creating a unique pathway to the behaviours in question. The assessment is about uncovering that pathway by exposing the connections between the different experiences, and explaining how they acted together to precipitate the sexual behaviours. Finally, in discussing the process of engaging a child or young person in therapeutic work, the chapter referred back to the practice framework from Chapter 2. The framework reminds the practitioner to address directly and specifically his or her power relationship with the child or young person. This necessitates an open and transparent approach to the work that maintains a high level of respect for the child or young person, whilst not losing sight of the need to challenge him about the harmful or inappropriate nature of the sexual behaviours he has committed.

CASE STUDY – NEIL (15)

Synopsis

Neil is a 15-year-old white British boy who lives with his mother Jan and his younger brother Ricky who is 11, and his sister Becky who is six. Jan was 16 when Neil was born. Michael, Neil and Ricky's father, died in an accident shortly after Ricky was born. From Michael's life insurance money, Jan was able to pay off the mortgage she had on their small house, but she was unable to work due to depression. Childcare commitments created additional barriers and forced the family to rely on state benefits. Four years later Jan met Ian, who at the age of 19 moved in with the family; he is the father of Becky. Jan described the family at this stage as being very happy. She saw Ian as having a good positive relationship with her boys; Neil in particular, who had been quite withdrawn since the death of his father, quickly became very close to Ian, who was Jan's first partner since Michael's death. Ian had a reasonably paid job with a local computer company; as a result the family were able to afford some modest holidays. Becky was born within 12 months of Ian joining the family.

Neil had a digestive complaint and bouts of chronic constipation and his mother took him to see the family doctor. Neil had to see a specialist for an examination, who raised concerns about the origin of scarring on Neil's anus. These concerns were referred to the Social Services Department. Following a planning meeting, the police and Social Services jointly interviewed Neil, whereupon he disclosed that Ian had sexually penetrated him. The sexual abuse was extensive and was sustained over a two-and-a-half-year period. Neil had been very reluctant to talk about what had happened to him. He did not believe that what had happened to him was sexual abuse; he described it as a sexual relationship that he felt he had instigated. He was nevertheless aware that what had happened was wrong. By this stage he had become very close to Ian, sharing many hobbies and interests. Jan had seen Ian as a devoted stepfather and was devastated by Neil's disclosure. Initially she reacted with disbelief – she simply could not believe that Ian would have done this. When the truth began to dawn on Jan, she responded by questioning Neil severely about how and why he had instigated the sexual behaviour. During the investigation, when the other children were interviewed, it was established that Neil had on several occasions exposed and masturbated himself in front of Ricky, and had engaged him in inappropriate sexual conversations. It also became clear that Ian had also spoken to Ricky about sexual matters in an inappropriate manner, and had shared some information about what he had been doing 'with' Neil. There was no evidence of Ian having any form of sexual involvement with Becky. Ian was convicted for the sexual offences he committed against Neil and received a six-year prison sentence.

Since Ian has left the family, Neil had become increasingly beyond his mother's control and had on three occasions been 'accommodated' by the local authority. Jan has expressed increasing concerns about Neil leaving the house and not returning until either very late, or sometimes the next day.

Jan has also expressed concerns about Neil continuing to gravitate towards his younger brother when he uses the bathroom, and that on some occasions, Neil had again exposed himself to Ricky and led him into inappropriate conversations about sexual matters. She expressed concerns about being able to keep Ricky safe from Neil. Additionally, there was a report from Neil's school about a series of incidents during a geography field trip, which led to rumours amongst the peer group, that Neil and his friend Barry had been having some undefined form of sexual contact. As a result of these rumours, Barry has broken off his friendship with Neil, who is becoming increasingly isolated at school, and is often absent.

Jan has often found Neil crying, and says that he has never really spoken to anybody about Ian, and often becomes more distraught when his name is mentioned. Neil has said that he feels responsible for Ian being sent to prison and that he feels that he should not have told anybody about the abuse.

Initial Analysis

• From the manner in which the sexual abuse was discovered, it is likely that Neil did not fully choose to disclose his abuse at this stage. He may have wished not to disclose the abuse at any stage. Telling about sexual abuse is often not a singular event, but a culmination of a lengthy process. When young people tell about sexual abuse, the telling is often preceded and contextualised by a period of high anguish, self-doubt and uncertainty, as the young person considers all the options and possible consequences of telling – Neil would have probably considered whether or not telling will be met with disbelief; the impact and family changes it will bring, both positive and negative; who would be the best person to tell and when; the possibility of others finding out, especially peers at school; what will everybody think of me; will people think that I am gay, and therefore blame me, etc. (Durham, 2003). Neil is now in the position whereby his disclosure has been as much a shock to himself as for everybody else. He may not be ready emotionally to cope with the consequences of the sexual abuse, or, as he saw it, the sexual 'relationship', being known about. Any approach to Neil must be very sensitive, as he may not wish to discuss the matter any further.

- Neil had lost his own father and had become very close to Ian – the abuse took place in this context, and was likely to have been planned and committed in a manner that made Neil feel that he was responsible. The evidence at the police interview suggests that Neil felt that he was in a relationship that he had instigated. If Neil believes this, then he may have fears about his mother's reaction to his betrayal of trust. The abuse was extensive and ongoing with Neil being set up to report for and ask for the abuse as much as being asked to do it – this is not uncommon in circumstances of abuse.

- It is likely that Neil will be very confused about many aspects of his life – family relationships and boundaries; how to trust people; when is a relationship abusive; his own sexuality – Neil is likely to be very confused about his sexuality – Neil may believe that he is gay, it may be that he *is* gay, always has been and that this made him more vulnerable to abuse. Equally he may well not be gay – this is an issue that will require sensitive exploration at Neil's pace, and consideration will need to be given as to who would be the best person to raise these issues with Neil.

- It will be important to be aware of the potential problem of conflating sexual abuse with gay sexuality – both for Neil and for those dealing with him – for example, responses at school to Neil will need to balance the risks between keeping everybody safe and not being oppressive towards Neil because he appears to be interested in boys. Insensitive approaches to these issues will further compound Neil's sense of being responsible for the abuse, and will further silence him, preventing him from finding true solutions to the problems and difficulties in his life.

- Neil may have worries about what will happen to Ian, and feel responsible for getting him into trouble. He may not wish for Ian to be punished, and may wish to continue to have contact with him. It may take some considerable time for Neil to accept that the relationship was abusive. This issue needs to be approached with an open mind as to how Neil may feel about Ian.

- Ian took over many aspects of the care and control of Neil (and Ricky) in a way that undermined his mother – Neil's mother finds it hard to manage Neil. Jan feels guilty for not spotting what was going on; her relationship with Neil will have been further strained by her initial disbelief and blaming of Neil. Neil may also believe that he has betrayed his mother, by having an 'affair' with her partner – fostering this belief may have been a deliberate tactic by Neil to prevent him from feeling able to tell anybody about what was happening. Both will require help in being able to see that they have both been victimised by the 'grooming' processes through which Neil was sexually abused.

- Neil must be responded to as being essentially a victim of sexual abuse, but it is important not to lose sight of his inappropriate sexual behaviours towards Ricky, and the potential of further inappropriate sexual behaviour towards others. An assessment of Neil must establish whether or not Neil's sexual behaviours are likely to fade, now that his own abuse has been disclosed. Balancing risks is about keeping Neil safe – protecting others from his potential behaviours whilst they are being addressed in therapeutic work. Neil will require help to bring his sexual behaviours under control; again this will need to be handled very sensitively, but in a very clear manner that confirms to Neil that sexual abuse is harmful, and re-establishes his understanding of appropriate family boundaries. This will be difficult if Neil continues to believe that being sexually abused himself was not harmful, or that it was primarily a result of his own actions. If Neil continues to believe that the sexual abuse was not harmful to him, then it will be more difficult for him to see how some of his sexual behaviours are harmful to others.

Case Plan

Neil – Post-abuse Counselling, Incorporating Therapeutic Work to Address His Inappropriate Sexual Behaviour

- Providing a non-judgemental opportunity for Neil to talk through his experiences, without immediately challenging misconceptions in his beliefs. The discovery of the abuse has been a trauma for Neil – it will be helpful for him to talk through everything that has been on his mind, and be given open opportunities to identify and express his feelings.
- Helping Neil to see and understand the abusive processes he has been through, placing blame and responsibility with Ian – tracing out the history of the abuse from Ian's perspective, speculating in detail how it was planned, using information from Ian's admission to the police, and, if possible, information from subsequent sexual offence specific work that may be undertaken with Ian. It will be helpful for Neil to be taken through Finkelhor's (1984) four preconditions of abusing – represented more simply as the 'Four Steps' – wanting to do it; thinking it is OK to do it; finding a time and place to do it; getting the victim to go along with it. When Neil understands that he has been exploited, and that what he considered to be a consenting relationship did, in fact, involve elements of sexual abuse – it is likely that he will in some way begin to feel the impact of being abused and will require significant support all round and during the therapeutic work – others will have to be informed about some of his struggles so as to be able to give that support.

- Helping Neil to understand that the abuse was not his fault, even though he may have asked for it to happen and experienced emotional, physical and sexual pleasure when it happened – disentangling the knot between Neil's feelings about his sexuality and sexual feelings and the abuse he experienced – helping Neil to cope with oppressive responses from others – clearing the ground as far as the abuse is concerned, so that Neil can think about his own sexuality in its own right.
- Assessing the ongoing impact on Neil of the trauma of the abuse and its disclosure – the extent to which Neil is troubled by flashbacks and intrusive memories, and the influences they have on how he feels about his sexuality and sexual behaviour.
- Sex and relationships education – an update and clarification of Neil's understanding and knowledge of sexual behaviour, sexuality and relationships, including issues about informed consent and the law – understanding the components of appropriate sexual behaviour – age, consent, responsibility, sexual attraction, sexual fantasy, etc. Helping Neil to explore and understand issues around gay sexuality, and if necessary help him to seek out appropriate further help from local gay youth networks. If Neil wishes, he can be provided with opportunities to meet other gay young people – youth groups, etc. – this would really need to come later on in the counselling when Neil is clearer about how he feels, and when he has had more time and information to think it all through. Generally making sure that Neil knows how to access local sexual health services. Neil may need reassurance about the confidentiality of this aspect of the work, with information only being shared with Neil's full agreement, the exception being information about someone, including Neil, being harmed significantly.
- Exploring and talking through in detail how, when and why Neil has been making sexual approaches to Ricky – analysing his thoughts and feelings before, during and after the reported incidents. Helping Neil to understand the impact this has had on Ricky – recognising the need to make a full apology to Ricky, thereby taking responsibility for his actions.
- Assessing the ongoing sexual risk that Neil may present to others. Providing Neil with techniques to manage his behaviours and keep him and others safe in the future. Neil needs to be assisted in becoming fully aware that sexual abuse is harmful. As stated above, some of this is closely related to helping Neil to understand how and why his experiences with Ian were sexually abusive, and that he was not responsible. It will also be necessary to explain to Neil how and why some of the rules of his household will be changed and managed, so as to set up safe boundaries and ensure everybody's protection. This will be sensitive, as Neil will be aware initially that he is the one being protected against. One of

the best ways to manage this is to get Neil to see that the changes are about undoing the problematic boundaries set up by Ian, and that Neil's acceptance of the changes is part and parcel of his recovery from being sexually abused.

- Exploring with Neil where he goes to at night-time and assessing how this may relate to his thoughts and feelings about the abuse and its consequences – explaining to Neil why this is causing concern, highlighting the potential risk he is facing, and helping him to seek alternative activities.
- Helping to raise Neil's self-esteem and confidence about being able to manage the aftermath of his sexual abuse and the impact it has had on his life and his family. Helping Neil to cope with the loss of Ian as a father figure, and exploring any resonance this may have with the loss of his own father. Helping Neil to find ways to heal his relationship with his mother, and to become more able to negotiate boundaries and conflict. Finding ways to find appropriate solutions to problems as they arise, and to ask for help when necessary.
- Assessing how Neil is feeling about his peer group experiences and how he is feeling about himself and his life in more general terms. Helping Neil to develop skills to solve his own problems, by breaking them down into small achievable targets. Helping Neil to identify and utilise potential sources of help and support in his daily life, identifying key people he can turn to for assistance. Pointing Neil towards activities that will help to raise his self-esteem and sense of being able to cope with and manage his very difficult and troubled circumstances.

Jan – Post-abuse Support, and Assistance in Managing Inappropriate Sexual Behaviours

- Setting up ongoing help and support for Jan in managing Neil, and being able to reinforce the messages he is receiving from the therapeutic work.
- Helping Jan to understand the nature of work being undertaken with Neil – both the post-abuse counselling, and the work on Neil's sexual behaviour. Also helping Jan to understand some of the potential issues Neil will be struggling with about his sexuality – emphasising the distinction between sexual abuse and gay sexuality. It may be necessary to help Jan come to terms with the fact that Neil is gay, and to understand how this may have made him vulnerable to being sexually abused by Ian. This work will have to be undertaken with full respect being given to the confidentiality of some of the work being undertaken with Neil.
- In a similar manner to approaches with Neil, helping Jan to understand the stages and process of sexual abuse, both in terms of Ian's 'grooming'

of both her and Neil, and possibly the rest of the family, and specifically concerning the sexual abuse committed by Ian against Neil. Jan must be left with no illusions about Neil being responsible in any way.

- Providing an opportunity for Jan to talk through the history of her relationship with Ian, and to discuss how she feels about the relationship now.
- Helping Jan to set up and manage safe personal and sexual boundaries in the household, so as to protect everybody from sexual abuse in the future. This is likely to involve developing a new set of house rules about bathroom and bedroom use, and setting up open opportunities for each member of the household to feel able to discuss any matter that concerns them, and to be able to report when they feel the rules have been broken or compromised. This will help all members of the family to feel safer, and to give an ongoing message to Neil that these issues can now be talked about openly. This work will inevitably involve some work with all members of the household, and will be an opportunity to discuss some of the relevant issues with Ricky and Becky (see Alan's case for a detailed example of a 'family safety plan').

Neil and Jan

- Sessions with Neil and Jan together to explore jointly some of the issues covered in their individual sessions, geared towards improving understanding and communication between them, and developing strategies to solve day-to-day conflict and other problems that may arise.

Outcome

Initially Neil was reluctant to undertake the planned work, and his circumstances at home deteriorated. In particular, his relationship with his mother Jan became very strained to the extent that the only communication that took place between them was conflict. Both Neil and Jan were independently feeling very guilty and responsible about the sexual abuse. This culminated in Neil having to leave the family home. On two occasions he was 'accommodated' overnight in foster care; on the third occasion that this happened, Jan refused to have Neil back home.

After three weeks in foster care, with Neil beginning to undertake the planned therapeutic work, alongside the work being undertaken with Jan, an agreement for his return home was achieved. Since this time, Neil continued to receive therapeutic work for a period of eight months, initially on a weekly basis, moving to fortnightly after three months. The full programme of work described above was completed.

Neil did have a strong belief that because he was gay, he had caused the abuse to happen, and that it was wrong that Ian had been punished. As Neil became more able to describe what had happened, it became clear Ian had fostered this belief in Neil. The abuse started by Ian entering the bathroom when Neil was in the shower, usually to either wash his hands or to get something. On some occasions Ian would get undressed in the bathroom, whilst Neil was in the shower, asking Neil to leave the shower on, so that he could use it straight after him. By doing this, Ian created opportunities to make sexual innuendo and eventually engage Neil in initially mild sexual activity, under the pretence that it was sex education and learning about growing up. At this early stage, Neil was told that his mother would be angry with him if she knew what he had been doing. Neil explained that he was particularly worried about this because from around the age of 11, he had often thought that he might be gay, and that what happened with Ian proved that he was. Over time, the sexual behaviour between Ian and Neil increased in intensity and frequency, with Neil fully confiding in Ian his feelings about being gay. All this was used to continual advantage by Ian, with Neil believing that he was the one who was instigating the sexual activity. By the time Neil was approaching 15, he was deriving a great deal of sexual pleasure from what was happening, and had absolutely no intention of telling anybody about it, least of all his mother.

When the abuse was discovered, Neil took the view that he had destroyed his family. Neil thought that he had wrecked his mother's life and destroyed her relationship. This was reinforced by some of the initial comments made to Neil by his mother Jan – she was also very confused and did not know what to think about Neil's sexuality and did wonder seriously whether Neil had started the sexual behaviour with Ian, especially as he behaves quite often in a very sexualised way – speaking in innuendo and exposing himself to Ricky.

As Neil's story unfolded it became clear that he was very uncomfortable and guilty about what had happened to him, but that he had great difficulty in disentangling this from the sexual pleasures he had experienced. Eventually Neil was able to accept that Ian had been his parent, and that it was wrong for this relationship to be sexual. Neil stated that deep down he had always known this to be the case, but that his guilt had not allowed him to accept it. As the work progressed Neil became increasingly aware that regardless of any physical pleasure he had experienced, the relationship had involved elements of sexual abuse.

As Neil began to understand and accept that what happened to him had been sexually abusive, he became more able to recognise the inappropriateness of his sexualised behaviours towards Ricky. From this point, these behaviours quickly began to subside – initially restricting and supervising the contact he had with Ricky had controlled them – over time Neil was able to demonstrate increasingly that he knew that his behaviours were wrong, and that he no longer had the motivation to commit them. Initially Neil had been resentful towards the idea of the new house rules, believing them to be unnecessary, but this changed as the therapeutic work progressed. Neil was able to take full responsibility for his inappropriate sexual behaviour towards Ricky and made a full apology to him – this was accepted and welcomed by Ricky, and the relationship between the brothers improved dramatically.

Both Neil and Jan were able to reunite with the belief that Ian had sexually abused Neil and that he was not responsible. With this belief, a great deal of the family conflict subsided, and there were improved family relationships all round. However, Neil continued to push the boundaries, and often stayed out late, occasionally overnight, but was much more able to account for his whereabouts.

One of the ongoing problems for Neil was that he had been immersed in sexual experiences (abuse) since the age of 12. On the surface these experiences had been increasingly pleasurable for Neil, leaving him with an appetite for more sexual experiences – he was nearly 16 and wanted to continue having sexual experiences. The task was to get Neil to appreciate how and why it would be better to explore this aspect of his life in a safe manner that did not lead to him being exploited again. In the individual sessions Neil confided that when he was 14, he had a brief unfulfilling sexual encounter with a girl in his school year, and that recently he had a short-lived relationship with a boy who was 17, but that they had fallen out before it really developed. Neil also stated that he did have an ongoing friendship with a male school friend that was becoming increasingly sexual, and that they had both on occasions managed to pass as 18 and gain admission to an adult gay nightclub. They were both secretive about this relationship at school, being afraid of the potential homophobic reaction of some of the other pupils.

As his school peer group was becoming quite hostile towards him, Neil welcomed the opportunity to join a local gay youth club, and took his friend with him, receiving support on a number of personal issues. Neil became increasingly clear within himself about being gay, he became happier, his relationship with his friend developed and improved, and Neil began to feel much better about himself. He was able to increasingly recognise by contrast the abusive aspects of the 'sexual relationship' set up with him by Ian.

7

EXPLORING PATTERNS OF BEHAVIOUR

INTRODUCTION

Many researchers and therapeutic practitioners in the field of sexual offending are in agreement about the relevance of cognitive behavioural methods (Salter, 1988; Marshall et al., 1990; Ryan & Lane, 1991; Araji, 1997; Calder et al., 1997; Hackett, 2004). These methods explore the connections between thoughts, feelings, physiological responses and behaviour; how behaviours are reinforced and what purpose or function they serve, or what need they meet in the individual. Therapeutic intervention, using these methods, seeks to assist the individual in understanding and developing a ready awareness of the interconnections between these processes, looking at thoughts, feelings and physiological responses before, during and after the behaviour being considered. The individual is assisted in identifying and recognising patterns of his thinking that have led to the problematic behaviour – how he perceived the outcome of his actions; how he justified the actions to himself; how he avoided information that may have prevented the behaviours from taking place. Most often these thoughts will include sexual fantasies that reinforced and increased the likelihood of harmful or inappropriate sexual behaviour taking place. The emphasis is on assisting individuals, in a very structured manner, to develop the skills to manage their behaviours in a wide variety of settings. The significance of 'victim empathy', the development of pro-social sexual values and attitudes, building self-esteem and more generalised social skills and the concept of 'relapse prevention' are closely allied to these methods and will be discussed in turn throughout the remaining chapters of the book. By presenting a range of useful practice materials, this chapter will specifically explore how the patterns of harmful or inappropriate sexual behaviour can be broken down into their component parts, and how doing this provides many opportunities for behavioural change – the 'Four Steps and Four Stops' is a child- or young-person-centred representation of Finkelhor's (1984) four preconditions of sexual abuse and 'Steps to Offending' is a further development of this; 'STFA – Situation, Thought, Feeling and Action' is a simplified behavioural chain; 'Patterns and Cycles' will explore some of the principles of sexual offence cycles, and will present a simplified offence pattern diagram that can be completed by children and young people, followed by a brief discussion of 'Thinking Errors'. The chapter will discuss finally the values and principles involved in helping young people develop appropriate sexual fantasies.

THE FOUR STEPS AND FOUR STOPS

The 'Four Steps and Four Stops' is based upon Finkelhor's (1984) four 'preconditions' model – developed further by Finkelhor et al. (1986) which was discussed in Chapter 2. The Four Steps are: (1) Wanting to do it; (2) Thinking it is OK to do it; (3) Finding a time and place to do it; (4) Getting the person to go along with it. These stages are illustrated in Figure 7.1, as steps on an ascending staircase.

The staircase is a helpful representation of these stages that can be used to assist the child or young person in understanding each individual step of his path to committing the harmful sexual behaviour. By using a page of flip chart or A3 paper for each step, a wide range of individual contributory factors can be listed or drawn. It is useful to keep these sheets available for future sessions, so as to be able to add on more details as more information emerges throughout the process of the work. Typically, wanting to do it (1) may have involved exposure to pornography; experiences of sexual abuse; distorted familial sexual boundaries; patterns of sexual arousal to other children; not being able to meet sexual needs – for a variety of reasons including lack of confidence or poor social skills, lack of sex education, peer pressures about sexual experience and sexual competence; unresolved feelings and anxieties – family based, for example, oppressive or violent par-

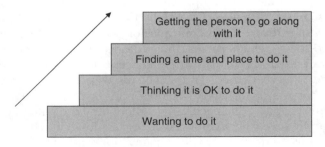

Figure 7.1   The Four Steps

enting; school or peer based, for example, displaced anger responses to being bullied. Thinking it is OK to do it (2) may have been influenced again by poor familial sexual boundaries; sexually abusive parental attitudes; sexualised family environment; beliefs about own experiences of being sexually abused; thinking errors employed to justify sexual abuse. Finding a time and place to do it (3) may involve being left to babysit; opportunities created by parental employment patterns; poor parental supervision; sharing bedrooms; loosely supervised shared play activities. Getting the person to go along with it (4) may involve being an older sibling or friend; being in a position of power; being a caregiver; victim characteristics, including disability, being scared; the use of bribes or threats; use of violence and intimidation. Whilst the Four Steps provide a useful framework, it is important to allow the young person's accounts to emerge as a reasonably free narrative, particularly at the early stages, rather than enforcing a structure on how the young person accounts for his actions. Once the young person has begun to feel comfortable in talking, the framework can then be used to guide and encourage further discussion. Once a picture has been built up of how the young person came to commit harmful or inappropriate sexual behaviour, the Four Stops can begin to be put in place to prevent reoccurrence of the behaviours in the future.

The most immediate stop would be to prevent the opportunities to abuse by providing close but subtle supervision and monitoring. By this stage of the work, this should have already been set in place. As the work progresses, the young person will hopefully become more aware of his risks and increasingly able to avoid such opportunities himself, alongside building up the other three stops.

The Four Stops are represented in Figure 7.2; these are essentially the inverse of the Four Steps – (1) Not wanting to do it, meeting my needs appropriately; (2) Knowing it is wrong to do it; (3) Avoiding situations where it could happen; (4) Knowing it would hurt my victim. In a similar manner to discussing the Four Steps, as a structured visual representation on large

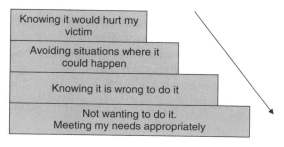

Figure 7.2 The Four Stops

sheets of paper, the Four Stops can be used to assist the child or young person in understanding the accumulating stages of an intervention programme – combining an analysis of all the factors that led to the harmful sexual behaviour with structured solutions of developing a better understanding of how to avoid and change these behaviours in the future. Not wanting to do it (1) may be achieved by not using pornography; assistance in recovery from sexual abuse; understanding appropriate sexual boundaries; sex and relationships education; changing patterns of sexual arousal and building social skills in being able to relate more effectively to other peers and to solve personal problems. Knowing it is wrong to do it (2) will overlap with some of this, and will involve having a better understanding of the impact of sexual abuse, breaking down 'thinking errors'. Avoiding situations where it could happen (3) will initially involve accepting and cooperating with close supervision and learning about situations that could lead to abuse and how to manage them. Knowing it would hurt my victim (4) is related to the other three factors and will involve having a clear understanding of when sexual behaviour is appropriate; issues of informed consent; and again, a very clear understanding of the impact of sexual abuse. Many of these factors will bear repetition throughout the course of the therapeutic programme.

STEPS TO OFFENDING

This is a further extension of the Four Steps, represented as a large staircase broken down into the individual statements – many of which would have been included in each of the Four Steps – combining circumstantial and family factors with individual thoughts and motivations as individual steps on a large staircase that traces in chronological order the individual steps that were taken by the child or young person towards the harmful sexual behaviours. This can include the young person's 'thinking errors' and inappropriate sexual thoughts or fantasies, alongside factors such as being bullied, or family problems, or any other relevant factor in the child or young person's life that can in some way be related to the harmful sexual behaviour. It is important to try to get these factors listed in their chronological order, with the thoughts and feelings adjacent to the various events. This allows the construction of a more unique and detailed pathway. Again it is helpful for the staircase – or alternatively a pathway or a spiral pathway – to be drawn out on a large-sized sheet of paper.

STFA – SITUATION, THOUGHT, FEELING AND ACTION

This is a cognitive behavioural chain that can be used to analyse the behaviours already committed by the child or young person, and also to assist him in avoiding particular behaviours in future, by becoming more aware of cues and triggers associated with the behaviour. The child or young person is asked to consider a particular situation that he may find himself in, or did find himself in, and to consider the interacting process of the thoughts and feelings that led to him embarking on a particular action. It is helpful to introduce and rehearse the process by using an example of a neutral aspect of behaviour, for example, the process of feeling hungry and eating, or not eating, as the case may be. So, after establishing what the young person's favourite food is, the situation is that he is walking down a road past a food shop that contains his favourite food, or that he sees an advertisement for the food – what does he think; what does he feel; where on his body does he have this feeling; and what action does he undertake based on this feeling? Alternatively the young person could be sitting in a classroom, experiencing feelings of hunger that lead to thoughts or fantasies about eating his favourite food, but because of being in the lesson, he is not able to take immediate action in response to his thoughts and feelings. There are some important points for consideration at this stage – whether the feeling or the thought comes first, why and how? How are thoughts and feelings related to each other? Why it is that thoughts and feelings cannot always be acted upon? Once these factors have been rehearsed with the young person, the concepts can then more easily be related to aspects of sexual behaviour. Again, it is helpful for the child or young person to be taken through some further rehearsal of the process by relating it to generic patterns of normal or neutral sexual behaviour – thoughts, desire, fantasies, physiological feelings and so on, before looking at the problematic sexual behaviours. Once the young person has demonstrated that he understands these processes, they can be applied to circumstances where he has committed harmful or inappropriate sexual behaviours or to potential circumstances where these behaviours could be committed in the future (see Chapter 11). STFA methods are closely allied to many of the other methods described in this chapter.

PATTERNS AND CYCLES

Sexual offence patterns and cycles of behaviour are also cognitive behavioural chains, involving the interplay between thoughts, feelings, physiological responses, inappropriate sexual fantasies, 'grooming behaviours' and thinking errors. The Four Steps and the Four Stops closely relate to the use of patterns or cycles, and both frameworks are often used in combination, and often appear side by side in the literature. The sexual abuse cycle has been described by Ryan and Lane (1991) as a sexualised expression of non-sexual needs at another's expense; a compensatory need to have power and control over another person in response to feelings of powerlessness elsewhere. Patterns of sexual arousal occur prior to the harmful sexual acts taking place. Being paired with abuse-related sexual fantasy and masturbation to orgasm most often reinforces this sexual arousal. The sexual excitement and anxiety reduction outcome of this process, alongside cognitive distortions or 'thinking errors', propels the individual towards setting up circumstances where the abuse can be acted out against a victim. Subsequently, further distortions and rationalisations allow the process to be repeated. The sexual offence cycle centralises issues of power, control and exploitation, and clearly locates conscious responsibility with the abuser. There is some suggestion of addiction and compulsion in Ryan and Lane's theorising, when accounting for how and why the cycle is repeated many times. Aspects of the sexual abuse cycle are very compatible with the practice framework of this book, which centralises issues of power, control, homophobia and compulsory heterosexuality, in its interrogation of masculinity.

When working with children and young people, rather than using the term 'offence cycle', it may in some circumstances be more appropriate to use the term 'offence pattern', particularly if the behaviour has been discovered at a very early stage. This avoids conveying inevitability that the harmful sexual behaviour will be repeated. It is also important to be very clear with the young person that the cycle of behaviour is an analytical tool that can easily be adapted to examine many other aspects of behaviour. As with SFTA, it may be useful to rehearse the process of the cycle or pattern in relation to another aspect of behaviour, for example, smoking, or taking food from the fridge that is meant for a family meal. Figure 7.3 presents a diagrammatic representation of a sexual offence pattern. The arrows between the main boxes represent 'thinking errors' that propel the individual to the next stage. The dashed arrow allows an option for the practitioner of using the framework as either a pattern, or a repeating cycle.

As with other materials presented in this chapter, the boxes can be drawn out on a large flip chart or A3 page, giving details of the specific informa-

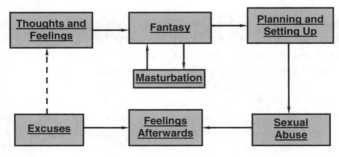

Figure 7.3   Sexual assault pattern (cycle)

tion provided by the young person. Again it is important to collect as much free narrative information from the child or young person about what has happened, before introducing the pattern as a means to shape and develop his account further, as a structure through which to develop his understanding of his actions, and provide important clues about how to avoid the behaviours in future.

Thoughts and Feelings – this box relates to the motivation to sexually abuse; the events and circumstances in a young person's life that precipitated the young person towards having the thoughts and feelings that led to him developing fantasies about sexual abusing. 'Thinking errors' form a bridge to the next box.

Fantasies – this box relates to the detail of the masturbatory sexual fantasies developed by the young person. 'Thinking errors' form a bridge to the next box.

Planning and Setting Up – this box explains precisely how the young person set up, or identified, circumstances that would provide an opportunity to sexually abuse without detection by others. This box will contain the details of what was said to the victim to get them to cooperate and not tell about the abuse. Thinking errors form a bridge to the next box.

Sexual Abuse – this box contains the full details of the sexual abuse that was committed, including how the victim responded to it. 'Thinking errors' form a bridge to the next box.

Feelings Afterwards – this box provides the details of how the young person felt immediately after having committed the abuse. Typically it will contain combinations of satisfaction and guilt. 'Thinking errors' form a bridge to the next box.

Excuses – this box will contain the post-abuse rationalisations employed by the young person to either repeat the behaviour, or make the decision to try to avoid repeating it, or perhaps to select another victim. Essentially, the young person will likely return to the thoughts and feelings he had at the beginning of the process, as the problems that existed at the beginning are in the main not likely to be solved by committing the abuse. The feelings gained by abusing will be mainly transitory, which explains why for some people the cycle of abuse escalates into many repetitions, only being stopped when the behaviour is detected and stopped, or hopefully when the victim tells.

From the pattern, some of the components of an intervention programme can be recognised: addressing the circumstances that led to the child or young person having the identified thoughts and feelings that led to his abusing, and helping him to respond appropriately to negative feelings in the future; assisting the young person in recognising and correcting the 'thinking errors' he employed to feel able to commit the abuse; helping the young person to develop age-appropriate sexual fantasies, and providing a comprehensive programme of sex and relationships education; helping the young person to accept close supervision and avoid circumstances where he could commit further sexual abuse; enabling the young person to be confronted with a full understanding of the impact of sexual abuse, both on his victims and also in a wider, more generalised sense; deconstructing any existing 'thinking errors' or post-offence rationalisations.

'THINKING ERRORS'

Much has been said already in this chapter about cognitive distortions or 'thinking errors'. These are essentially statements made by the child or young person to himself that excuse or justify committing harmful or inappropriate sexual behaviour. These excuses relate to underlying beliefs of the young person, and may play a direct part in the committal of harmful sexual behaviour. Some of these beliefs may relate directly to a particular aspect of behaviour, or a particular victim. Others will involve wider beliefs about sex and sexuality, beliefs about peers, beliefs about women and about masculinity, sexual entitlement and so on. These beliefs allow the young person to overcome his inhibitions and, as stated above, propel him towards committing sexual abuse. Most people who commit sexual abuse will know that it is wrong and harmful, and will therefore employ 'thinking errors' to make themselves feel better about what they are about to do, or about what they have already done. Typical 'thinking errors' include statements such as:

- I didn't mean to do it
- Just the once
- They agreed to do it
- I didn't use force
- It didn't hurt him/her
- They didn't say no
- It was only like a game
- It just happened
- I couldn't help myself
- I wasn't thinking when I did it
- They didn't tell on me
- They could have stopped me
- All girls have to learn about sex sometime
- It was like giving a lesson about sex
- I didn't fully penetrate
- I only touched them
- They did it to me
- They made me do it

- It happened to me
- It was very loving
- They liked it really
- They owed it to me
- It made me feel good
- It made me feel like a man
- Rape is only when they say no
- They were going out with me
- He's gay so he wanted me to do it

These statements can be listed or printed on to sort cards for the young person to select and place in order of relevance and significance. They can be used as statements to write alongside the connecting arrows on the offence pattern diagram. It is important to include some blank cards, or some space on a list for additional comments that may not have been included. Again, as with many of the materials in this chapter, it is important to allow the young person to explain his own thoughts associated with the harmful sexual behaviour, before using the cards, or the list, to prompt further discussion. Once these 'thinking errors' have been listed or chosen, the meaning behind each one can be discussed, challenged and corrected to compile a list of *thinking truths* along the line of:

- It was harmful
- I did hurt them
- They didn't have any choice
- They were too scared to tell
- I forced them into it
- I knew what I was doing
- I wanted to do it for me
- I knew it was wrong
- They did not agree
- It was rape
- It was my fault, not theirs
- There was no excuse for what I did

CHANGING SEXUAL FANTASIES

This chapter has established that sexual fantasies can play a very significant part in the process of sexual offending; when paired with the physiological response to masturbation they can provide a very powerful behavioural reinforcement that is sufficient to propel a young person into setting up circumstances and acting out the harmful sexual behaviours featured in the fantasy (Calder et al., 1997). From my own therapeutic practice experience of talking to many young people who have been through this process, I am aware that quite often these fantasies will have been masturbated to, possibly many times, and will be deeply ingrained into the memory of the young person. Even after being caught, and suffering all the negative consequences of their behaviours – perhaps including extreme consequences such as family rejection and having to move into public care – these fantasies will persist, and will be triggered by subsequent feelings of sexual arousal and other factors associated with the sexual abuse that has been committed, for example, a television news feature about paedophiles or child sexual abuse. It is important to ensure that the young person understands that it is critical that he no longer engages in masturbating to inappropriate sexual fantasies, as these are the precursors to acting out further harmful sexual behaviours. It is therefore important that he is taught how to manage these fantasies, by pairing them with negative consequences – for example, a memory and associated feelings of the police interview about his abusing, or school friends walking in on the sexual abuse scene featured in the fantasy – and developing alternative age-appropriate positive sexual fantasies that are able to meet his sexual needs.

The young person will be aware that there are social taboos about discussing these issues, which is why it is important at the early stages of the work to fully inform the young person and his parents or carers about the explicit nature of some of the work that needs to be undertaken, and why it is necessary. It is also important for practitioners to be working under a framework of formally endorsed protective agency policies that recognise, in a generalised sense, the explicit nature of the work that needs to be undertaken in assisting children and young people to avoid repeating harmful or inappropriate sexual behaviours.

Many young people will find this area of the work difficult to talk about, and may be reluctant even to admit to masturbation, yet alone talking about their sexual fantasies, particularly those that are abuse-related. It is important to inform the young person that masturbation and sexual fantasies are natural, particularly during adolescence, and that they happen to most people. The young person will ideally be helped to understand that appropriate and positive sexual fantasies are mutual and consenting, and that they involve behaviour with people of a similar age or older than the young person. These fantasies must continue to have meaning for the young person and will therefore need to be sexually arousing for him. It does not really matter whether the fantasies are impossible – pop stars, etc. – or whether they are achievable – about somebody in their class at school. The components of an appropriate fantasy will need to match sexual behaviour that is appropriate and legal, and will ideally include details of a scenario and a relationship history, rather than focusing purely on sexual activity. The sexual activity itself will need to be mutual, and attention must be paid to consent, communication by body language, and relationship building. The fantasised sexual activity itself should involve varied roles of initiation and non-initiation. It is helpful to give permission to the young person to fantasise about either gender. These fantasies must not include any aspects of violence, abuse, non-consenting or age-inappropriate relationships and behaviour. If the young person has understanding, and a repertoire of effective positive sexual fantasy, he has something to replace those fantasies that led or are likely to lead to harmful sexual behaviours.

CONCLUSIONS

This chapter has explored a range of cognitive behavioural interventions for children and young people who have committed harmful or inappropriate sexual behaviours. It has presented a range of useful practice materials that have allowed patterns of harmful or inappropriate sexual behaviour to be broken down into their component parts, providing opportunities and ideas for assisting children and young people to engage in behavioural change – the 'Four Steps and Four Stops' was a child- or young-person-centred representation of Finkelhor's (1984) four preconditions of sexual abuse and 'Steps to Offending' was a further development of this; 'STFA – Situation, Thought, Feeling and Action' was a simplified behavioural chain; 'Patterns and Cycles' explored some of the variations of sexual offence cycles that have been developed. This was followed by a brief discussion of 'Thinking Errors', followed by 'Changing Sexual Fantasies' which discussed the values and principles involved in helping young people develop appropriate sexual fantasies. The chapter has emphasised that it is important to locate these methods within the wider practice framework of the book, so as to maintain a positive engagement of the child or young person, and not to lose sight of the wider influences on children and young people's decisions to engage in harmful or inappropriate sexual behaviours.

CASE STUDY – TONY (14)

Synopsis

Tony is a 14-year-old white British boy who lives with his mother, Linda, his father, Mark, his twin sisters Sally and Susan who are 21, and his younger sister Helen who is seven years old. The family live in a small rural town. Linda and Mark work together for a domestic products distribution company and work long hours. They are often away from home until late into the evening. During term time, Sally and Susan live away from home at college, and Tony is often left to look after Helen; he often cooks her tea, entertains her and puts her to bed before her parents return from work. Tony's maternal aunt contacted the Social Services Department to report that Helen had told her that last weekend, when her parents were out and Tony was left in charge, he had taken his clothes off and lay down on top of her. Helen said that Tony had done this several times before and she had told her mum and dad about this, and they had 'told Tony off'.

Helen was jointly interviewed on video, by the police and Social Services. At this interview she became very upset, and said that she did not want to get Tony into more trouble, but eventually she was able to talk about what had happened to her. She described how Tony had committed sexual acts against her on at least five occasions. These acts included Tony encouraging Helen to watch pornographic films and getting her to masturbate him and suck his penis, and simulating intercourse. She said that last Easter (nine months ago), she had told her parents about what Tony had done, and that her father had shouted at him and punished him by taking away and selling his possessions, and smacking him. Helen has said that she loves Tony, and that most of the time he is kind to her, and continues to look after her when her parents are at work.

Helen's parents do not deny being told about these behaviours by Helen before, and admit that Mark took matters into his own hands and punished Tony. They believed that at this point the matter was closed and that there was no need to involve others from outside the family. Tony's father, Mark, described not being able to trust Tony outside the house, as he often mixes with the 'wrong sort of people'. Eighteen months ago, Tony was caught trying to steal a packet of biscuits from the local shop. Mark knew the owner of the shop and there was no involvement of the police. Since this incident, Mark says that he has felt even more justified in keeping Tony in, to prevent him from getting a criminal record. As a result Tony spends most of his free time either in the house or in the garden, rarely seeing his friends. Mark explained that he had a great deal of conflict with Tony, often about Tony not doing household jobs, and 'answering back'. Tony's mother Linda has a better relationship with him, but has said very little during the investigation, apart from that she has tried to persuade Tony not to annoy his father, and to do the jobs he asked him to do.

Tony was interviewed by the police and admitted committing the offences, saying he did not mean to hurt his sister and that he was sorry. Tony explained to the police that he had been watching explicit pornographic films at home, which he had taken from his father's collection, some in the lounge and some from his father's bedroom. Tony described these films as involving explicit sexual acts and sometimes sexual violence and sexual scenes involving animals. Tony also admitted to watching pornographic material on the internet at home. He said that he believed his father also watched internet pornography, as he had found sites listed in the computer's history, and that his dad does not know enough about computers to know how to delete them. Tony was distraught, and after the interview he refused to return home, saying that his father would kill him, now that he has admitted using the computer and going into his father's room, which was strictly forbidden.

Upon hearing that Tony had admitted the offences, Mark has said that Tony could no longer live with them at home, and that very soon, when the twins leave home, the family will be moving to a smaller house in another town, and there will no longer be room for him. Mark said that he always knew it would only be a matter of time before Tony did something else wrong and that he was ashamed to call him his son. Initially Mark denied having pornographic films and, in confirmation of what Tony had said at his interview, became very angry when he heard that Tony had been in his bedroom. At this point Mark said that if he saw Tony again he would 'go for him'. This prompted the police to warn him that they were aware that he had threatened his son with violence, and that they would take action against him should he carry out his threat. When the police later asked to see the pornographic films, Tony informed them that they had all been destroyed. The police examined Mark's computer and found some of the materials described by Tony. There were no files found that could lead to a prosecution, but some of the material dated back three years, which was before the period when Tony would have had use of the computer. Mark denied looking at this material, as he had denied ownership of the pornographic material, saying that Tony must have brought them into the house.

Tony was 'accommodated' under the Children Act 1989 by the Social Services Department and placed in foster care in a nearby town. Tony continues to attend his school where he is reported to be a model pupil, having very good relationships with staff, and reasonable academic attainment. However, it was reported that his self-esteem was low, and that there have been problems in relation to his peer group. Tony has on several occasions been bullied, and is often called names to the point that he cries. Tony said that one of the reasons why he had watched pornography and wanted to have sex was to have something to say about himself to earn more 'respect' from some of the people that were bullying him. Tony went on to say that he is always being called 'immature' and 'little boy', and that some of the bullies say that he will never get a girlfriend. The school have never been able to engage Tony's parents in assisting them with this problem.

Tony is quite small and immature for his age, and until 12 months ago had a bed-wetting problem. He is distraught at having to live away from his mother and sister, but is relieved to be away from his father, who he feels he has never really got on with, particularly since the birth of his sister. Tony has described his father as being volatile and having a violent temper, saying that, until recently, his father quite frequently smacked him, sometimes across the face. Tony said that two months ago he had asked his father if he could have a paper round, and had gone for an interview and been given the job, which he did for a week up to the point when his father kept him in again and he lost the job. Tony has said that his father has told him that he is not good at anything and will never be able to get a job or look after himself when he is older. Tony says that he dislikes his father and is afraid of him. Tony says that his mother would let him have the freedom to do more things, but that she is also afraid of his father and has also been hit by him. Tony says that he has never seen Mark hit Helen, and that he does not believe that he would, as he calls her 'his little princess' and favours her above everybody.

Helen has told her parents and the police that she does not wish to go to court and speak against Tony. Tony was charged and was convicted for the offences after pleading guilty in court and was ordered to sign the sex offender's register for two and a half years. He received a community-based order, on the basis that he will receive specialist therapeutic help from the Social Services Department, which will challenge and explore his sexually abusive behaviours. The court was informed of Tony's family circumstances and his recent move into foster care.

Initial Analysis

● Tony has committed a range of very serious sexual offences against his sister, and now has a permanent criminal record. Under the Sexual Offences Act 2003 he would have been charged with 'rape', because of the oral penile penetration. He will require a full programme of therapeutic work, looking at both offence-related matters and the wider issues in his family that will have inevitably influenced his behaviour.

● Mark and Linda failed to report the first incident of sexual abuse to the authorities, and failed to adequately protect Helen, by allowing Tony to continue to look after her on his own, and by not seeking help and advice in response to her being sexually abused. The punishment given to Tony was unhelpful and inappropriate, as it in no way addressed any of the issues behind his behaviour.

● There are serious child protection and domestic violence issues in the family that need to be addressed, alongside the need for work with Tony.

● Tony has witnessed and experienced violence and cruel emotionally abusive treatment from his father over a long period of time. The issue of

Mark's power and control in the family was epitomised by his disproportionate response to hearing that Tony had been in his bedroom. This
reaction may also have been related to Tony disclosing that his father had
a collection of explicit pornography in the house.

- There is evidence that Tony's sexual offences may have been a retaliatory
  response to this violence. Tony may have sought revenge against his
  father by sexually abusing Helen. Mark has made it clear to Tony that he
  favours Helen.
- The sexual abuse was planned and executed at a time and place to avoid
  detection. Prior to committing the abuse, Tony had been watching pornography – suggesting that this fed into his sexual arousal, perhaps giving
  him some of the ideas he carried out in the abuse. Tony also used the
  pornography to introduce and 'normalise' these ideas to Helen.
- Tony has been exposed to a role model of male behaviour based on exercising power and control through fear and violence. This may have influenced Tony's beliefs and understanding about his own masculinity, and
  may have had an influence on his beliefs and understanding of sexual
  behaviour. At every point in Tony's life it appears that he has been put
  down and criticised by his father. This appears to have impacted significantly on his self-esteem and confidence.
- Tony has been kept inside and not allowed to mix and experience normal
  relationships and friendships with his peers. This will have restricted the
  development of his social skills, and reduced his confidence in being able
  to make intimate relationships. Tony will require help in building up his
  self-esteem and developing social skills.
- Tony potentially presents significant sexual risks to other children, and
  has now been placed in foster care. Until these risks can be assessed and
  addressed, Tony must not be allowed to have unsupervised contact with
  other children.
- Tony's foster carers will require help and guidance in understanding
  young people's sexually abusive behaviours, and will need to have full
  information about what has happened and the nature of the risks presented by Tony. They will require ongoing help and support throughout
  the placement.

Case Plan

Mark and Linda

There are many outstanding issues relating to Mark and Linda's parenting
of Tony and Helen. Work will need to be undertaken with them to explore
why they decided not to report Helen's sexual abuse when it first happened,

and whether or not they would report it in the future. There are domestic violence issues that need to be handled very sensitively. Linda will need to be asked in confidence about what Tony has said about her being hit and the extent to which this is happening.

Both Mark and Linda will need to be told about what Tony has said in his interview about the pornography. Discussions will have to take place about the link between the pornography and the sexual abuse, alongside a consideration of the potential impact on Helen, of having pornography in the house, should she discover it, or become aware that it is being watched.

There will also need to be discussions about Mark's disproportionate parenting and violence towards Tony. Although Mark has said that he wishes to have no contact with Tony, this is an area that will need to be worked upon. There may be improvements with the passage of time. There are therefore no immediate plans for Tony to return to live with the family.

Mark and Linda will need to be advised about how they can now best help Helen in her recovery from the sexual abuse. It will be important for them to remember that Helen is still very fond of Tony and will miss him, and will possibly be blaming herself for him having to leave the family. They will also need to reassure Helen that she can still tell them about anything that makes her feel uncomfortable or unhappy.

It will also be important to remind Mark and Linda that Helen's perception of the sexual abuse will be very different from theirs, and to help them understand the implications of this in terms of making developmentally appropriate responses, and of concealing their anger and anxieties from her. Equally Mark and Linda need to be aware that Helen's understanding will move closer to theirs as she get older and begins to understand more about sexual behaviour.

Therapeutic Work with Helen

A separate plan of therapeutic support will need to be offered to Helen, whereby she will be helped to talk through her memories and express her feelings, and receive comforting information about keeping safe in the future. This approach of this work will be similar to that described in the work for Paul, Stuart and Louise in Alan's case (see also Durham, 2003). This work is somewhat complicated in that Mark and Linda have already failed to protect Helen, and the 'keeping safe' information will be contradictory to how they responded when she first reported being sexually abused by Tony. This will have to be talked through with Mark and Linda, who will need to then further help Helen, by supporting and reinforcing the new 'keeping safe' messages being given to Helen.

Foster Carers

The issues for foster carers who look after children with sexual behaviour problems are discussed fully in Chapter 5 and practice issues are discussed more fully in Stephen and Graham's case. The most important point for Tony's case is that the carers are provided with adequate information about the circumstances of his harmful sexual behaviours. The placement agreement described in Chapter 5 will need to be completed and liaison work will need to be undertaken with the foster carers to ensure that they are kept fully up to date with the therapeutic issues being worked through with Tony, and how they can reinforce his learning through their day-to-day interaction with him. At this stage, Tony will need to be placed in a foster home where there are no other children. This placement will be very difficult for the foster carers, as the risks presented by Tony will need to be managed at all times. A completed placement agreement would look like this:

Details of Inappropriate Sexual Behaviour(s)

(Details of inappropriate or harmful sexual behaviour in terms of: (1) number of incidents; (2) age, relationship and gender of victim(s); (3) nature (detail) of incidents; and (4) the situation in which the behaviour(s) occurred.)

Tony has sexually abused his seven-year-old sister on at least five separate occasions. All of these incidents occurred when Tony was left alone to babysit Helen in the house. Some of the incidents occurred in the lounge and some in the bedroom. The sexual abuse involved Tony encouraging Helen to watch pornographic films and getting her to take off her clothes and masturbate him and suck his penis. It also involved 'simulated sexual intercourse' – whereby Tony lay on top of Helen whilst they were naked. It is not thought that vaginal or anal penetration took place.

Legal Consequences

(Details of police, court and youth justice involvement, etc.)

Tony was convicted in magistrates' court and was sentenced to a 12 months referral order. He will initially be visited weekly and will undertake work as requested by the Youth Offending Team. This is to be carried out by a local specialist (see intervention details below).

Details of Supervision within Placement

(Details of special arrangements within placement, for example: house rules; special arrangements as regards contact with family members, child relatives, other children; the extent to which this is to be supervised.)

- Tony must not be left unsupervised with any child younger than himself at any time.
- Tony's contact with same-age children and above will need to be closely monitored.
- Foster carers will as far as possible need to be informed by Tony of his whereabouts at all times.
- Tony must have no contact with his family without the involvement of his social worker.
- Tony's use of the computer must be supervised.

Other People Who Need to Know

(Details of other people who for child protection purposes need to know that the child or young person has initiated inappropriate sexual behaviour.)

A key person – Mr Smith (Tony's form tutor at school, – has been informed about Tony's offences and his move into foster care and he is the contact point with the school for all matters. No other people should be informed about Tony's sexual offences without the involvement of Tony's social worker or other members of the Social Services Department.

Intervention Details

(Details of intervention to be received, frequency, location, name and contact point for specialist worker.)

Tony will meet with the specialist worker once a week at Smith Street Offices to undertake therapeutic work that will work through issues of Tony's sexual offending and future management of risk, and other related issues, particularly in relation to his family.

Does the Child or Young Person Agree to Cooperate with the Intervention Plan?

Yes.

Any Other Relevant Information

Tony's father has said that he does not wish to see him again and has threatened to hit Tony if he sees him. Any contact between Tony and his family must be arranged through his social worker.

Signatures

Child or Young Person:
Specialist Worker:
Social Worker:
Carer(s):

Tony – Therapeutic Offence-related Work Incorporating Work Looking at Wider Personal and Family Issues

The therapeutic plan for Tony will involve all of the following components:

- Tony's explanation of the sexual abuse he committed, and how this compares to the account given by Helen – challenging Tony over any serious inconsistencies, denial or minimisations and promoting his acceptance of full responsibility for his actions.
- Exploring Tony's sexual history and level of sexual knowledge, and how it was obtained, identifying attitudes to sexuality, sexism, sexual stereotyping.
- Detailed exploration of Tony's sexually abusive behaviour using cognitive behavioural analysis to explore his predispositions to sexual offending, his offence patterns, his 'thinking errors' and supporting sexual fantasies – thoughts and feelings before, during and after the offences – (see 'outcome' below).
- Exploring the significance of Tony's use of pornography prior to his sexual offending.
- Helping Tony to fully appreciate the impact of his sexually abusive behaviour on Helen, and how she may view this in the future.
- Exploration of Tony's own victim experiences, and responses to trauma and stress, in particular his relationship with his father.
- Comprehensive sex and sexuality education – establishing a baseline of age-appropriate sexual knowledge, exploring sexism, gender and sexual stereotyping; sexuality, sexual identity and sexual orientation.
- Examining appropriate sexual behaviour, informed consent and the law.
- Exploration of Tony's current sexual motivations, interests and fantasies.
- Exploring issues of power, control and masculinity and how they may influence sexual relationships.

- Exploration of Tony's friendships, peer relations and feelings about intimate relationships.
- Family relationships and dynamics, and patterns of attachment, again particularly focusing on Tony's relationship with his father, but also helping Tony explore how his father's control of the family influenced the relationship he had with his mother.
- Problem solving, anger management, feelings recognition and positive thinking – building on personal strengths to raise self-esteem.
- Encouraging Tony to become more open and to express his feelings more accurately.
- Helping Tony come to terms with leaving his family and living in foster care.
- Relapse prevention – identifying and avoiding high-risk situations; changing or modifying fantasies – practising self-management.

Outcome

Offence Analysis

Tony was encouraged to look at the circumstances of his sexual abusing using some of the offence-specific materials described earlier in this chapter:

1. Four Steps and Four Stops
2. Steps to Offending
3. Situation; Thoughts; Feelings; Action
4. Offence Pattern Diagram
5. Thinking Error Cards
6. How My Victim Felt When I Offended Sort Cards
7. How I Felt When I Offended Sort Cards

Offence Pattern Diagram

As an example of how these materials are used in practice, I have detailed below the contents of one of the offence pattern diagrams completed with Tony.

1. Circumstances – Thoughts and Feelings

Feeling at the bottom of the pile at home; always dumped on and criticised by Dad. Always made to look after Helen, even though Dad knew I wanted to go out. Not being allowed to see my friends. Not allowed to work. Feeling angry and wanting to get one over my dad. Feeling sorry for myself and resentful of my family for having a better deal.

Beginning to be more interested in sex, masturbating a lot, wanting to have a girlfriend and have sexual experiences like my friends at school. Finding Dad's films and looking at girls on the internet, and masturbating even more.

2. Sexual Fantasies

The sex films are teaching me some good ideas about what I could do. Firstly I used to think about being with the people on the film and having sex with them. Then I used to think about girls at school, but I hardly know them. Eventually I began to imagine myself being with Helen and her doing to me what was happening in the films. I began to think more and more about having sex with Helen – she was there and I knew there were lots of times when we would be on our own for hours.

3. Planning and Setting Up

Watch Mum and Dad's car go down the road. Call Helen into the lounge and flick through the channels on the TV remote. See how she acts when the porno stuff comes on. Ask her if she wants to watch it – keep flicking back, eventually leave it on. After this I ask Helen if she wants to play the same game and took some of my clothes off – my top and my trainers and socks. Helen copied me and took off most of her clothes.

4. Abuse

Here was a detailed description in Tony's words of all the sexual acts that took place . . .

After this I told Helen that it was really important to keep this as a big secret, because she would be in trouble with Mum and Dad if they found out. We both agreed not to tell anybody. Helen then went upstairs to her room. Next day I did the same again, but in her bedroom without the porno film. She knew what to do this time.

5. Feelings Afterwards

Relieved; happy; worried; excited; wanted to do it again; scared; powerful; at last something that I really wanted to do that Dad can't stop me and does not know about. Feeling angry towards Dad for leaving me here with Helen. I always knew it was wrong, but it was really his fault because he never listens to me or lets me do what I want and he left me alone all this time and they were his films. It was still quite good though, and it was sex really; I was feeling that I am now a man.

6. Excuses

We've done it once and next time I asked Helen, she wanted to do it because she did not say no – she wanted me to do it. Nobody knows, so I'll never get caught and Helen won't tell, not now that she likes what I was doing. I didn't hurt her and I didn't go inside, it was just like giving her a lesson really, she will have to learn anyway so I am really helping her.

'Thinking Errors'

There's not much of an age difference between us, Dad's seven years older than Mum, so it won't really matter.

If I don't actually go inside her and if I don't cum, it won't really be like having sex and so it won't really be bad.

I'll make it like a game so that Helen wants to do it. If she sees people doing it on the films, she will actually want to do it like I do.

Dad won't know – it will be my secret – that makes me feel good. I will be able to tell my friends at school that I have had sex.

I can't help myself any more, I know I'm going to do it and I won't get caught.

Once this was completed, Tony was taken through each stage and challenged about the true nature of what he was doing and how he was misusing his power and control over Helen, and how his expression of anger towards his father was misplaced. This was a very difficult phase of the work for Tony, because he knew from the start that what he was doing was very wrong and would be harmful to Helen.

Tony described himself as at the time lacking the self-confidence to engage in age-appropriate sexual relationships with his female peers. Around this time, Tony had heard a great deal of talk about sex and relationships amongst his peers. He had also discovered pornographic videos in his father's bedroom – he had also viewed pornography on his father's computer. Tony estimates that he had watched around 30 hours of pornography. He developed a habit of watching these films on his own and masturbating. These films encouraged Tony to develop a powerful sexual appetite which, beyond masturbation, he felt unable to fulfil. Eventually, Tony developed the sexual fantasies about his sister Helen, which ultimately led him to committing the abuse.

The circumstances and process of Tony's sexual abusing also appear to be strongly associated with the very difficult and troublesome relationship he has with his father. Tony had accumulated strong resentment towards his father, because of the way he treated him, and that privately, any opportunity to get back at him was a bonus – discovering his father's video tapes and watching them without him knowing it being an example. As can be seen from the offence pattern, these feelings of resentment contributed to Tony's decision to sexually abuse Helen.

Tony believes that the difficulties he had with his father date back from around the time when Helen was born, and he had to take second place. Tony believes that his father has always had expectations of him that he could not live up to. Tony states that he has never really got on well with his father, who would always be the parent who punished him. Tony would receive praise from his mother, but, where possible, would always hide his achievements from his father, with an expectation of not being praised. Over time, and possibly always, Tony has developed the capacity to hide his feelings and present as being content and happy. He feels that he has always received inconsistent and contradictory messages from his father. Tony has stated that he loves his father, but that often he does not like him. Tony also began to develop some resentment towards Helen, partly because of her having the relationship with her father that he wanted, and partly because of having to babysit for her, and often finding her difficult to manage, and his own free time restricted.

To summarise, Tony committed these sexual offences after extensive viewing of and masturbating to 'hard core' pornography, causing an intensive build-up of sexual feelings, but without the self-confidence to consider entering into appropriate relationships with his female peers. At the same time, Tony had an accumulating resentment towards his father over many issues. In response to the intersection of these factors, Tony began to develop masturbatory fantasies towards his sister Helen, and eventually took advantage of an opportunity to carry these fantasies forward into sexually abusing Helen. Tony always knew this would be harmful to Helen, but, as shown above, employed 'thinking errors' to put this detail aside. Predictably, after the first incident was discovered, despite the punishment, and in the absence of appropriate therapeutic intervention, Tony's sexual fantasies towards Helen continued, and it was only a matter of time before a further sexual offence was committed.

The practice framework detailed in Chapter 2 informed the therapeutic intervention provided for Tony. There were some very powerful peer influences on Tony's behaviour that were reinforced by some of the pornographic material that he was watching – that masculinity and sexual behaviour is about being in control and feeling powerful. The role model that Mark presented to Tony was about the head of the household being in charge and always having his own way, that cannot be challenged. These attitudes were tinged with violence – both real and feared by probably all members of the family. The work with Tony took him through an examination of these attitudes and representations of masculinity and explored how they were reinforced in wider society, and in particular by his peer group experiences. He was the victim of quite a violent pecking order; he felt that he needed to brag about his sexuality and about having sex with a girl to earn respect and stave off some of the bullying he was being subjected to. What made it worse was that for a short time he did feel that he had begun to earn some respect by being able to show that he knew about sex by talking about what he had seen in the pornographic films and by talking about his new 'girlfriend'. These wider influences alongside the power imbalances at home ultimately directed Tony to feeling able to justify sexually abusing Helen. The framework provided a map through which to explore with Tony the origins and influences of the power relationships in his life, and to help him to develop new ways of thinking about himself and his life. The full programme of therapeutic work described above was completed with Tony, and lasted for 18 months – he still maintains sporadic contact with his specialist worker.

Sadly Tony remained estranged from his family who refused to cooperate with the Social Services Department. An approach was made to Linda by the domestic violence team, but she never took it up. The family did move to another area and shut Tony out of their lives completely. Tony has some contact with both sets of his grandparents, and some of his uncles, who are close to him in age. He also has occasional contact with his twin sisters who now live away from home. Recently he has begun to receive letters from his mother, but she has asked him not to let any of his relatives know that he has heard from her, as his father was not aware that she had been writing, and that it would cause problems for her if he found out. Tony continued to live in foster care up until past his eighteenth birthday, and had many positive experiences. He now lives independently; there have been no reports of Tony committing further sexual offences. He maintains appropriate friendships and relationships with his peers, and works full-time in a print shop.

8

VICTIM EMPATHY

INTRODUCTION

Most therapeutic programmes for children and young people who have harmful or inappropriate sexual behaviours will have a component that focuses on the issue of 'empathy' – the ability to perceive another person's perspective, and recognise the feelings this produces and to have compassionate responses as a result. This is important because of the mutuality that is needed for healthy relationships with peers, particularly sexual relationships that are based on understanding and mutual consent. If a child or young person has sexually victimised another person, it is important that he is helped to fully understand the impact of his behaviour – how it was experienced and felt by the victim, and the impact it has had and could have on his or her life. This is often referred to as 'victim empathy' work, and most practitioners and researchers will agree that this is an important component of the work (Araji, 1997; Hackett, 2004). However, there are a few important points to note: firstly, that not all people who lack empathy commit inappropriate or harmful sexual behaviours. Research has shown that a lack of empathy is not in itself a significant predictor of future harmful sexual behaviours (Calder et al., 2001). Secondly, some people may in many aspects of their lives demonstrate a high degree of empathy, and yet still commit harmful sexual behaviours, in which case the question becomes: why or what caused, in this particular circumstance, this person to become able to withhold his empathy? Thirdly, adolescence is for many young people a time of change and uncertainty, with all efforts being needed to manage and cope with new independence, and perhaps new identities, etc., in a context of enormous social and developmental pressure (Moore & Rosenthal, 1993). Consequently, some young people, particularly adolescents, may not on the surface express a significant degree of empathy. Fourthly, some people may commit sexual offences with an express intent to harm their victim. If they are subsequently confronted with the extent of that harm, their behaviour may as a result be reinforced. Fifthly, some people may simply not see their behaviours as being in any way harmful to the victim, so an absence of empathy does not come into play. This chapter will explore the concept of victim empathy, and explain why for most people who have sexually harmed, victim empathy is a valuable component of an intervention programme, not least because it can lead to improvements for the victim – for example, by leading to a person who has abused to openly accept responsibility for his actions. The chapter will discuss the process of undertaking this work, presenting a range of practice techniques. There will also be an exploration of how this aspect of the work may lead a child or young person who has sexually harmed towards coming to terms with his own victim experiences. The main themes of the chapter will be drawn together in the conclusion, before presenting some additional victim empathy exercises.

VICTIM EMPATHY

In simplistic terms empathy is best understood as process of feeling for another, and can be considered in terms of *thinking*, *feeling* and *doing* – being able to cognitively and emotionally perceive another person's perspective, to recognise the feelings invoked by this perception and to express a compassionate response based on those feelings and that perspective. Empathy has the capacity to have a profound influence on human interactions and relationships. The expression of empathy is a socially desirable behaviour that can encourage positive relationships. When people do not have or express empathy, others can see them as cold, detached and self-centred – these are not the ingredients of popularity and friendship. Secure attachments with others are based on feeling comfortable about oneself and others, and feeling that others are comfortable with us. When we do not feel comfortable with others, or about ourselves, we are, logically, less inclined to make relationships with them, and less inclined to be concerned about how they may feel. Many of the young people featured in the case studies of this book had difficulties in forming appropriate and positive relationships with others and felt very uncomfortable about themselves. By developing improved capacities for understanding, feeling and expressing empathy, both in a global sense and in a specific sense towards their victims, they were assisted in feeling and being able to move on. Knowing that what they have done was wrong was very uncomfortable for them, causing a level of empathic distress and negative self-appraisal, causing some of them to become highly motivated towards denying or minimising their harmful sexual behaviours. To be assisted in becoming able to come to terms with the impact of the harm they had caused, and to be assisted in expressing remorse, sometimes directly to the victim, led to improved self-appraisals, improved self-esteem and a belief that they could move away from their harmful sexual behaviours. Furthermore, they had generally improved understandings of how to make positive relationships, and a potential to become more able to meet their needs appropriately, without harming others.

Victim empathy work takes the young person beyond an intellectual understanding of the harm they have caused, by bringing emotions and feelings of the victim into the equation, and encouraging the child or young person who has committed the harm to have appropriate feelings about their actions. Victim empathy work allows the young person to remember the trauma he has introduced into another person's life. Victim empathy work invites the young person to keep the victim in mind, as a reminder of the harm he has caused, and as a reminder not to commit further harmful sexual behaviours. The process of this work will assist in reducing the young person's cognitive distortions or 'thinking errors', and will further break down his denial or minimisation. It will lead to positive improvements in relationships and can be used to assist the young person in developing positive sexual fantasies and patterns of sexual arousal.

Victim empathy work is quite often a challenging, stressful and sometimes painful stage of the work, and therefore needs to be carefully timed. The young person will require substantial support in being able to take on the potentially traumatic understanding of his behaviours. It is important to have a sufficiently established therapeutic relationship, so as to be able to support him through the discomfort that the work is intended to invoke, as part of the process of getting him to understand and feel the impact of the harm he has caused. It is best for this work to take place after an analysis of offence patterns, which will have enabled the child or young person to give detailed descriptions and explanations of his behaviours, thus providing the information necessary for the victim empathy stage of the work.

PRIOR EXPERIENCES OF HAVING BEEN SEXUALLY ABUSED

When focusing on the suffering of the victim, issues relating to the child or young person's own sexual victimisation may surface. Any denial by him of the impact of being sexually abused, or statements of feeling responsible for being abused, must be explored and challenged. When a young person has himself been sexually abused, it is important to emphasise to him that most people who have been sexually abused *do not* go on to sexually abuse others and that why this has happened in his case needs to be explored. There has been a great deal of discussion in the literature about whether or not a prior experience of sexual abuse can be seen as an explanation of subsequent harmful sexual behaviour. My previous study (Durham, 2003) was critical of the direct link between abuse and abusing implied by some of these studies, referring to it as a mythology and concluding that a prior experience of sexual abuse was neither necessary nor sufficient as an explanation of sexually abusive behaviour. Many other factors that interacted with the abuse experience were cited, for example, the absence of supportive adults in the child's life, experiences of domestic violence and a discontinuity of care – leaving restricted opportunities for the child to recover from the abuse, being left alone to make his own sense and meaning of the experience, possibly remaining exposed to the distorted rationalisations of the abuser.

When the child or young person has been sexually abused himself, the decision about when to address the impact of this really depends upon the individual circumstances. For some children and young people, prior experiences of sexual abuse will limit their capacity to undertake therapeutic work in relation to their own sexual behaviours – attempts to talk about any aspect of sexual behaviour may invoke traumatic memories. For many reasons, including guilt, shame, embarrassment, feeling responsible, fears about being blamed or disbelieved, a child or young person will not readily disclose that he has been sexually abused – even though logically to an outsider this may appear as a perfect excuse or justification that can be offered to explain their subsequent harmful sexual behaviours. It is therefore important from the outset of the therapeutic work for the practitioner to remain alert to the possibility of these processes taking place. It may become necessary to change the direction of the work to alleviate some of the child or young person's distress by addressing some of his sexual victimisation issues – if this is the case, it is important to explain that this is part of the process of addressing his own harmful sexual behaviours. The memory of a young person's own victim experiences can be used to enhance an empathic understanding of the harm he may have caused to others.

TECHNIQUES FOR ENHANCING VICTIM EMPATHY

Discussion of the Impact of the Sexual Abuse

This involves detailed discussion with the child or young person about the impact of his harmful sexual behaviour on the victim – how he or she might have felt at the time of the abuse, and how s/he may be feeling now. The child or young person can be invited to consider where the victim is at the moment – for example, in a lesson at school – and how s/he may be thinking about what has happened to her/him; what s/he may have said about the abuse; what factors may remind her/him of being abused; how this may have affected her/his friendships; how s/he may feel about her/himself and so on; how s/he would feel if her/his friends knew about what had happened; how s/he may feel about the child or young person who abused her/him; the changes in her/his life as a result of the abuse; what help s/he needs to assist her/his recovery; how long s/he is likely to remember the abuse.

Stories from Other Survivors

Reading and discussing detailed quotes and stories from other survivors of sexual abuse, for example, using *Out in the Open* by Bain and Sanders (1990) or *Young Men Surviving Child Sexual Abuse* by Durham (2003).

Perspective-taking Exercises

Encourage the child or young person to consider many of his interactions with others in his life, trying to understand how the other person thought and felt during these interactions. For example – today you were with a group of other young people during the school break – try to remember what you did, and what you talked about – how did these people respond to you? Ask the young person to name these people and in turn pretend to be each one of them and describe what they thought and what they felt, including how they thought and felt about the young person. Take the child or young person through a similar process with other people in his daily life, for example, about how his teacher may have felt and thought in front of his class; how somebody who had to be reprimanded about something may have felt; how somebody who scored a goal or won a prize or was praised may have felt and so on; how his foster carer may have felt about him at breakfast time, etc.

Another perspective-taking exercise is role swapping – ask the young person to exchange roles with yourself. Ask him (the young person as the practitioner) a range of questions about yourself (practitioner as the young person) – for example, opinions about how he or she feels about your harmful sexual behaviour, how he feels about your progress with the work, how he generally feels about you as a person, etc. Ask the young person (as the practitioner) questions such as how he feels he can help you change your behaviour, whether he believes that you can change, and encourage him to ask as many questions as he can think of about you. This exercise, aside from allowing the young person to practise seeing a situation from another's perspective, will produce additional insight into the progress and thinking of the young person. Once the role swapping has ceased – at your or his request, or both – discuss with the young person, firstly how he felt about the exercise, and what he may have learnt or understood differently. Secondly, discuss with the young person any additional issues or information the exercise may have produced – in the exchanged role the young person may have said something quite new and unexpected.

Addressing the Victim in the Room

Ask the child or young person to imagine that the victim is present in the room and speak to him or her about the sexual harm he committed against him/her. This is an opportunity for him to demonstrate the progress he has made, for example, whether or not he easily accepts responsibility for his actions, and how he phrases this in what he says to the victim. In some circumstances it is appropriate for the young person to meet with the victim, particularly if he or she is a relative or close family friend. This must, of course, only take place if it has been assessed as being beneficial for the victim, and if he or she agrees, and adequate preparation for the meeting must have taken place with all parties involved. This exercise will be a good rehearsal for such a meeting and will allow the practitioner to be sure that nothing harmful will be said. In most circumstances it is beneficial for the therapeutic practitioner to attend the meeting with the young person. Sometimes, the child or young person will have continued to live in the same household as the victim; in these circumstances it is particularly important for the meeting to take place, with the young person admitting responsibility for his actions and making an unreserved apology. In these circumstances, protective supervision procedures should have already been established.

Letter of Apology to the Victim (Sent or Not Sent)

Whether or not the letter is actually sent, this is a useful exercise to encourage the young person to express his feelings, again providing useful assessment information about his progress. It can be repeated at different stages of the work, as a means of assessing changes in feelings, understanding, attitude, etc. Ask the young person to write a letter to the victim, explaining how he feels about the harm he has caused, and how he feels about the victim now. This letter should have meaningful content, unique to the addressee. The letter must not ask questions or expect anything of the victim and must emphasise that he or she has choice about reading the letter, and is therefore now in control of the process of the young person's relationship with him or her. The letter should emphasise that the abuse was not the victim's fault, and that he or she had no choice in the matter, and was right to tell (if appropriate). The letter should explain that the young person understands that he has hurt the victim; that his behaviours have caused harm. The letter should contain a clear and unreserved apology to the victim, with a statement of hope about the victim's recovery. The letter should close with a statement containing positive aspirations about the victim's future life.

Victim Empathy Sort Cards

These are two sets of cards with lists of feelings, one set for how the victim felt at the time of the abuse and another set for how the child or young person who committed the behaviour felt (Cook & Taylor, 1991). The following five steps explain how the cards should be used:

1. The young person is asked to select the cards he feels appropriate to him or his circumstances. This selection should then be noted down, and the young person can be asked to explain his understanding of the cards and discuss his selection more fully.
2. The young person is then asked to explain what he understands by the cards he did not select, and explain more fully why he did not select them. With clarification, it may be that the young person changes his mind and selects additional cards. If this happens, the reasons for the change should be noted.
3. The young person is then asked to arrange all the cards as best he can in a continuum or an order of importance to himself. The young person can then be asked to explain his ordering.
4. After a full discussion of the issues raised by the selections, rejections and orderings, the young person can then be invited to reselect the cards. Any differences in selection should also be noted.
5. At a later stage of the intervention programme, as an evaluative measure the exercise can be repeated, in order to identify shifts of attitude and so on, when compared to the earlier selection.

It is important to use the blank cards alongside the sets to allow the inclusion of other issues not referred to on the cards; these issues may be raised by either the child or young person or the practitioner. An easy way to keep a record of the selections is to group the cards together and photocopy them. It is useful to see the layout of the cards altogether, and analyse with the child or young person the interconnections between the selections. It is also useful to compare selections or the two sets of cards side by side. The feelings printed on the cards should include:

How I Felt When I Sexually Abused

Lost	Sexual	Satisfied
High	Confident	Cool
Proud	Angry	Terrified
Powerful	Secretive	Guilty
In Control	Planned	Determined
Macho	Out of Control	Happy
Loving	Ashamed	Strong
Caring	Worried	Scared
Boastful	Turned On	Like an Adult

How My Victim Felt When I Sexually Abused

Weak	Betrayed	Seemed OK
Angry	Hurt	Playful
Sick	Disgusted	High-spirited
Nervous	Out of Control	In Control
Unable to Tell	Terrified	Turned On
Confused	Tense	Sexual
Dirty	Alone	Cheerful
Anxious	Embarrassed	Panicked
Frightened	Ashamed	Agreeable
Threatened	Powerless	Resisting
Scared	Guilty	Childish

CONCLUSIONS

This chapter has explored the concept of victim empathy, and explained why, for most people who have sexually harmed, victim empathy is a valuable component of an intervention programme, not least because it can lead to improvements for the victim – for example, by leading to a person openly accepting responsibility for their actions. The chapter noted that there were some exceptions to this, identifying circumstances where victim empathy work would either be counterproductive, ineffective, or would need to be tackled in a different manner, perhaps linked with other aspects of an intervention programme. An example of this was where there were clearly sadistic elements to the young person's harmful sexual behaviours, or where the young person simply did not see or believe his actions as being in anyway harmful. It was also noted that victim empathy work was not a stand-alone intervention, and needed to be provided as a well-timed component of a wider intervention programme. The chapter discussed the process of undertaking victim empathy work, and presented a range of practice techniques. There was also an exploration of how victim empathy work may lead a child or young person who has sexually harmed towards disclosing and/or coming to terms with his own victim experiences, and how this should be managed in the wider context of an intervention programme.

POSTSCRIPT – LETTERS EXERCISE

Read through the two examples below of letters written from young people to the victims of their harmful sexual behaviours, and based on the content of this chapter, see if you can recognise some of the reasons why they are problematic.

Martin's Letter

Martin is 15 years old, and has received a Referral Order for sexually abusing his 11-year-old sister. There was a very close bond between the brother and sister, especially as they have experienced quite severe problems. Their mother has had a series of life-threatening operations, and both parents have experienced long-term unemployment. The children have often been victimised and bullied at school. Martin has been temporarily accommodated and has been receiving therapeutic work for three months. He was asked to write a draft letter to his sister and bring it to the next session.

Hi Stephanie,

Just thought I'd write to say hello and let you know that I've been getting some help about what happened. I now know that it was wrong and I wanted to say that I know it will never happen again. I hope one day that you will be able to forgive me, because I never meant it to happen the way it did. I know I'm to blame, but I still miss all the other games and times we had together, I often look back to good times.

I think the help has made me be a better person and I think I will be able to get on better with everybody at school, because you know how difficult that used to be for me. I still miss being with Mum and Dad, I hope you all enjoyed the holiday last month. I look forward to when we can put everything behind us and get back to where we were. I know that things will never be the same, but I still think they can be OK between us. Mum and Dad are coming to see me next week, I'm looking forward to that.

If there's anything I can do for you let me know, at least that's one thing that hasn't changed, I will always stand up and protect you, I hope you're not getting bullied at school any more, I often wonder about that. Now that I'm at a different school it worries me.

Anyway this has been a hard letter for me to write, and I look forward to hearing from you as soon as you can write back. I know that you might not feel like writing back, but that's OK, it's your choice, but I hope you can do it. I hope you're OK, and getting on with your life.

With love from your brother,

Martin

Eric's Letter

Eric is 14 and has received a Final Warning for sexually abusing his 10-year-old cousin Paul. Paul used to enjoy staying at Eric's house for most weekends, whilst his parents worked away from home. He would spend large amounts of time playing with Eric, to the extent that they became more like brothers. Eric has been receiving therapeutic work for the past three months. He was asked to draft a letter of apology to Paul and bring it to the next session.

Dear Paul,

How is it going? I know how you must feel about me and I'm sorry you have to feel that way. If there is anything I can do to repay you for all the trouble you've gone through I'll be glad to help out. I know this may sound weird, but I'm glad you told on me. It's made me a better person. I've been having counselling for some months and it has helped me be a better person, I have learned a lot. Since it happened, I have found out that there are lots of other kids who have the same problem as me, so I am not alone. I have been taught to be open about my offences, it was hard at first, I have been taught to look for ways to solve my problems, and I think it is working for me.

I know we won't be able to have the same kind of relationship as we had before, but I guess that's the way things will have to be. I always wanted to say I'm sorry for what happened, as you might know I was punished and had to go to the police station and now I have a supervision order.

I want you to know that I wish this never happened and that it won't ever happen again. Also if it wasn't for you, I wouldn't have got the help I'm now having. I hope one day I will be able to face you in person and tell you I am sorry and give you a big hug, but the way things are now, that just can't happen. Better be off now.

Yours

Eric

Clearly both of these letters are very self-centred and are casual and indirect in their references to the sexual harm caused – 'what happened', 'the trouble you've gone through'. No direct apologies have been made and any hint of regret or apology has been qualified by information about the author's life. Both letters make requests of the addressee, and indirectly blame him/her for their continued separation.

CASE STUDY – ALAN (15)

Synopsis

Alan is 15 years old, of white British ethnicity and until recently lived with his father John and his relatively new partner Jilli, who is black African, and her two sons, Paul aged five and Stuart aged seven; both have the same white British father, Simon, who is now separated from Jilli and has little contact with them. John and Jilli have been in a relationship for just over three years. Jilli and her two boys have lived with John and Alan as a family for just over two years.

Alan's mother Erica has a long-term heroin addiction, and is now critically ill. When Alan visits her, he finds it very difficult to accept his mother's illness and addiction and often blames her for the difficulties in his life, and for not being available for him as a mother throughout most of his life. His contact with Erica is now infrequent, and is always very distressing for him when it happens. Alan's parents John and Erica divorced four years ago, but have lived apart for over six years.

Prior to Jilli moving in to live with John, with plans to get married, Alan had lived with different family relatives over the past four years – with aunts and uncles, paternal grandmother and sometimes with one of his two adult brothers. For many years Alan's father has worked away from home, often travelling and staying away for several days on business trips. It is known within the family that John has had affairs with other women whilst he was married to Erica. There has always been conflict in their relationship, and historically, John has relied heavily on the support of his own parents, and his sister, in bringing up all of his children – he has often managed the situation by being absent. By his own admission, John has tried to compensate all of his children for his regular absence and unavailability – by this John recognises that in many ways, due to the difficulties in his marriage, he has been emotionally unavailable to his children, but less so to Alan – by providing material comforts, excessive pocket money and expensive family holidays abroad.

At the age of 15, Alan received a police Final Warning for sexually assaulting Paul (aged five) and Stuart (aged seven). This sexual abuse came to light when Alan was caught attempting to touch the genitals of his female cousin Louise (aged four) during a family visit. Louise's mother reported her concerns to the Social Services Department, as she was absolutely certain that without her interruption, by walking into the room, her daughter would have been sexually assaulted. After initial inquiries, the police and Social Services Department held a strategy meeting that led on to an investigation that involved separately interviewing Paul and Stuart. For extra pocket money, Alan had regularly looked after Paul and Stuart at night-time, when Jilli and

John went out. The children were asked questions about their relationship with Alan and how they spent their time together. The children were also asked if anything had happened to them that they were not happy with, or that they wished to speak about. Both Paul and Stuart described Alan regularly being left to look after them and that generally they liked this. They stated that they really liked Alan, but eventually they stated that they did not like it when he came into the bathroom and got into the bath with them. They also stated that they did not like some of the 'games' he played with them when they were getting undressed for bed. Paul and Stuart described Alan kissing them in between their legs and being made to do the same to Alan. They also described Alan being naked and masturbating in front of them, and that he had told them that these were secret games for children and that adults should not find out about them.

The abuse of Paul and Stuart initially took place 15 months ago, when Alan was 14. This abuse remained undetected for nine months, and only came to light when the police and Social Services investigated. The last time it took place was during a family holiday, when the three boys shared a room. Alan sexually abused Paul and Stuart on a regular basis over a period of three months. After these three months, Alan stopped abusing them for six months, after which he then started to abuse them again. This was around the same time that he attempted to touch Louise down the front of her trousers and was caught by his sister-in-law. Both boys are really fond of Alan and cannot fully understand why he is not allowed to come and visit any more. It does not appear that any of the abuse involved an overt use of force.

Since the sexual abuse came to light, Alan has lived with his father's sister Alice, who is single and up to this point was living alone. She has always been fond of Alan, and has on many occasions looked after him in the past. In recent months, Alice has found Alan to be very difficult to live with and there has been a great deal of conflict. She often states that Alan cannot be told anything and always believes he is right. In tandem with this, Alan has had significant problems at school, and has received a series of short-term exclusions. Alan is above average intelligence and performs well at sports. Until recently, he was in the top grade for all his major subjects, but has now been moved down to the second grade for maths and science. At school, for many years, Alan has had difficulties in making and keeping friendships. He has many possessions and often has the most up-to-date computer games. These possessions initially attract friendships, but many of Alan's friends find him to be moody and sometimes arrogant, and quite quickly break off their contact with him. Alan often states to Alice that he is lonely and has no friends. John and Jilli did have a long-term hope that they can live as a family with Paul, Stuart and Alan together, but now they are uncertain about this, and recognise that there are pressing limitations on how long Alan can live with Alice.

Initial Analysis

- Alan has had significant disruptions in his parenting over a number of years. There has clearly been a great deal of family conflict and both parents have been unavailable to Alan in different ways. He appears to have resentment towards both of his parents – his mother for her addiction and his father for his absence.
- An absence of consistent parental affection appears to have been compensated by the provision of material comforts and an abundance of money. This seems to have allowed Alan to develop a pattern of behaviour whereby he likes to be in control. Alan is likely to be aware that his father feels guilty for his persistent absence in Alan's life. These attitudes have not only affected Alan's family relationships, but his peer and school relationships have also suffered from this outlook.
- Alan's developmental history has many of the typical factors associated with harmful sexual behaviour in young people. These include experience of emotional abuse and neglect, family breakdown and discontinuity of care, attachment difficulties, school problems, social isolation and a sense of being different from his peers.
- All of Alan's sexually abusive behaviours have been directed towards children under seven, and he may therefore not present significant risk to his peers – this will need to be assessed.
- Alan may be resenting the time that his father is now spending with Jilli, and that he has to share his attention with an additional two children.
- Loneliness, an absence of affection and resentment are likely to be key elements in Alan's sexually abusive behaviours. It is also important to consider the possibility of racist dimensions to Alan's behaviour.
- Alan's approach to social interaction and his subsequent reputation may be hindering his ability to make intimate relationships. Added to this, there is evidence that Alan will be either insecure or frightened about his sexuality.
- Alan has sexually abused Paul and Stuart through a process of friendship and play – by engaging them in 'games' that are likely to make them feel guilty and possibly responsible for the sexual behaviour. Alan is likely to have employed 'thinking errors' to allow him to believe that by committing sexual abuse in the context of a game, it was less harmful. There is evidence that Alan is sexually aware and certainly that he knows his behaviours were wrong, and needed to be concealed from adults.
- Despite the inconsistencies and disruptions in his life, there is evidence that Alan has significant family attachments and loyalties, and that he seeks family attention and approval, particularly from his father. Helping Alan to find ways to manage these and other relationships better will be a key aspect to helping Alan move away from the attitudes and

beliefs that have led him to sexually abuse. It will also be very important to assist John and other key family members in having a better understanding of Alan's needs. This will be difficult, given how they are likely to be feeling about Alan, having discovered that he has sexually abused Paul and Stuart. Nonetheless, both John and Jilli will be key players in the plan for Alan, and in the plan for Paul and Stuart's recovery from sexual abuse.

- It is imperative that Paul and Stuart receive an offer of therapeutic assistance in their own right, in parallel to any plans for therapeutic work with Alan.

Case Plan

Therapeutic Work with Alan

- Comparing Alan's description of the sexual abuse he committed with what was reported by Paul and Stuart – challenging Alan over any serious inconsistencies, denials or minimisations and promoting his acceptance of full responsibility for his actions.
- Offence-specific work – cognitive behavioural analysis of Alan's sexually abusive behaviour, similar to the work described in Tony's case, and detailed in Chapter 7 – helping Alan to identify the patterns of his behaviour in terms of his thoughts and feelings before, during and after the abuse. This will also involve an exploration of Alan's power relationship with Paul and Stuart, looking at dimensions of age understanding and ability, and whether or not there were racist dimensions to Alan's behaviour, both in terms of Alan's general attitudes towards Paul and Stuart as black children, and also in relation to how Alan being white may have in itself influenced the power relationship, and the extent to which Alan utilised this, or was aware of its potential.
- Sex and relationships education including an exploration of Alan's sexual history (see Chapter 9). In particular, this will involve an exploration of Alan's sexual thoughts and fantasies and his use of pornography. It will look at media images of masculinity and femininity that may have influenced Alan's behaviours and beliefs about sexuality. This will also involve an exploration of power and consent in sexual relationships.
- Victim empathy – helping Alan to understand the actual and potential impact of his sexually abusive behaviour on Paul and Stuart.
- Constructing a 'lifeline' to assist exploring Alan's social and family history, looking at his experiences of abuse and neglect. It will also help to explore Alan's attachments, relationships and peer experiences. Helping him to better understand some of the patterns in these relation-

ships, and building his self-esteem and confidence to improve his social competence (this will be paralleled with equivalent work being undertaken with Alan's parents and other carers to help them appreciate the impact of Alan's life experiences on his behaviours and attitudes, and for them to be able to understand and manage him better).

- Setting up a relapse prevention plan that helps Alan to challenge and interrupt his 'thinking errors' and inappropriate sexual thoughts and fantasies, and helps him to manage risk situations. Given the long-term aim of Alan returning to live with his father, Jilli, Paul and Stuart, this will be incorporated into a wider 'family safety plan'.
- Ongoing assessment and evaluation of Alan's overall progress, and his acceptance of a continued need to employ risk management strategies.
- Generally helping Alan to rebuild his life with an improved self-esteem and social competence, and assisting him in developing appropriate peer networks and friendships, so as to be able to meet his needs more appropriately, without hurting others. This will also involve helping him to better manage the areas of conflict in his life. Importantly he will initially need to work towards improving his relationship with Alice, as she is an important attachment figure in his life, and in the immediate term his main carer.

Therapeutic Work with Paul and Stuart (and Louise)

A separate plan of work to help Paul and Stuart recover from the sexual abuse they have experienced, helping them to be able to feel and keep safe and to be able to speak to a range of adults in their lives about anything that bothers them. This work will essentially praise and encourage them for being able to talk about their abuse and will clarify for them that Alan was responsible for what happened and not them. At some stage, and when they are ready, it will be helpful for them to hear this directly from Alan. The extent of this work will depend on individual assessments of Paul and Stuart and will closely involve working with Jilli to develop her skills and understanding of their needs in respect of the abuse and in keeping them safe in the future. It will be helpful for Paul and Stuart to have opportunities to talk through their experiences and express their thoughts and feelings.

It is important that this work attempts to see the situation through the eyes of Paul and Stuart, and for it to be pitched at their level of understanding of sexual behaviour. As with Alan, the work with Paul and Stuart will be linked to the 'family safety plan'. It is essential, throughout all of the work, that Paul and Stuart's needs and wishes, as far as possible and realistic, remain paramount.

Assistance for Alice

As in the immediate term, Alice will be looking after Alan, and has stated that she is finding it difficult; she will need help and support in managing Alan, both in terms of his general behaviour management, but also specifically in ensuring that he does not commit any further sexual offences. This will involve discussing with Alice the nature and process of Alan's sexual offending, and identifying potential circumstances of risk in Alan's life. There will also be a need for work to be undertaken with Alice and Alan together, to discuss ways to reduce the conflict between them.

Assistance for John and Jilli

Work with John and Jilli will initially focus on maintaining the safety and recovery of Paul and Stuart, and the protection of others from Alan. The protection plan for Alan will involve very close supervision that will continue until work with Alan has progressed to the point that it is assessed that he has become able to manage some of his own risks. It is important that John and Jilli receive help in understanding the nature of the work planned for all of their children. In relation to Paul and Stuart, Jilli will have a key role in assisting their recovery from sexual abuse. It is important that Jilli understands the necessity of not allowing her understandings and anxieties about sexual abuse to be conveyed to Paul and Stuart, and that she is helped in appreciating that their comprehension of what has happened to them will be very different from hers, particularly as they were abused in a context of play and cooperation, without any significant instillation of fear. Both Paul and Stuart remain very fond of Alan and have stated that they miss him; it will need to be reinforced that his absence from their lives at the present time is not their fault. John and Jilli will both have key roles in the 'family safety plan' described below, and will have to be schooled in the principles behind the plan.

Family Safety Plan

The family safety plan is a set of routines to ensure the safety of Paul, Stuart and Alan, and any other child that enters the household, and as far as possible, by virtue of the work undertaken with Alan, any child outside the household. Its general principles are to support Alan in taking responsibility for ensuring that he keeps to its provisions, and does not have unsupervised contact with Paul and Stuart; to ensure that Alan is aware that Paul and Stuart will be asked regularly about how they are and how they feel about life at home, and in particular their relationship with Alan, and what contact they have had with him, and whether or not there is anything inappropriate happening, or anything that has made them in any way feel uncomfortable. The plan is accompanied by a set of house rules, and definitions of behaviours or circumstances considered to be 'risky'. A 'risky' behaviour or situation is one that could lead to sexual abuse or inappropriate sexual behaviour. In operating the plan, the family will hold 'meetings' every two or three days – these meetings will need to be incorporated into the family lifestyle, for example, they could take the form of an after teatime discussion, or an evening discussion in between television programmes. The important point is that the children are asked regularly about their safety in the presence of Alan and also without his presence. By being present, Alan will be reminded regularly about the safety issues, and that there are clear opportunities for Paul and Stuart to report anything that concerns them, and he will be reminded that they will also be having private opportunities to talk. The purpose of this is to reinforce Alan's risk management, directing his thinking away from seeking opportunities to engage in harmful sexual behaviours. Alan, Paul and Stuart will all have regular individual discussions about these matters with John or Jilli. Initially, when first operating the plan, references to the prevention of sexual abuse will be regular and overt, and will involve the presence of professionals, but with a successful outcome, these references can become more euphemised with the children being asked in less direct terms about 'feeling safe', 'getting on well with Alan' and being asked whether or not anything has happened to upset them. At the early stages it is important for there to be clarity about the precise nature of behaviour and actions that should not take place. Once it is clear that everybody has the message, it is important for Paul and Stuart particularly not to have the issue of sexual abuse discussed every time the family meets. The success of this plan is closely related to the progress of the individual work with all parties involved. An outline of the 'family safety plan' is detailed below.

Introduction

- This safety plan has been devised so as to enable Alan to return to live with his family – John, Jilli, Paul and Stuart.
- It has been specifically devised to prevent any recurrence of sexual abuse.
- It has also been devised to assist John and Jilli in providing care and safety for all the children in the family.
- The plan involves a series of planned meetings, mainly involving members of the family on their own. The meetings will enable John and Jilli to

monitor the safety of their children, and ensure that they have a regular opportunity to talk about anything they are unhappy with.
- The family social worker and Alan's specialist worker will attend some of the planned meetings. At these meetings, the overall progress of the safety plan will be reviewed, and advice will be offered.
- Detailed plans for all the meetings, alongside house rules and a statement about 'risky' behaviour, will be provided for the family.
- Initially the plan will entail a high level of professional involvement, but it is intended that over time, the family will operate the plan on their own.
- Alan's return to live with the family is conditional upon a successful operation of this plan.

'Risky'

The word 'risky' has special meaning for Alan, and can be used as a buzz-word to remind him of the behaviours he needs to avoid:

'I think that might be a little bit "risky".'
'Don't you think you were being "risky" when you . . . ?'

'Risky' behaviour is often quite a few steps away from actually abusing somebody, but once a first step has been made, the second step is there for the taking. The tactic is to spot the first step and challenge Alan, so that it serves as a reminder for him to manage his own risks. If Alan is resistant, he should be reminded that challenging him is about caring for him.

'Risky' refers to any act, thought or situation which *could* lead to sexual abuse:

- Any time spent by Alan with Paul or Stuart that is not supervised by an adult.
- Alan entering Paul or Stuart's bedroom.
- Paul or Stuart entering Alan's bedroom.
- Alan entering the bathroom when Paul or Stuart are occupying it.
- Alan, Paul or Stuart getting up at night-time and wandering about the house.
- Alan not wearing appropriate clothing, or in any way exposing his private parts to other members of the household.
- Alan, Paul or Stuart engaging in explicit sexual jokes, conversation or innuendo.
- Alan having thoughts or fantasies about sexual contact with Paul or Stuart or any other young child. Also includes engaging in aggressive sexual fantasies.

- Alan playing with younger children, or deliberately spending time in places where younger children play.
- Alan not asking for help when he needs it, not talking about problems, and in particular not being able to talk about risky thoughts.

House Rules

- Alan is not allowed to enter Paul and Stuart's bedroom, without an adult present.
- Paul and Stuart are not allowed to enter Alan's bedroom, without an adult present.
- Alan must not be in the bathroom at the same time as Paul or Stuart.
- After bedtime, nobody is allowed to leave their bedroom unless they are ill, upset or need to use the bathroom.
- Alan must not be in an undressed state in the presence of Paul or Stuart.
- All children must sleep in their own beds.
- No sexual contact with or between children is allowed.
- Alan must not engage in any 'rude' (sexual) conversation with Paul or Stuart.
- All 'risky' behaviour must be reported to Jilli or John.
- Any breaking of these rules must be reported as soon as possible and must be discussed at the family meeting.

Family Safety Meeting

(Twice weekly – involving John or Jilli with Alan, Paul and Stuart)

Parent introduces the meeting reminding everybody that the purpose is:

1. To make sure that *everybody* is happy and that nothing 'risky' has happened.
2. *Everybody* should feel safe to tell about anything.

Parent asks each family member to say:

1. How they feel about the week.
2. If they feel that anything 'risky' has happened (such as: has anybody broken the rules about bedrooms and bathrooms, getting up at night, making sexual comments or sexual touching?).
3. If anything has happened that has made them feel unsafe, unhappy or annoyed.

Parents state:

1. They are pleased/not pleased with how everybody has done, giving examples of why.
2. Remind the family about sticking to rules.
3. Remind everybody that they may speak to John or Jilli on their own (in private) if they wish.
4. Thank you to everybody for taking part in the meeting.

A Social Services professional will attend one of the meetings each week.

Individual Safety Meetings – Paul and Stuart

(Weekly and separately)

John or Jilli to ask:

1. How they feel about the week.
2. If they feel that anything 'risky' has happened (such as: has anybody broken the rules about bedrooms and bathrooms, getting up at night, making sexual comments or sexual touching?).
3. If anything has happened that has made them feel unsafe, unhappy or annoyed.

Individual Safety Meetings – Alan

Listed below are some helpful questions that serve to create opportunities for Alan to talk about his feelings and progress. The questions progress to a focus on Alan's potentially abusive thoughts and behaviours. The list of questions should be used in progression. These questions will provide opportunities for Alan to discuss appropriate responses to the daily difficulties or problems that may occur in his life, and will remind him of the importance of responding appropriately to inappropriate thoughts or fantasies, and of avoiding high-risk situations.

(Twice weekly)

John or Jilli to ask Alan:

General

1. How he feels about the week.
2. If anything 'risky' has happened (such as: has anybody broken the rules about bedrooms and bathrooms, getting up at night, making sexual comments or sexual touching?).
3. If anything has happened that has made him feel unsafe.

Anger

1. Has anything annoyed you today/this week?
2. How did it make you feel?
3. What did you do about it?
4. Is there anything you want to do about it now?

Problems

1. Have you had any problems today/this week?
2. What did you do?
3. What happened as a result?
4. How do you think you managed?

'Risky' Thoughts

1. Have you had any 'risky' thoughts or feelings today/this week?
2. How did they make you feel?
3. What did you do about it?

'Risky' Situations

1. Have you been to any 'risky' situations or places this week?
2. How did you decide to end up in that situation?
3. What happened?
4. How did you feel?
5. How did you manage?
6. What will you do next time to avoid a 'risky' situation?

Parents' Meeting

(Weekly for the first month, then fortnightly – a professional with John and Jilli)

1. To review the working of the family safety plan.
2. To monitor family and individual meetings.
3. To discuss any circumstances where it has been reported that the family rules have been broken.
4. To offer advice and support about maintaining the family safety plan.
5. To offer more general family support advice.
6. To present an opportunity for all parties to air grievances.
7. To monitor and assess the ongoing risks that Alan presents.
8. To review and plan future ongoing contact with the family.

Outcome

After initial reluctance, Alan cooperated well with therapeutic work. He was helped to recognise the pattern of his behaviour, and has admitted to having frequent prior and ongoing masturbatory fantasies about Paul and Stuart – before and throughout the initial time he was abusing them, and also throughout the intervening six-month period before he sexually abused them again. Alan admitted that he derived sexual pleasure from the abuse, and that this caused him to want to do it again. He managed to convince himself that he would not really be doing Paul and Stuart any harm because it had always happened in the context of a game. He was able to abuse them by setting up a series of 'games', which involved removing clothes, masturbating each other, sometimes oral genital contact and on three occasions he attempted to anally penetrate Stuart, but that he was unable to do this, and so instead simulated intercourse. Alan stated that he remains very fond of both boys and that he knows he has done harm and that he deeply regrets what he has done. He said that whenever Paul or Stuart gave any indication of resistance or unhappiness, then he stopped.

Over time, and with help, there was evidence that Alan was able to replace his deviant sexual fantasies with more age-appropriate sexual thoughts and fantasies. Alan often had flashbacks about abusing, and was helped to avoid being aroused by these thoughts by being able to pair them with thoughts of being back in the police station having to account for his actions. Alan explained that when he attempted to sexually abuse Louise, he had acted on a passing thought and that he had considered doing this in the past, and he had been trying to stop himself. Alan said that he was pleased that he was initially able to stop abusing Paul and Stuart of his own accord, and that he always knew it was wrong, but that he continued to want to do it and as his sexual fantasies increased he managed to again convince himself that it would not hurt them. Alan was able to additionally rationalise in his own mind that he had done it before and that they still liked him and appeared not to mind.

Alan has said on several occasions that he believes that if his family had paid more attention to him, then none of this would have happened. There was a level of anger and possibly retaliation in Alan's sexual offending. He explained that for several months, he felt a high level of power and control over his father and Jilli, as he knew what he had been doing and they did not. Alan states that initially he was angry with his father and Jilli and wanted to do something to get back at them. Once he started the abuse, he became used to the sexual pleasure involved and carried it on. The sexual abuse had featured strongly in Alan's sexual thoughts and fantasies for some considerable time.

Alan stated that he does not believe that he is gay, and that he has had 'mild' sexual experiences with female peers. He says that there has always been a problem at school with his peers calling him 'gay Al', which he says has come from a TV series. The name seems to have stuck and causes Alan to become involved in fights. Despite this, Alan believes he remains very popular at school. He says he often helps his friends with homework, and is good at football. He also admits that he often loses friends and that he cannot explain why this happens. Alan was frightened that since the abuse, members of his family, including his father, believe that he is either gay or perverted. Alan stated that when he was 11, he went through a stage when he was able to watch his brother's pornographic films. He continues to have an interest in pornography; in some ways this has allowed him to feel that he is a 'normal heterosexual male'. Alan's father has reported that Alan has in the past accessed gay pornographic sites on his computer, but Alan has vehemently denied this. As these issues were discussed more fully with Alan, he admitted that when he was 13 he engaged in some sexual experimentation with a male friend whom he refused to name. He said that it was more a game of 'dare', and that he believes that somehow this had been discovered at school, and that this is where the initial name-calling came from. The work with Alan has helped him to analyse these issues and has challenged his understanding and beliefs about masculinity, sexuality and racism and has helped him to recognise how anger and the desire for power, control and revenge contributed to his sexual offending.

Work with Alan lasted for almost 18 months, as these issues were tackled and revisited several times. Initially Alan refused to show remorse in his family, although appropriate and genuine remorse was expressed during the therapeutic sessions. Eventually these and the many other identified issues in Alan's life were worked through and with the operation of the family safety plan, Alan was allowed to return to live with his family. There were no reports of Alan committing further sexual offences.

9

SEX AND RELATIONSHIPS EDUCATION

INTRODUCTION

Sex and relationships education is a lifelong learning process of discovering and acquiring information, developing knowledge and skills and forming attitudes about gender, sex, sexuality, relationships and feelings. Children usually begin to learn informally at home, from indirect messages given by their parents, carers or perhaps older siblings, and from their own observations start to develop a sense of the different expectations of girls and boys. This learning is later reinforced, or perhaps challenged, by peer experiences, and a developing awareness of media messages. As children and young people's bodies develop, they experience changing feelings that direct them towards new curiosities that will lead them into their initial sexual experiences. Most young people will explore their sexuality with or without adult approval; it is helpful if they are encouraged to feel comfortable with their growing sexuality, so that they can develop their self-esteem and have a positive self-image, and feel comfortable about making their own decisions. To do this, all children and young people need to have access to age-appropriate sex and relationships information and advice. If a child or young person has been exhibiting inappropriate or harmful sexual behaviour, then it is particularly important that he receives an assessment of his sexual history and, based on this assessment, some formal sex and relationships education as part of a wider programme of addressing these behaviours, and helping him to develop the knowledge and skills to meet his future needs appropriately. The timing of this work in the programme will generally depend upon the needs and circumstances of the individual, but it is important at an early stage to open up a dialogue with the child or young person about sex and relationships issues, as a basic foundation for the work to follow. This will usually be done when the child or young person's sexual history is taken, as part of the initial assessment. This chapter will discuss the components of a comprehensive programme of sex and relationships education, exploring some of the values involved, acknowledging that they will vary between different individual, cultural and religious perspectives. It will also explore issues relating to informed consent and peer pressure, sexuality and sexual oppression, including homophobia and pornography. The chapter will also signpost the reader towards a range of sex and relationships education resources, including information about contraception and sexual health.

RETURNING TO SEXUAL HISTORY

By this stage of an intervention programme, there will be some established knowledge of the young person's sexual history, and possibly of the gaps in his knowledge. In moving on to consider formal sex and relationships education, there will be an opportunity to revisit, clarify and build upon the earlier assessment. By this stage it is likely that the practitioner will now have a more fully established therapeutic relationship with the child or young person. This should be utilised to enhance greater openness and comfort for the young person in discussing these issues at greater depth. In approaching this sensitive topic, perhaps made more sensitive for the young person by his harmful or inappropriate sexual behaviours, many of the issues about initial engagement discussed in Chapter 6 continue to be relevant. Essentially the child or young person needs to be assisted in feeling comfortable and being able to discuss some very personal and private issues, which under general circumstances he would have probably been unlikely to discuss in such detail with an adult, or perhaps with anyone. A very open and transparent approach is needed to safeguard the child or young person, and ensure that he understands precisely why these personal questions are important. The child or young person should be asked questions about some or all of the areas detailed below, depending upon his age and understanding.

SEX AND RELATIONSHIPS EDUCATION SCHEDULE

To inform the operation of this schedule, a comprehensive list of sex and relationships education resources is provided at the end of the chapter.

- *Prior sex and relationships education* – whether or not the child or young person has had any formal sex and relationships education, at what ages this took place, who presented it and in what context – school, outside

school, and what he feels he learnt from it, and how he feels this could
have been improved.

- *Puberty and sexual development* – depending on age, how the child or young
  person discovered, or what he knows about, the changes that take place
  during puberty for both boys and girls; the differences between boys and
  girls; the reasons for these differences – biological and social information.
- *Conception and childbirth* – biological information.
- *Contraception* – full discussion of a range of contraceptive methods.
- *Sexually transmitted diseases* – factual information about a range of sexually transmitted diseases and how to access appropriate sexual health
  services.
- *Sexual intercourse* – whether or not the child or young person understands
  what is meant by sexual intercourse, and again how he found this out.
  Whether he understands the difference between vaginal and anal intercourse – biological and factual information.
- *Masturbation* – what the young person understands about this, whether
  or not he considers it to be acceptable behaviour, and at what age he may
  have started doing this, how often in the past and how often now, where
  he does it, etc. Some discussion could be included about cultural variations and how the myths he may have been told about masturbation can
  lead to shame and guilt. It would also be helpful to provide some information about why people engage in masturbation, and the most appropriate context – time and place, i.e. privacy, etc. – for it to be done.
- *Other sexual behaviours* – his knowledge of other sexual behaviours including kissing, massage, oral sex, and again how he found out about them –
  social, cultural and factual information.
- *Sexual fantasies* – whether or not the young person has sexual fantasies,
  what they are, and whether or not they are associated with masturbation.
  This should include information about the links between fantasies and
  behaviour – see Chapter 7.
- *Sexual relationships* – whether or not the child or young person is able to
  associate intimate and social relationships with sexual behaviour. Feelings, emotions and sexual relationships – encouraging him not to consider
  only the physical and genital aspects of sexual behaviour.
- *Past sexual experiences* – history of intimate and sexual relationships –
  'normal' sexual experiences – intimate or sexual relationships with others,
  at what age these started and what sexual experiences were involved –
  genital and non-genital. It may be helpful to construct a timeline of these
  experiences, perhaps alongside other experiences in the child or young
  person's life.
- *Sex and the law* – full exploration of issues relating to sex and the law,
  including the age of sexual consent, and what types of sexual behaviours
  are illegal, for example, between siblings. This should include a detailed

exploration of scenarios of sexual behaviour, including circumstances where behaviours may be illegal, despite there being consent.

- *Informed consent* – full exploration of issues relating to informed sexual consent, and the appropriate steps to be taken in making and developing relationships that may become sexual. This should include an exploration of the power relationships involved in sexual behaviour, and how they are determined – age, knowledge, gender, ability, sexual orientation, physical size, physical ability, intellectual ability, race, status amongst peers, etc.

- *Unwanted sexual contact and sexual abuse* – whether or not the child or young person has experienced unwanted sexual contact or sexual abuse. (It is particularly important to revisit this topic at this stage of the intervention, as there may be many reasons why the child or young person up to this point has still felt unable to disclose experiences of being sexually abused. By this stage, possibly after some of the victim empathy work, if the young person has already been opened up to a dialogue about more generalised sexual behaviour, and has a more established relationship with the practitioner, he may feel more able to discuss these issues.) Following these questions, a full exploration of what his understanding of sexual abuse is, and whether or not he has ever discussed it before, or knows about anybody else who has been sexually abused.

- *Exposure to sexual behaviour* – whether or not the child or young person has seen others engaging in sexual behaviour, and to what extent, whether or not it was mutually consenting; whether or not there was force or aggression involved. This should include a full discussion of why a pairing of anger or aggression and sexual behaviour is highly problematic and dangerous.

- *Pornography* – history of the young person's exposure to and current use of pornographic material – on paper in books or magazines, on film, DVD or video, text messages, phone calls, chat lines, etc., on the internet – and whether or not this is used for masturbation, when and to what extent. Discussion of the young person's feelings and attitudes about pornography and the extent to which it is related to his inappropriate or harmful sexual behaviour. Whether or not he believes that there is exploitation involved in pornography – full discussion of issues concerning the links between pornography and sexual abuse and sexual exploitation.

- *Sexuality* – full discussion with the child or young person of issues relating to sexuality – including the differences between sexual identity, sexual orientation and sexual behaviour – attitudes towards gay sexuality, bisexuality, celibacy, understanding of homophobia, whether or not he has had sexual experiences with other boys or young men, or has considered doing so.

- *Sexual oppression* – gender roles, sexism and sexual oppression, peer pressures, general attitude towards women and girls. Whether or not the young person himself has experienced oppression based upon his sexuality. What the young person understands about masculinity and femininity, and what he understands about the social expectations of being a boy or a young man – what types of behaviours are considered to be acceptable and by whom; what types of behaviours would invite social censure and why.
- *Prostitution* – issues relating to prostitution, children sexually abused through prostitution. Whether the young person has been involved with prostitution in any way – what the young person believes and understands about prostitution; whether or not he considers that there is exploitation involved.
- *Young person's level of sexual knowledge* – what overall the child or young person feels about his level of knowledge and understanding of sexual behaviour, and whether or not he feels he needs more information, and if so in which particular areas.

SEXUALITY, VALUES AND OPPRESSION

The term 'sexuality' can be broken down into three component parts – sexual orientation, sexual behaviour and sexual identity. Sexuality is about our sexual feelings towards others, and how we feel about ourselves. It is about sexual attraction to others. It is also about our sexual identity – how we portray ourselves to others and the messages we give out about our sexual interests. Sexuality is really about everything in our daily lives that makes us sexual human beings – our sexual feelings, thoughts and desires, as well as any sexual contact from holding hands, kissing and sexual touching to sexual intercourse. Sexual orientation is about the nature of a person's sexual attraction to others, and whether they are heterosexual, homosexual or bisexual. In our society, where heterosexuality is oppressively policed, gay, lesbian and bisexual people often feel forced to conceal or suppress their sexual orientation (Steinberg et al., 1997; Durham, 2003).

In helping young people understand issues about sexuality and sexual behaviour, it is important to have clearly stated values that take a holistic view of sexuality. Children and young people should be encouraged to understand that sexual behaviour is not just about physical or genital contact, but includes physical, mental, emotional, individual, social, cultural, religious and political components and that it is not necessary to have sex in order to express sexuality. They should be helped to understand that as a practitioner you are able to consider that all forms of sexuality are valid:

heterosexuality, lesbian and gay sexuality, celibacy. In discussing these issues, it is important to challenge oppression, misinformation and stereotyping, whilst acknowledging that not everybody has the same attitudes towards sexual behaviour, and that there are huge variations in attitude and acceptability between different cultures and religions. It is therefore important to have an understanding of the child or young person's religious and cultural background, as an important aspect of the context for undertaking this work. It is also important to state that sexual behaviour is regulated by the law, and that this is the framework by which we must all abide. It is important for the child or young person to be made fully aware of these laws and the potential consequences of breaking them.

It is also important to assist the young person in understanding that there are widespread oppressive attitudes towards certain types of sexuality, particularly gay sexuality – homophobia, etc. – and also sexist attitudes towards women. Indeed, some of these attitudes may have been a significant contributor towards the young person's harmful or inappropriate sexual behaviours. It may be that some of these oppressive attitudes are readily expressed by members of the young person's family, and that he may need help and assistance in negotiating and responding to them. In undertaking this work, the practice framework from Chapter 2 can both provide theoretical underpinnings for the practitioner and be used as a direct work tool with the young person. Using the framework, the practitioner can draw out a specific configuration of the young person's own beliefs and feelings about his gender and sexuality, possibly accompanied by looking through and discussing images in newspapers and magazines. In doing this, the young person can be helped to develop a more critical approach to gender and sexuality. Specifically, and importantly, the framework can be used to help young men explore their beliefs and understandings about their masculinity, how this relates to their sexual behaviour and how it may shape their understanding of femininity. As we have already discussed in Chapter 2, this is closely related to the social generation of homophobia and compulsory heterosexuality, particularly in male adolescent peer relations. An antihomophobic approach to sex and relationships education, which acknowledges all aspects of sexuality and sexual feelings, will assist the young person in feeling able to challenge some of these images and received beliefs. It is important to acknowledge that young people are often oppressed into being afraid to admit that they have not had many sexual experiences and may therefore overstate their knowledge and competence, believing that having the right image is more important than being truthful about what they need to learn.

Similarly, the framework could be used to explore the influences on peer relations, exploring the origins and perpetuation of social oppression and power differentials in interpersonal relationships, taking in issues of oppression and pressure, based on age, class, gender, sexuality, racism and disability. In looking at issues of power, the young person needs to understand the concept of 'informed consent'. To give informed consent to a sexual act, a young person has to be old enough to understand what they are consenting to; have enough knowledge and information; be in a situation where it is just as easy to say 'no' as it is to say 'yes', and not feel under any pressure. The issue of pressure will also need to be fully explored, especially in the context of the young person's peer experiences, where image and identity are particularly significant and can therefore potentially lead a young person into making mistakes that could lead to inappropriate or harmful sexual behaviours (Moore & Rosenthal, 1993).

CONCLUSIONS

This chapter has explored a range of issues relating to sex and relationships education, arguing that this is a very important component of a programme of therapeutic work for children and young people who have committed inappropriate or harmful sexual behaviours. The chapter established that sex and relationships education will build upon other aspects of the therapeutic programme to provide the young person with the knowledge and understanding to build the necessary skills to become more able to meet his sexual needs appropriately. The chapter has provided guidance for a comprehensive programme of sex and relationships education. There was an exploration of sexual values with an emphasis on their variation between different cultures and religions. There was a discussion of sexual oppression, with reference to homophobia and oppressive forms of masculinity. The chapter also drew attention to how the practice framework presented in Chapter 2 could be used to help both the practitioner and the young person, in terms of understanding and explaining the origins and processes of these social oppressions.

RESOURCES

Books

Davies D & Neal C (eds) (1996) *Pink Therapy – a Guide for Counsellors and Therapists Working with Lesbian, Gay and Bi-sexual Clients.* Buckingham, Open University Press.
Fenwick E & Walker R (1994) *How Sex Works – a Clear and Comprehensive Guide to Growing Up Physically, Emotionally and Sexually.* London, Dorling Kindersley.
Fisher N (1991) *Boys about Boys – the Facts, Fears and Fantasies.* London, Macmillan.

Fisher N (1994) *Living with a Willy – the Inside Story*. London, Macmillan.
Harris RH & Emberley M (1994) *Let's Talk about Sex – Growing Up, Changing Bodies, Sex and Sexual Health*. London, Walker Books.
Mayle P (1973) '*Where Did I Come From?*' – *the Facts of Life without any Nonsense and with Illustrations*. London, Pan Macmillan.
Meredith S (1985) *Growing Up – Adolescence, Body Changes and Sex*. London, Usborne.
Meredith S & Gee R (1985) *Understanding the Facts of Life*. London, Usborne.
Pavanel J (2003) *The Sex Book – a No Nonsense Guide for Teenagers*. Cambridge, Wizard Books.

Leaflets

AVERT (1985) *Young Gay Men Talking*. Horsham, West Sussex, AVERT.
FPA (1995) *Is Everybody Doing It? – Your Guide to Contraception*. London, FPA.
FPA (2002) *4 Girls – A Below-the-Bra Guide to the Female Body*. London, FPA.
FPA (2003) *4 You – Growing up – What It's All About*. London, FPA.
FPA (2004) *4 Boys – A Below-the-Belt Guide to the Male Body*. London, FPA.

Videos, DVDs and CD-ROMs

Blake S & Orpin L (2003) *Sense Sex and Relationships for Young People Aged 14–16. Interactive CD-ROM and Teacher's Support Manual*. Robertsbridge, Sussex, Sense Interactive CDs Ltd and London, National Children's Bureau.
Video – *Sex – a Guide for the Young – Colourful Animation with Humour and a Frank Approach Are the Elements Used to Introduce a Difficult Subject – the First Sexual Experience*. Harrow, Middlesex, Educational Media Film and Video Ltd.
Video – *Safe for Life – the Most Deadly Sexually Transmitted Disease of Our Time – AIDS – What It Is and How to Prevent It, an Entertaining and Informative Approach*. Harrow, Middlesex, Educational Media Film and Video Ltd.
Video – *You, Your Body and Sex; Kylie's Private World; Jason's Private World – Three Animated Sex Education Videos for People with Learning Difficulties*. London, Life Support Productions. Highlights available in DVD format – DVD – *You, Your Body and Sex*. London, Life Support Productions.

Websites

www.avert.org   Avert (AIDS Education and Research Trust) – provides information about HIV/AIDS and other aspects of sex and sexuality. Targets young people and has downloadable resources.
www.fpa.org.uk   FPA (formerly Family Planning Association) – provides information on contraception and sexual health.
www.brook.org.uk   provides a wide range of useful leaflets about sexual health and sexuality for young people and general sex education materials, contraceptive advice, etc.
www.ruthinking.co.uk   sexwise – information on a wide range of sex and relationships issues for young people.

CASE STUDY – LUKE (15) AND JON (15)

Synopsis

Luke and Jon are 15-year-old black Afro-Caribbean non-identical twin brothers. They were born in a small English town where they have lived all their lives on their neighbourhood estate. Their mother and father, Marcia and Simon, were also born in England, where they have lived all their lives, moving into their current house 16 years ago, 12 months before they were married. Jon and Luke also have a younger sister Sonia, who is 10 years old. Both sets of maternal and paternal grandparents originated from Barbados, and have lived in England for over 40 years. Marcia works as a classroom assistant in the local secondary school attended by Luke and Jon. Simon works as an assistant promoter connected to a local music retail business, and occasionally has to work away from home, for several days at a time. There have been some difficulties surrounding Luke; he has been quite disruptive at school, and has on some occasions been bullied and called racist names. The head teacher had invited Marcia and Simon in to discuss this, and some extra support was organised for Luke.

Luke and Jon are very close friends with their neighbour and school friend Colin, who is a white British boy, also 15; they have known each other all their lives, their parents are also close friends. The boys would regularly sleep over in each other's houses for most weekends. On one particular occasion when Colin had been staying over, he had woken up to find Jon and Luke in one bed, engaging in sexual activity. This shocked Colin, and Jon pleaded with him not to tell anybody. For several weeks Colin kept this to himself, but was very confused and concerned by what he had discovered. He was aware that Luke had some problems at school; he was often bullied and victimised by homophobic name-calling, which up to this point he had not really paid much attention to, apart from defending and supporting his friend. Colin continued his close friendship with Jon and Luke, still sleeping over regularly. On one night when Jon was up late and Luke was asleep, he woke up Colin and asked him if he would like to get into his bed; he felt quite pressurised and agreed to do this for a short while. Jon's mother Marcia heard a disturbance and entered their bedroom, to find Jon and Colin in bed together.

When Marcia questioned the boys, Colin explained that Jon had begged and persuaded him to get into his bed, especially as now he knew what had been happening with Luke. Jon initially completely denied this, but Luke did not want Colin to get into trouble and disclosed to his mother that he and his brother Jon had been engaging in sexual activity with each other for over nine months, and that at the beginning he told Jon that he did not want to do it, but Jon had persuaded him by offering him money and computer games. He explained that when Colin had found this out they had sworn him to secrecy. Luke also said that he had wanted to tell his mother for a long time, but was very scared about being 'accused' of being 'gay', especially as he knew that his father Simon had strong opinions against this. Jon refused to speak to his mother about any of this and became quite angry, because he thought he was being blamed. He begged his mother not to tell anyone, especially his father. Marcia did speak to Simon about the situation when he returned from his work trip; he was very confused, concerned and angry about what had happened. They also spoke with Colin's mother, who was also concerned for all the boys. They all agreed that nobody should fall out over what had happened and that they should seek professional help for the boys. The following morning Marcia telephoned the Social Services Department and explained the whole situation.

At an initial meeting, Simon was initially very angry with Luke and Jon, and stated that he wanted the Social Services Department to sort his boys out and make sure that his boys were not homosexual, saying that he was prepared to accept that what had happened had been an experiment, but that nothing like this could ever happen again. He was concerned about the family's reputation, and his own reputation at work, in the neighbourhood and with his friends. Simon also stated that the boys' grandparents would also be very disapproving of homosexuality. Marcia was able to persuade Simon that the boys needed help more than blame or punishment. The family were initially alarmed to hear that what had happened would have to be discussed with the police.

When the situation was discussed at a police and Social Services planning meeting, concerns were expressed about the potential degree of pressure being exerted by Jon, and it was agreed that all three boys should be interviewed under the Child Protection Procedures, so as to establish a clearer context to the behaviours. When Luke and Colin were each interviewed, they more or less repeated the same account they had given to Marcia, leading the interviewers towards an understanding that the sexual behaviours had been initiated by Jon, and that he may have pressurised Luke and Colin into taking part, although Colin had said that deep down he feels that he agreed because he was a very close friend to both boys, and was curious, and had been persuaded because he knew already that they had been having sexual activity with each other, and he had been thinking about it over a number of weeks. Overall Colin was very confused about whether he had consented or not. Luke described a range of sexual behaviours taking place between him and Jon over a number of months. He was very anxious and confused about what had been happening; he, like Colin, was also unsure about the extent to which he had consented or not, and had wanted to tell someone about it for a long time. He was very clear about wanting it to stop, and expressed anxiety about other pupils at his school finding out about what had happened. He also expressed anxieties about getting Jon into trouble as he was his twin brother, and they were very close.

Jon was very afraid, and initially refused to speak about what had happened, but with persuasion eventually confirmed the accounts given by Luke and Colin, admitting that he had started the sexual behaviour by asking and persuading Luke to take part. Jon was physically smaller and weaker than Luke, but had a stronger and more confident personality. He was adamant that he had never used threats of physical force, but he had initially persuaded Luke by offering him material possessions, but after the initial few times the behaviour became habitual. This was consistent with the account given by Luke. At a subsequent planning meeting, it was agreed that practitioners from the Social Services Department should seek to engage all three boys and both sets of parents in further work, and that Jon in particular should receive therapeutic work to explore his sexual behaviours. On balance, and in accordance with the Sexual Offences Act 2003, the police decided that with therapeutic work in place, it would not be in the public interest to charge any of the boys. Some consideration was given to Jon receiving a Final Warning, but it was finally agreed that he should be spoken to informally by the police about the consequences of non-consensual sexual behaviour in the future.

Initial Analysis

- The sexual behaviours have clearly been initiated by Jon, and there has at least been a level of persuasion bordering on pressure. Both Luke and Colin have indicated that they were not happy with what Jon had asked them to do. The balance between consent, cooperation, pressure and force will need to be fully assessed and explored with all three boys.
- Jon states that he believes that he did not use 'force', but in holding this belief he may be employing 'thinking errors' (see Chapter 7); he was unhappy at the suggestion that Luke and Colin may not have given their consent. However, he has admitted getting Luke to cooperate by offering him material possessions.
- Luke has been having difficulties at school – the homophobic name-calling has probably escalated because of his reaction to it. His reaction will have likely been fuelled by his private anxieties about what Jon was doing to him, and fears about his own 'cooperation', especially as the sexual behaviour has taken place on many occasions.
- Both Jon and Luke are aware that their father Simon would not approve of homosexuality, and will be anticipating considerable difficulties over this. On the other hand their mother Marcia has shown more understanding and may be able to have a positive influence, mediating some of

Simon's possible reactions. The family should be offered some support in this area.

- It will be helpful for Jon and Luke to be offered an opportunity to explore their experiences as black boys growing up in a predominantly white culture. Luke has already reported that he has been victimised by racist name-calling. It also needs to be established whether or not either of them see being black as having any significant influence on how they feel about the sexual behaviours and people's likely reaction to it. Simon has indicated that he is concerned about his and the family's reputation. It will be helpful to explore this more fully, as it will clearly have an influence on Jon and Luke.

- Jon in particular may need to have safe opportunities to discuss his sexuality; he may need some support in coming to terms with being gay, and how to manage this in relation to his father's stated views. Again it will be important to explore the racial dimensions to this.

- Jon and Luke are very close as twin brothers, and will want to continue to spend a great deal of their time together. They both wish to maintain their friendship with Colin. They will therefore need to be given advice on how to manage this and draw a line under what has happened between them. Jon and Luke as twins will continue to have close feelings for one another. They are likely to need help in understanding how these feelings will need to be delineated from feelings of sexual attraction.

- Colin will also need to be offered an opportunity to talk about what has happened, and possibly to be given advice about how to manage his future friendship with Luke and Jon.

- Colin and Luke have both stated that they do not want Jon to get into trouble; this will have influenced the police decision not to criminalise the situation by giving Jon a Final Warning.

- Given the nature and circumstances of the reported sexual behaviours, there does not appear to be any significant risk towards Sonia, but the potential of this must not be ignored, and her safety needs to be assured.

- It is important to be clear that the concerning issue is not about gay sexuality, but about informed consent and pressure in sexual relationships, and the issue of sexual contact between family relatives.

Case Plan

Marcia and Simon

- Provide a supportive opportunity for Marcia and Simon both together and separately to talk through their feelings and concerns about the current situation. This will include a discussion of their feelings about the homosexuality and the possible influence their feelings will have on the boys. Simon in particular will need to be asked to explain and discuss more about both the basis of his personal concerns and his concerns about the family's reputation. Marcia and Simon may need to be given opportunity and support in exploring how they would feel if Jon told them he was gay. Simon in particular may need support over this, if he is to be able to preserve a positive relationship with his son.

- A family safety plan will need to be drawn up to ensure that no further sexual behaviour takes place between any of the siblings. There needs to be agreements about bedroom and bathroom use, and circumstances that could lead to further sexual behaviour taking place. A set of 'keeping safe' rules will need to be identified between the siblings, with Sonia being given sufficient information to enable her to understand why they are necessary. It will not be appropriate, in view of her age, to tell Sonia the full details of what has happened. Marcia and Simon will need to establish frequent patterns of communication with each child, providing them opportunities to talk about or report anything that they feel uncomfortable about, or any breaking of the house rules.
- Getting Marcia to agree to attend a meeting facilitated by Jon's therapeutic worker, attended by Colin's mother, Colin, Luke and Jon, whereby Jon will take responsibility and apologise for his actions, and make agreements not to repeat the behaviours.

Colin and His Mother

- Providing a therapeutic opportunity for Colin to talk through his experiences with Luke and Jon and identify any particular needs that he feels he may have.
- Attend a meeting with his mother, Jon, Luke and their mother, to hear Jon's statements of apology, and to clarify the basis of their future friendship.
- Providing an opportunity for Colin's mother to discuss how she feels about what has happened, and how she sees the future between the families.

Luke

Therapeutic work with Luke, exploring the process of Jon's sexual behaviours, providing supportive opportunity for Luke to express how he feels about what has happened, and how people have reacted to it. It is important that Luke, who is essentially in a victim position, is offered a choice about the extent to which he wishes to discuss these very personal matters.

- Discussing with Luke how the sexual behaviour first took place, how Jon persuaded Luke to take part, and how Luke felt about it.
- Full exploration of the issue of informed consent in sexual relationships, helping Luke to understand how it may have been difficult for him to refuse, placing responsibility for what happened with Jon.
- Comprehensive sex and relationships education, based on an assessment of Luke's current level of sexual knowledge, including information about sex and the law.
- Comprehensive discussion about sexuality and sexual attraction, including an exploration of Luke's anxieties about his own sexuality, related to his feelings of having cooperated with Jon's requests, including an exploration of the extent to which Luke may have experienced sexual pleasure. Providing reassurance to Luke that he is only 15 and that his future sexuality will be based on how he thinks and feels about others.
- Helping Luke to manage his relationship with his parents, particularly with his father Simon, in view of his initial reactions to the sexual behaviour.
- Preparing Luke for a meeting in which Jon will formally take the responsibility and apologise for his actions.
- Giving Luke advice about how to manage his future relationship with Jon, helping him to delineate his continuing feelings of brotherly closeness and possible continuing feelings of sexual attraction.
- Exploration of Luke's peer experiences, exploring some of the origins of racism and homophobic name-calling. Identifying key support people at school, and encouraging Luke to share some of his experiences with his parents.

Jon

A full programme of therapeutic work with Jon to address his inappropriate sexual behaviours, and the impact they have had on others, incorporating opportunities for Jon to fully discuss his sexuality.

- Jon's account of the inappropriate sexual behaviours he has committed – checking how this compares to the accounts given by Luke and Colin, challenging Jon over any inconsistencies or minimisation.
- Assessing Jon's sexual history and level of sexual knowledge, identifying his attitudes towards sexuality, sexual behaviour, consent, etc.

- Detailed exploration of Jon's inappropriate sexual behaviours, exploring Jon's thoughts and feelings before, during and after, identifying precursors and accompanying sexual fantasies.
- Jon's explanation as to how he feels he obtained consent, exploring the 'thinking errors' he employed, confronting him with what really took place.
- Helping Jon to fully understand the impact of his behaviours on Luke and Colin, informing him how they feel about what he did.
- Helping Jon to prepare appropriate apologies to be given to Luke and Colin, at a formal meeting attended by their mothers.
- Comprehensive sex and relationships education exploring a range of issues from basic factual information to exploring issues around sexuality, sexual identity and sexual orientation. Also including information about informed consent, appropriate sexual behaviour, sex and the law, etc.
- Exploration of Jon's peer and school experiences, and whether or not they have had any bearing on his sexual behaviours.
- Exploration of Jon's perceptions of the impact of growing up as a black boy in a predominantly white culture, and whether or not he identifies any particular issues for discussion.
- Providing specific opportunities for Jon to discuss and explore issues around his own sexuality – whether or not he believes that he is gay, and his anticipations about people's reactions to this, especially his father. Further work to be based upon Jon's wishes and feelings about this issue, possibly including an exploration of how Jon will be able to meet his future social and sexual needs.

Outcome

At the initial stages, a great deal of discussion took place with Marcia and Simon, who continued to be anxious about the situation. They were able to convert a small upstairs boxroom into an extra bedroom to allow Jon and Luke to have their own rooms. Following the apology meeting, and seeing the repairing relationship between Jon and Luke, the family became increasingly confident that the sexual behaviours would not be repeated. Marcia and Simon increasingly suspected that Jon was gay, but it would be some time before Jon would be able to discuss this with them. Simon remained uncomfortable about this, and did not want Jon to be open about this outside the family, and was eventually able to come to terms with continuing to accept Jon as his son, with the subject of his sexuality not being discussed. Over time there were improvements with this, but Simon always remained uncomfortable about it.

When Colin was spoken to again, he explained that he was still very confused about what had happened, because prior to discovering Jon and Luke having sex together, he had never really considered the possibility of having any form of sexual contact with boys, and that his only previous sexual encounter had been with a girl at his school; this had been a very short-lived relationship. Colin presented as being quite sexually naive. After talking to Jon and Luke he had begun to wonder about why they were doing sexual things together, as they were brothers. He had wondered whether or not it would get them into trouble, as he knew it was wrong. At the same time he reasoned that by being curious and slightly aroused by what had happened, he did not think that it would have really mattered if the situation between him and Jon had gone further, had it not been interrupted, and had nobody else found out about it, notwithstanding feeling slightly pressurised by Jon. On balance he was relieved that nothing sexual had really happened, because he did not believe that he was gay, or wanted to be gay. He was now strongly of the opinion that Jon was gay, because of the content of the conversation that led to him getting into his bed. He did not have a problem with this, but said that he was worried about Luke, because he knew that Luke liked girls, but was having trouble at school with being called names. He was very keen to remain friends with both twins, and was very clear about not speaking to anybody else about what had happened. After this discussion, and attending the meeting with Jon, Luke and their mother, both Colin and his mother stated that they felt that their individual and joint follow-up sessions had helped them. Colin was very clear in saying that he did not feel he now needed any further help.

Luke was very distraught during the early stages of the work with him, expressing a great deal of anxiety about having sexual contact with his brother, and that he knew this would seriously upset his father. He said that he did not know whether or not he had wanted this to happen, because he did not say no to Jon when he first asked him. He said that his father had hardly spoken to him since the sexual behaviour had been discovered. He was adamant that he would never do anything sexual with Jon again, and that he was not interested in having sexual relationships with boys, and that he liked girls. He was worried about how he was now going to get on with Jon, because they were still very close and, as twins, would be likely to continue spending most of their time together. Luke was agreeable to receiving help in exploring these issues in more detail, and also asked for his father to be spoken to. He was also to keen to receive help in relation to being bullied at school. The programme of work with Luke was fully completed over several sessions, as described above. Parallel work with his parents led to improved relationships, and although Luke always felt that for a long time he would have to live with his father's disapproval, he was always aware that the situation was much worse for Jon, who he now understood to be gay. In some ways the fact that Jon eventually told him that he was gay helped him to understand that what had happened was not his fault, even though he did experience a level of sexual pleasure and feels that he had eventually cooperated with Jon's requests more willingly. Luke was adamant that no further sexual behaviour would take place with Jon, and that he was fully confident in being able to say no or if necessary to physically stop Jon. He did not feel that this would ever be necessary, as he had sorted out his relationship with Jon and they were fine and very supportive with each other. As time progressed and Luke moved further away from his anxieties about what had happened, his confidence improved, and he was able to avoid being bullied at school. He was very clear that this had been a situation that he had needed to sort out for himself, saying that the previous intervention of staff at school had in some ways made the situation worse.

Jon was very welcoming of therapeutic support, and was able quickly to own up fully to starting the sexual behaviour both with Luke and with Colin. Jon said that he had come to believe that Luke truly wanted to take part in the behaviour and that on some recent occasions Luke had made hints to go upstairs to the bedroom. Jon was able to recognise that he dominated his relationship with Luke, and that Luke would often do things to please him. Jon stated that if he had known how unhappy Luke had been, he would not have done anything sexual with him, or would have stopped when he found out. Jon stated that he and Luke had spoken briefly about what had happened and have both agreed never to do it again. Jon explained that he and Luke would often exchange possessions in return for favours, and that this was the context in which he had initially offered money and Playstation games in return for Luke's cooperation. Eventually Luke began to cooperate without anything being offered in return. Having said this Jon stated that deep down he always knew that it was wrong to offer material things in exchange for sexual favours, and that Luke was his brother, and that he knew that eventually this would land him in trouble. Jon was also fearful of his situation, because he was fully aware that what he had done with Luke was illegal; he was very relieved by the police decision not to charge him. In discussing these issues confidentially, Jon eventually stated that he believed that he probably was gay, as he had never had any sexual feelings towards girls, and often found himself looking at other boys at school. He felt that he could never tell his parents about this, as he knew that he would not be accepted by the rest of his family. At this point he became distraught; he also stated that he thought that 'people' will think that he is a 'pervert' if they ever found out about his sexual behaviour with Luke. He was worried about Colin knowing what had happened, in case he spoke to other boys at school, and he was worried about losing Colin's friendship. He was also concerned that should his younger sister Sonia find out about what had happened, she would not be able to keep quiet about it, and would not fully understand the reasons why she should not talk about it. Jon volunteered that he needed to make apologies to both Colin and Luke. He was very keen to have more discussions about his situation, as he did not feel he could talk about it to anyone in his family.

The plan of work described above was completed with Jon over several months. Towards the end of the work Jon began to speak much more openly about his sexuality; he was engaged in lengthy discussion about this and was given access to a wide range of resources, including the Avert website. He was reluctant to attend any gay youth network events, as he was fearful of friends at school finding out, and because of his father. For a long time, only Colin and Luke knew about Jon being gay; eventually Jon made the decision to have some discussion with his parents, initially his mother. Marcia told Jon that she had suspected that he was gay and that this was acceptable to her. Simon was for a long time not able to accept that his son was gay and asked him not to tell anybody else about it, hoping that Jon was wrong and would grow out of it. Soon after Jon was 16, he moved from school to college and began to make connections with other gay young people in the wider community, partly through college contacts and the gay youth networks that had previously been identified for him. At this stage the therapeutic work with Jon came to an end. There were no further reported concerns about Jon's sexual behaviours.

10

SELF-ESTEEM

INTRODUCTION

The case studies in this book and other studies (Araji, 1997; Calder, 2002; Hackett, 2004) have shown that children and young people who commit inappropriate or harmful sexual behaviours often have multiple difficulties in their lives, and quite complex needs. Holistic approaches to therapeutic work recognise the importance of addressing these wider needs and will seek to build upon children and young people's strengths, competences and self-esteem, so that they become more able to meet their needs appropriately, and live positive lives without harming others. If a child or young person does not value himself, he is not likely to value others and is therefore more likely to treat others badly, either intentionally or unintentionally. In meeting these needs it is helpful for a child or young person to have a sense of self-worth, alongside a feeling of being valued by others, and to be able to develop his emotional and interpersonal skills to become more able to communicate his wishes and feelings. This is particularly important in sexual relationships, especially if the young person has already made mistakes, but it is also important in wider day-to-day social relationships. It is important for the child or young person to be able to express himself to others, and to be open to receiving positive expression from others in return. It is also important for him to be able to manage and respond to negative appraisals from others, especially in a peer context, as they will have the potential to escalate if mishandled. It is not uncommon for children who have committed harmful sexual behaviours to have a history of peer-related difficulties ranging from name-calling to physical confrontation – being bullied or bullying. This brief chapter will explore issues relating to self-esteem and will discuss and signpost some practical ways of addressing the wider needs of children and young people who have sexual behaviour difficulties – raising self-esteem, developing positive friendships, improving family attachments, developing positive problem solving, managing peer conflicts and achieving positive life experiences.

SELF-ESTEEM

Having self-esteem is having an unconditional sense of self-worth that is enhanced by a sense of purpose and belonging, a sense of capability and self-acceptance, a sense of safety and security, a sense of responsibility and integrity and generally positive life experiences. It also involves recognition of weaknesses, and a positive acceptance of the limits to one's capabilities and abilities. The list of positive words and phrases below represents many different aspects of self-esteem, and can be used as a checklist. When considering the life of a child or young person who has committed inappropriate or harmful sexual behaviour, which of these aspects are present, and which are not, and why?

- Praise – receiving praise and being able to give praise.
- Clarity, awareness, a sense of purpose and belonging – a sense of being wanted.
- Friendship and love – a range of positive interpersonal relationships including positive family attachments, good peer friendships, and, depending on age, potential to become able to develop and maintain close intimate or sexual peer relationships.
- Caring and being cared for – at home, school and elsewhere.
- Achievement, confidence, enjoyment, happiness, communication, celebration and creative expression.
- Responsibility, contribution, assertion and participation.
- Integrity and independence.
- Safety and security.

There are a range of psychological questionnaires and inventories that can be used to assist an assessment of a child or young person's self-esteem (Calder et al., 2001). However, a great deal of information will have been gathered during the overall assessment process, and it is really more important to use the therapeutic sessions to engage the child or young person in telling you about his life and circumstances, and to be aware that his circumstances and his self-esteem will have likely been changed by his committal of harmful or inappropriate sexual behaviours. At the early stages of an intervention, a child or young person's self-esteem is likely to be influenced significantly by the reactions of others to his behaviours. Psychological questionnaires and inventories are less reliable on their own, and should really be used as a supplement to therapeutic interviewing (Babiker & Herbert, 1996).

BUILDING SELF-ESTEEM

Attachments and Relationships

Chapter 2 recognised the significance of poor or disrupted attachments as a significant feature in the lives of many children or young people who sexually harm. When children or young people have not had experiences of positive attachments, they are likely to have deficits in understanding intimacy and mutual caring, which is potentially problematic for their future relationships. In fact many of the areas identified on the list above may be absent or in short supply. It is therefore important to explore and assess this aspect of the child or young person's development and to establish an understanding of the nature of past attachment difficulties, and how they may be having an impact in the present. It may be necessary to undertake specific work between a parent and a child or young person, or perhaps with other family members, looking at their past and present relationships. Sometimes, in these circumstances parents may reject a child or young person, through not being able to come to terms with the news of their inappropriate or harmful sexual behaviours. It is quite likely that the child or young person will have some fears or worries about this happening. This may amount to a breakdown of a secure attachment, or a reinforcement of a previous poor attachment. Either way this will have a significant negative impact on the child or young person's self-esteem, and will affect him in many ways. In these circumstances therapeutic support can become very important, and very much needed. It is not unusual in these circumstances for a child or young person to feel isolated and unloved. Without appropriate support it is easy for this to develop into a spiral of increasing negative self-appraisal, possibly exacerbated by additional negative peer experiences, which may be invited by the child or young person's low or moody disposition. Sometimes children and young people in these circumstances are removed from their peer group altogether by a school exclusion, as educators begin to feel uneasy about the risks being presented. It is easy to see in these circumstances how many aspects of the above checklist can be disrupted. Whatever the particular circumstances of the child or young person are, they will need to be addressed and worked through as an essential part of the therapeutic programme, alongside the offence or behaviour-specific work. There needs to be a fine balance between addressing specific behavioural risks and meeting these wider needs.

THE CHILD OR YOUNG PERSON'S ACCOUNT OF HIS PAST AND PRESENT

A range of therapeutic methods, including timelines, eco-maps, genograms, life story and autobiography, can be used in facilitating a child or young person's account of his personal, family and social history.

Timelines

Timelines are constructed by locating dates and life experiences on a line in chronological order, identifying key events and noting associated past and present thoughts and feelings alongside. These can be augmented with cartoons and drawings as necessary or relevant to the child or young person's age, understanding or chosen mode of expression. Whilst there may be difficult or negative aspects to the timeline, it is helpful for there to be celebratory aspects, no matter how big or small. Timelines can be used in different ways at different stages of the intervention, initially as an assessment tool for gathering information, and comparing a child or young person's view of his past with that reported by others. They can also be used as a means of expression and processing difficult memories, or distorted impressions of the past. They can be used as a means to highlight many other wider and varying aspects of a child or young person's life and achievements, as compared to current difficulties.

Eco-maps

An eco-map is a drawing or map with the child or young person placed at the centre, with drawn lines reaching out to people, places and experiences in his life, highlighting key attachments, friendships and supporting people at home, in the neighbourhood and at school.

Genograms

A genogram is a detailed extended family tree that is used to map out family relationships and attachments. The family tree is mapped out across at least three generations; circles are drawn for females and squares for males. Once the genogram has been constructed, relationship lines can be drawn between family members – three lines for strong bonds between family members, reducing to one line as appropriate, and a dotted line to represent relationship difficulties or conflict.

Life Stories/Autobiography

Life stories and autobiographies are chronological accounts of the child or young person's past, identifying key events and other significant aspects of his history. They can be constructed verbally, using a voice recorder, or as a video diary, or can be written out as a narrative, alongside collected photographs and items of memorabilia, or even drawn as cartoons linking captions and phrases.

PROBLEM SOLVING

It is important for the child or young person to be helped to develop a range of problem-solving skills, and to be supported in addressing specific day-to-day problems in his life, by being given opportunities to discuss them at length, explaining their history and how he has attempted to solve them to date. This will have a direct link to some of the offence- or behaviour-specific work that will have already taken place, where links were made between thoughts, feelings and action, and ranges of alternative responses (stop and think) were established. Certainly the child or young person will need to learn alternative responses to those that were harmful to others, and many aspects of this work will transfer across to other circumstances of his life. Some of these responses will have included asking for help, which will mean identifying significant adults, and possibly peers or older siblings; considering different options; being aware of the responses and feelings of others and so on. Other problem-solving methods can include cognitive reframing – techniques to replace negative self-appraisal and a sense of inevitable failure with positive self-statements. For example, a child or young person having not been invited by his friends to join in a game could think 'nobody likes me because I am no good' or, alternatively, 'they did not choose me because they do not know what I am able to do', etc. Generally the child or young person can be encouraged to scrutinise his own thoughts and feelings and let go of those that are negative or self-defeating and replace them with positive thoughts; these will need to be rehearsed. It may be helpful to encourage him to list his abilities and achievements – this can be done as an overall list, and also as part of a 'this week's news' section at the beginning of each session. Problem solving may include a specific focus on conflict resolution, and possibly anger management, which will again have links with other aspects of the therapeutic work. It can also include relaxation techniques that could lead to a child or young person having better self-control, and improved patterns of sleep. These problem-solving techniques will accumulate to encourage assertiveness and participation, and will build resilience and self-esteem. Every opportunity should be taken to encourage the child or young person to believe that he is capable of having a positive life, despite the setbacks he may have experienced or caused.

SOCIAL SKILLS

Initial assessments will have considered the child or young person's social interactions and his social skills, and will have identified areas for support and development; these are likely to relate closely to the sex and relationships education needs identified in Chapter 9. Building social skills is likely to feature throughout most aspects of a therapeutic programme. It will involve helping a child or young person develop communication skills – listening and responding; understanding body language and people's sense of personal space; developing self-awareness and an understanding of other people's feelings and perspectives; identifying and understanding different feelings and learning how to express them; managing peer and family relationships; understanding friendship; conflict resolution; anger management and assertiveness training; taking part in age-appropriate social and leisure activities; understanding and managing the changes of puberty through adolescence into adulthood. A great deal of information about social skills training is available elsewhere in the literature, and will not be listed here. It is important that the tasks involved in social skills training are generally small and achievable in the child or young person's actual life. It will be helpful to discuss circumstances and scenarios with him during the therapeutic sessions, but he will also need to be supported through both his achievements and his possible setbacks, by those around him in his day-to-day life.

CONCLUSIONS

This chapter has explored the concept of self-esteem and has considered its place in a programme of therapeutic work for children and young people who have displayed harmful or inappropriate sexual behaviours. It was recognised that because of these behaviours, there may be many reasons and circumstances that will be challenging to the child or young person's self-esteem. His life will have changed and on the surface will have become more difficult, particularly at the early stage of the discovery of his behaviours. Raising and maintaining the child or young person's self-esteem was considered to be an essential task of therapeutic intervention, but one that must be balanced with identifying and managing areas of potential risk or harm. The chapter identified a range of issues important for building self-esteem and presented and signposted a range of methods and techniques that could be used in practice. It was emphasised that any tasks or targets set should be realistic and achievable, and that the child or young person should have access to day-to-day support in managing both successes and difficulties. It was recognised that building self-esteem permeates the whole intervention programme and is an essential ingredient to engagement and positive change.

CASE STUDY – MARK (9)

Synopsis

Mark is a nine-year-old white British boy, slightly below average size, and has above average learning abilities, although it is reported at school that academically he significantly underachieves. In the mornings at school he is often tired and grumpy, and is known to verbally and physically lash out at other pupils. His teachers have reported that Mark finds it hard to concentrate and often leads classroom distractions, which inevitably involve other pupils. There have been many occasions when Mark has been found taunting and bullying other pupils. For some time, special arrangements have been made for Mark to go to the deputy head teacher's office for the first half-hour of the day. On some days, Mark spends large portions of his break-times and lunchtimes with teachers, in isolation from other pupils. This had begun to happen with increasing regularity.

Mark has had a disrupted life; his parents, James and Angela, separated when he was four. At this time he lived for 15 months with his father in a one-bedroom flat, sleeping on a sofa-bed. Mark has no birth siblings. For the past three years, Mark's father has settled into a new family, with his new wife Jane, who has two children from a previous marriage – Stephen aged six and Jill aged four. Mark initially had regular contact with his father and his new family. Increasingly there was considerable conflict between Mark and his stepmother, with arguments mainly pivoting on Mark's relationship with Stephen and Jill, who were becoming increasingly frightened of Mark. Often Jane would enter the room to find one or both of them crying, after having been on their own with Mark for less than 10 minutes. The outcome of this was that Mark was eventually only allowed to stay with the family for limited periods of time. During this period, Mark was living partly with his mother Angela, and partly with his paternal grandmother, Helen.

Mark's mother, Angela, has bouts of severe depression and has an alcohol problem. Since separating from Mark's father, James, she has had several unhappy relationships with men. For 18 months she lived with a man named Michael, who was physically and sexually violent towards her. Mark has witnessed a great deal of this violence. On three occasions she has spent time in a woman's refuge, on two of these occasions she took Mark with her. On some occasions Michael was physically violent towards Mark, often blaming him as being the cause of the adults' problems. On other occasions Michael was kind, and spent time with Mark, taking him to football matches and on fishing trips. After this relationship finally broke down, Angela lived alone with Mark. By this stage Angela was drinking large quantities of alcohol, and was often away from home until late at night. On many occasions Mark was left in the care of teenage babysitters. On these occasions there would be many young people at the house. Again Mark witnessed sexual activity, drinking and sometimes drug taking, and was often heavily chastised by the babysitters for refusing to stay upstairs. During this period he spent long weekends with his father and stepmother and spent some of the school holidays with his paternal grandmother. Mark has always stated that he would like to live with his father.

Mark now lives on a permanent basis with his paternal grandmother, spending occasional and sporadic nights with his father's family. Mark's mother lives alone in temporary accommodation, and has severe alcohol problems. Mark sees her occasionally, but rarely stays overnight with her. Mark's grandmother has asked the Social Services Department for assistance, as she is finding Mark to be increasingly aggressive and finds him difficult to manage. More recently Mark has been refusing to go to bed on time, and has on some occasions stayed out of the house until after dark, with his grandmother reporting him missing to the police. On several occasions Mark has stolen small amounts of money from her, and has adamantly denied it when challenged. There have also been times when she has had to use quite severe reprimands in getting Mark ready for school on time. On several occasions she has received letters, phone calls or been called in to the school to discuss Mark's aggressive behaviour. Increasingly Mark is refusing to accede to his grandmother's wishes. On one or two occasions he has come close to physically threatening her.

Mark's grandmother was at a complete loss when it was reported to Social Services that, at school, Mark had lifted a girl's dress and put his hand down her pants, and had asked her to suck his penis. Prior to this there had been ongoing concerns about Mark's general demeanour at school, and about a number of incidents of suspected inappropriate sexual behaviour. Three weeks ago, a boy and a girl from the same class as Mark reported that he had touched their genital region, over their clothes, on more than one occasion. They both felt that these acts had been deliberate and were upset. It was not clear whether or not any other pupil witnessed this behaviour. There was no teacher present when it happened, and Mark adamantly and convincingly denied the accusation, saying that he was always being picked on by other boys and girls in the class, and that nobody would be his friend.

When the teacher questioned Mark, he became annoyed that he had been accused of something he did not do. He explained that the three of them and one or two others had been playing a game of 'tag', and that there had been some pushing and pulling when they were trying to get back to 'base' where they couldn't be 'on'. Mark said that he had been picked on because of a dispute about him refusing to be 'on' after being tagged. The other pupils were spoken to, and reported that there had been a bit of a fight, and that Mark had fallen out with the boy and the girl. These other pupils reported no immediate problem with Mark. At this stage the matter was considered resolved, with all pupils being reminded about privacy and safety.

Some time later on the same morning, a further pupil walked into the staffroom, in tears, and stated that when she had been in the school play-ground, Mark had threatened her to go behind the kitchens, and had put his hands down her pants, and had exposed his penis and told her that she had to suck it. When this incident was investigated by the Social Services, after a long period of denial, Mark admitted that the girl was telling the truth. Two weeks later, there was a further Social Services investigation into his-torical reports that Mark has forced his four-year-old stepsister Jill to suck his penis. It was also reported that Mark forced his stepbrother Stephen to lie on top of Jill, both without clothes on. Again, after a lengthy period of denial, Mark admitted that the reports were true. A multi-agency meeting was called to discuss the risks presented by Mark and plan a programme of intervention for the family.

Initial Analysis

- Mark has committed a series of serious sexual offences, but he is below age of criminal responsibility, and will therefore not be interviewed by the police. In a matter of weeks he will be 10 years old, so any future offences are likely to result in police action. There is therefore a risk that Mark could end up having a criminal record for sexual offences.
- Mark is very bright and aware of many of his actions, and has proved himself to be adept at explaining himself, and causing diversions to conceal his actions. This increases significantly the risk he presents to other children.
- Mark's behaviours are best described as being sexually aggressive, and they are extensive and varied, across a range of different settings at home and school. There are many potential reasons why Mark has been engag-ing in these behaviours, all of which must be identified and addressed by therapeutic work.
- Mark has witnessed and experienced domestic violence.
- Mark has witnessed aggressive sexual behaviour directed towards his mother from some of the men she associated with – in particular from Michael, who had an ambiguous and unpredictable relationship with him.

- Mark has witnessed teenage sexual activity and discussion and has seen pornographic films.
- It is likely that Mark feels that nobody really likes him or wants him apart from his grandmother. Most of Mark's attachments have been frag- mentary and ultimately disrupted. He has little investment in letting himself become attached to others, as he believes he will be let down – this has been his life experience. Mark has developed patterns of nega- tive thinking, and is probably fearful of rejection, both at home and at school.
- Mark has some good days with his grandmother, but repeatedly tests out this relationship – as if he cannot believe that it will last.
- Mark appears to have a deep resentment towards his father's new wife and other children – he probably feels that they are in his place. It is there- fore quite likely that Mark will interpret this as evidence of a rejection by his father.
- Mark is likely to believe that his mother no longer cares about him and does not really care about her any more – he sees himself mainly as part of his father's family.
- Mark does not believe that his grandmother really has that much of a right to tell him what to do. He feels in a similar way about his teachers at school.
- Mark's life has at times been completely out of control and unstructured, giving him both freedom and quite extreme vulnerability.
- Mark has sexually abused several children – all in circumstances of put- ting himself in a powerful and controlling position.
- Mark's behaviours are likely to have become sexual because of what he has seen and witnessed and because he has learned that these behaviours put him in a controlling position and generate a 'buzz' around him – drawing a great deal of attention.
- Mark may have learned that his sexual knowledge has a high currency amongst some of his peers and puts him in charge.
- Some of his behaviours appear to have been committed to hurt others, both the victims directly and others associated with the victims – his father and stepmother.
- Mark's behaviours are likely to continue at least initially in the face of therapeutic work, as they are purposeful, deep-rooted, multi-faceted and functional to his life. He is likely to be committing these behaviours to address personal feelings of being out of control and to feel good about himself in a life where he often feels sad and rejected. Some of the pat- terns of his behaviours have been learned from the adult male role models he has had – sexual aggression, violence, controlling attitudes.
- As Mark gets older, the sexual aspects of his behaviours will have increased potency, and will be an added drive to his behaviours.

Case Plan

All parties agreed to a plan of Mark remaining in the community, living pre-dominantly with his grandmother Helen. A programme of therapeutic work was set up for Mark, alongside regular support for Helen – Mark's grand-mother. Work was also undertaken with James and Angela – Mark's parents – to allow them to make a more positive contribution to Mark's care.

Immediate Safety and Protection

It was recognised that until Mark can be helped to bring these behaviours under control he will require substantial supervision and support – both at home and at school. 'Safety plans' were therefore drawn up with Mark and the adults across the various settings of his life to ensure that wherever pos-sible his contact with other children was supervised. These plans clearly identified circumstances of potential risk, and provided scripts for the various adults involved to ask Mark specific questions about how he was managing to keep to the plan, and how he was feeling about it. The purpose of this was to encourage Mark – who was a very articulate boy – to express his feelings, and in particular his daily anxieties, in words, rather than allow-ing him to build up anger and resentment. These discussions provided Mark with regular opportunities to receive positive support and attention, and find appropriate solutions to the problems in his life, as they arose. The format of this plan was similar to the 'family safety plan' detailed in Alan's case study. Importantly, as with that plan, the concepts 'risk', 'risky feelings' and 'risky situations' were clearly defined and shared with all parties. Sets of questions were designed to structure conversations between Mark and the various adults – mainly Helen – that would allow recognition of how he was managing these situations and feelings.

Written agreements were signed, and regular meetings were called to monitor their progress and fine-tune identified difficulties. In some ways this was very restrictive for Mark, but it also provided him with structured care, and guaranteed his own safety. It has to be remembered that at this stage Mark was presenting a range of very high risks – the safety plan was set up to prevent Mark from hurting others and from landing himself with a crimi-nal record that would have a negative effect on him for the rest of his life.

Mark – Therapeutic Programme to Address Mark's Sexually Aggressive Behaviour

There are many problems in Mark's life that need to be addressed, but most importantly, he first needs assistance in bringing his sexual behaviours under control. Without this immediate help, it is likely that he will commit further sexually aggressive behaviours. The immediate safety and protection plan will provide some initial assurance and security, and will reinforce the early stages of the work. A therapeutic programme for Mark will involve:

- Collection of detailed information about the circumstances of all Mark's known sexually harmful behaviours.
- Securing Mark's engagement and agreement to undertake therapeutic work to bring his sexually aggressive behaviours under control, and to help him find solutions and better ways of managing the many problems and difficulties in his life. Helping Mark to appreciate the importance of the work, and the potential personal, legal and social consequences for him and others, of committing further sexually aggressive behaviours (see Chapter 6).
- Comparing Mark's description and explanation of his behaviours with the details in the investigation reports, challenging inconsistencies and denial up to the point of there being an accurate description and some initial ownership of his sexually aggressive behaviours.
- Helping Mark to agree to a plan of supervision at home and school, to ensure the safety and protection of others and of him.
- Helping Mark to begin to identify his thoughts and feelings before, during and after his sexually aggressive behaviours, and developing his early basic understanding of how these relate to his safety plan. This will also involve helping Mark's early recognition and management of circumstances of risk.
- Helping Mark to construct a timeline of his life, setting out a chronology of significant life events from his perspective. Again this will need to involve a comparison with his known personal, family and social history.
- Exploration of Mark's sexual history and level of sexual knowledge, and how it was obtained. Embedding, as far as possible, neutral questions about whether Mark himself has been sexually abused. It is known that Mark has experienced an abuse of his sexuality and sexual development (Bolton, Morris & MacEachron, 1989), but it is important to establish whether he has experienced contact sexual abuse, how this has affected him, and how he views it.
- Detailed examination of the patterns or cycles of Mark's sexual behaviours, exploring his thinking errors, supporting thoughts or fantasies, and how he managed to get others to go along with his behaviours – what he said to them, and whether or not he threatened them if they told. As this work progresses, and Mark becomes more familiar with the process of the work, it will be possible to more fully challenge him about finer details and any minimisation or shifting of responsibility onto others (see Chapter 7).

- Helping Mark to fully appreciate the impact of his behaviours on others, in particular those he has directly hurt. The work needs to establish for Mark a full understanding of the impact of sexual abuse. This understanding will in the long run need to be demonstrated by Mark in terms of his thoughts and feelings, and his subsequent actions. It may be appropriate to assist Mark in making full and meaningful apologies to his step-siblings. If Mark has been sexually abused himself, it is important that he is guided towards an appreciation of the impact of this on himself, through being encouraged to talk about his experiences in detail (see Chapter 8).
- Providing Mark with a comprehensive programme of sex and relationships education, to replace the inappropriate knowledge and beliefs he will have likely gathered from his experiences and behaviours. Also, as suggested by the practice framework in Chapter 2, looking at the role of power in relationships, exploring how Mark sees himself as a boy and the images of masculinity he has received, using the 'Man's World' board game and other materials. Also work on understanding peer relations, making and keeping friendships, etc. (see Chapter 9).
- Helping Mark to talk through his family and life experiences and assisting him in repairing his family and peer relationships. Helping Mark to appreciate that adults have let him down, and that much that has happened to him in his life was not his fault, and was beyond his control. A balance needs to be maintained here, as it is important not to allow Mark to let these negative life experiences become excuses for his sexually aggressive behaviours. Through building on his attachment to his grandmother, Mark can be helped to re-establish other family attachments and make an investment in peer friendships. This will include helping Mark to appropriately express and manage his feelings towards others.
- Setting up additional positive experiences for Mark with a male social support worker. This will be important in terms of providing respite for Mark's grandmother, particularly in the interim period of trying to re-establish a positive relationship for Mark with his father, and in the longer term with his mother. Mark will need to have some longer-term assistance in enhancing his social skills, and in finding positive solutions to problems and difficulties. It will be helpful if he is guided towards recognising his personal strengths and building his self-esteem, both through his achievements in completing this therapeutic programme, and through wider experiences with the social support worker.
- Helping Mark to find ways to demonstrate that he is being able to manage his risks and avoid circumstances where he could abuse, by helping him to develop age-appropriate relapse prevention techniques (see Chapter 11) – for example, 'stop and think' techniques, 'avoidance and escape strategies', changing thoughts and fantasies, and importantly being able

to identify people in his life who will support him in his plan not to commit further sexual abuse, and how to contact them and ask for help. Also to prepare Mark for the possibility of receiving further help at a later stage of his development, possibly when he goes through puberty.

- Finally, an assessment and evaluation of Mark's overall progress and identification of potential future risks, and how they need to be managed.

Helen – Regular Support and Assistance in Understanding and Managing Mark's Behaviours

- Recognising the importance of Mark's attachment to his grandmother, and his need for consistent care, an intensive package of immediate support was provided.
- Carrying out an assessment of Helen's awareness of Mark's sexual behaviours and sexual development. This assessment will also need at least to involve Mark's father, and ideally his mother, as they will at some point in the future be involved with Mark's supervision, and may also have important further historical information. The immediate need is to establish these details from Helen, as his primary carer.
- Regular social work contact, providing ongoing help and support in managing Mark, providing basic information about how to manage the risks he presents to others.
- Helping Helen to understand the nature of work being undertaken with Mark, explaining how he thinks and feels about his circumstances, and how he translates these feelings into 'risky' behaviours including information about the process of abusing – wanting to do it; thinking it OK to do it; finding a time and place to do it; getting the victim to go along with it.
- Helping Helen to understand and implement Mark's safety plan.
- Provision of holiday-type respite breaks and regular contact with a male support worker – providing a positive male role model and engaging Mark in appropriate leisure activities and helping him to develop age-appropriate interests.

James and Angela – Mark's Parents

- Counselling to be undertaken separately with both James and Angela, to help them to gain a better understanding of Mark's perception of his life and how and why he has been engaging in sexually aggressive behaviours.
- Ensuring that they both understand the importance of managing the risks presented by Mark when they have contact with him.

- Assisting James's family in recovering from the sexual abuse their children have experienced. This will also include an offer of individual post-abuse counselling for Stephen and Jill. Ideally to be offered by other practitioners through separately allocated case work.
- Helping and encouraging James and Angela to become more able to offer positive support to Mark and have more regular contact with him.

Outcome

The programmes of work were carried out more or less as described. Some of the progress was hampered by changes of professionals involved, but Mark had the same specialist practitioner working with him directly throughout an 18-month plan of therapeutic work. Initially Mark was resistant to therapeutic help and minimised his sexually aggressive behaviours – he was a very unhappy boy. He attempted to blame others, rather than take responsibility for his actions. With a persistent response from those around him, and from the approach of the therapeutic work, Mark was enabled to accept the seriousness of his circumstances, and began to own his sexual behaviours.

Mark was helped not to feel responsible for his rejections and the bad things that had happened to him. Alongside this he was helped to understand the impact of his behaviours on others, and why they were wrong. Although Mark had on several occasions witnessed sexual violence towards his mother, he was very clear in stating that he himself had not experienced contact sexual abuse.

It took some considerable time before Mark could regain enough trust to be relied upon to keep to his safety plan without intensive supervision. Eventually he had to change his school, which at the time was difficult for all parties, but in the long run allowed him to build a better reputation for himself with his peers. Mark had some periods of time in respite foster care – the foster carers had attended a specialist training course and a placement agreement detailing the risks presented by Mark was completed. These were very carefully managed with Mark being fully aware that it was for a short break with a return back to his grandmother – she needed the breaks, and this kept the situation from breaking down.

As described in the programme, this work looked specifically at the sexually aggressive behaviours Mark had committed, analysing their process, using cognitive behavioural techniques to explore them and give Mark ways to avoid them in future. Alongside this a great deal of work was undertaken with Mark allowing him to explore his past experiences, his feelings of rejection, and the resentment he harboured towards both his mother and father, and his father's new family – working towards a reconciliation with his father – eventually he had renewed contact with his father and daytime visits (very closely supervised) to the family. Mark also renewed contact with his mother – it was made very clear to Mark that he would continue to live with his grandmother and that living with his mother or father was not an option – but that ongoing contact and a good relationship with them was an option.

As time passed, and with Mark making good progress with the therapeutic work, it was possible for some of his supervision to become less intense. He was able to make apologies to his step-siblings, and showed himself increasingly able to manage and evade potentially risky situations. There were no reports of Mark committing further sexual offences. When Mark was approaching 13, he returned for some further work. This was mainly based around sex and relationships education, and revisiting some of the issues around his past sexual behaviours. This was chiefly in response to changes in his understanding of sexual matters, due to the onset of his puberty – the need for this was predicted and planned for.

This case study was an example of a complex and long-term intervention involving many people forming a team around Mark to prevent further abuse. At the time Mark demonstrated strong motivation to abuse – the cause was multi-faceted and required a wide-ranging intervention. The role of the specialist help was to provide the therapeutic work to Mark and ongoing consultation and support to other parties involved – carers, and other professionals who could then cascade the knowledge down to other professionals, such as schoolteachers and classroom support workers.

11

RELAPSE PREVENTION

INTRODUCTION

One of the major objectives of the therapeutic work described in earlier chapters has been for the child or young person to be able to demonstrate that he is able to identify and understand the patterns or cycles of behavioural steps and associated thoughts, feelings and fantasies that led him to committing harmful or inappropriate sexual behaviours. Once this has been achieved it is important that the child or young person becomes able to apply his learning to new situations and circumstances in the real world. There will be many circumstances where he will be faced with decisions, the outcome of which will take him either towards or away from further harmful sexual behaviours. This stage of the work is often referred to as 'relapse prevention' and is a modification of a model that was originally used to strengthen the self-management skills of substance abusers (Gray & Pithers, 1993). This chapter will outline briefly the main principles of the relapse prevention approach, and will discuss a range of practical techniques for helping a child or young person avoid committing further harmful or inappropriate sexual behaviours. Some of these techniques and applications will be carried out by the young person himself, others will be related to those who will support him in his day-to-day life. It is important for these methods to be realistic and achievable, and tailored to the specific needs of the individual child or young person in a manner that addresses his unique pathway into committing the sexual behaviours in question. It is also important for relapse prevention work to be conducted in a context of building and developing children and young people's strengths, competencies and abilities to be able to meet their needs appropriately in a positive manner that enhances their self-esteem and enables them to recognise the needs and wishes of others.

OUTLINING THE RELAPSE PREVENTION MODEL

A key assumption of the relapse prevention model is that (apart from behaviours that have for various reasons been established as being more or less purely impulsive, perhaps for medical or psychiatric reasons) harmful or inappropriate sexual behaviour will occur as a result of an accumulation of thoughts, feelings, fantasies and behaviours over time, moving closer and closer towards high-risk situations. 'High-risk' situations are stimuli associated with past or future harmful sexual behaviours – it may be a time or place, a particular aspect of behaviour, or it may be a thought or a harmful or inappropriate sexual fantasy. A lapse is when a person engages in thoughts, feelings, fantasies or non-abusive behaviours that are precursors to harmful or inappropriate sexual behaviours. A relapse is when harmful or inappropriate sexual behaviour is actually committed. A person can move into increasingly 'risky' circumstances by making a series of 'Seemingly Unimportant Decisions' (Gray & Pithers, 1993, p. 295). Taken one by one the decisions may seem irrelevant or unconnected, but taken together they accumulate to precipitate the person into committing a harmful act. Isolated aspects of behaviour may seem safe, unimportant or irrelevant to previous harmful sexual behaviours, but when considered on a continuum of other thoughts and behaviours they may be a significant contributory factor to a relapse into further harmful sexual behaviour. For example, a boy may on a Friday morning choose not to plan to go to the cinema with friends on the following Saturday afternoon, knowing that his aunt will be visiting his house with his younger cousin, alongside another decision on Friday afternoon to get some old toys out of the loft – toys suitable for a much younger child. With these decisions made, on the Friday night the boy may then start to have sexual thoughts or fantasies about his younger cousin, and begin to think about how they will be able to play together on the Saturday. By this stage the boy has moved significantly along a pattern or cycle of behaviour that has led to him planning a harmful sexual act, and will probably already be employing 'thinking errors' – thinking that his cousin will be happy playing with his old toys, and therefore will go along with what other 'games' he may suggest, especially if he is allowed to keep some of the toys. A relapse prevention plan will help this boy to be able to recognise and understand how the connections between these individual decisions and actions could precipitate him towards committing a harmful sexual act. It will provide him with a series of alternative responses and reactions to his thoughts, which will lead him in an opposite direction.

RELAPSE PREVENTION WORK

Relapse prevention work is about assisting and maintaining the changes established by previous therapeutic work – transferring the learning out of the therapeutic context into the real world. It will assist the child or young person in identifying which decisions and situations could precipitate inappropriate or harmful sexual behaviour, helping him to develop methods and techniques to cope more effectively with circumstances of risk – self-management that enables him to avoid high-risk situations, and make the right decisions that will prevent him from committing harmful sexual behaviours. One of the difficulties with this – particularly after several weeks or months of therapeutic work – for many children and young people, and sometimes parents and carers, is having to accept the possibility of a relapse – the possibility that the child or young person could commit further harmful sexual behaviours. Practitioners in the field will be familiar with statements along the lines of: 'I know now that what I did was wrong and I therefore know that I won't do it again.' Did this young person ever really think that what he was doing was right? If so, why, for example, did the behaviour take place when his parents went out, and why did he ask his sister to keep it secret, etc.? Many of these challenges to the young person will have already taken place during the early stages of the work, but they are likely to resurface during these later stages. Children and young people will naturally want to know that they are OK and will therefore have at least a level of resistance to the need to learn about taking control and managing lapses. They will be helped if they can get to the position of thinking that they are OK because they have accepted the possibility of risk, understand the relapse process, and have learned how to manage lapses at an early stage, long before they become relapses. It is helpful to mention that everybody in some way has to exercise self-control, and that many people have urges and thoughts that they know they would never want to act out in reality.

It is important for relapse prevention plans to be tailored to the needs of the individual child or young person, and be closely related to his pathway into committing harmful sexual behaviours. It is helpful to inform the young person that recurring memories or fantasies related to his past harmful sexual behaviours are very likely, and that what is important is how he reacts to them, and that he learns to see a lapse as an opportunity to practise self-management and take control of his life. In this way lapses are reinterpreted as positive opportunities to learn, as opposed to being incidents of failure. To do this the young person will need to be assisted in building on his existing and newly learnt personal and social coping skills. This will involve learning how to recognise and acknowledge the antecedents of harmful or inappropriate sexual behaviours, and to have a continuous awareness of potential risks; important decisions to avoid risks; knowledge of high-risk situations; knowledge of strategies to avoid risks; programmed coping responses to known and potential risk situations; techniques for coping with inappropriate sexual urges or inappropriate sexual fantasies – pairing them with negative stimuli and/or replacing them with appropriate positive fantasies; developed problem-solving skills – being able to stop and think about lapses or other problems, and plan more positive responses; learning about when to ask for help from others. One of the best ways to help a young person avoid harmful sexual behaviours is to help him to develop the competence and ability to perform positive behaviours and meet his needs appropriately, and to have experiences that will naturally build and develop his self-esteem, and allow him to feel able to meet his sexual needs appropriately. These issues were discussed in the two previous chapters and are crucial to positive relapse prevention.

RELAPSE PREVENTION TECHNIQUES

Relapse prevention techniques are mainly extensions and summaries of previous work that will have been undertaken, for example, as described in Chapter 7, helping a young person to identify his pattern or cycle of behaviour; work on Situation–Thoughts–Feelings–Action; the Four Steps and Four Stops; Steps to Sexual Offending and work on developing appropriate sexual fantasies. Gray and Pithers (1993, pp. 301–307) have identified a 16-stage plan which breaks down as follows:

Stage 1   Explanation of the RP model
Stage 2   Identifying risk factors
Stage 3   Recording risk factors
Stage 4   Individual review of risk factors
Stage 5   Identification of the most common risk factor
Stage 6   Cue identification
Stage 7   Analysis of cues
Stage 8   Identification of coping responses
Stage 9   Brainstorming of coping strategies
Stage 10   Analysis of coping strategies
Stage 11   Review of optimal coping strategies
Stage 12   Preparation of reminder card
Stage 13   Processing other risk factors
Stage 14   Testing preparedness
Stage 15   Analysis of effectiveness
Stage 16   Informing the prevention team

Importantly this plan concludes with reference to a prevention team, this being a group of people, usually adults, who will assist with various stages of the plan. The 'prevention team' – perhaps better referred to as a 'support team' – will comprise nominated people who are part of the young person's day-to-day life and will have knowledge of his circumstances, and of the plan. They will assist by monitoring and supervising the child or young person's progress, and will be there to give reminders and direction as necessary. It is hoped that as the plan progresses over time, the role of the support team will diminish, with the child or young person taking on an increasing amount of self-monitoring and self-management of lapses, avoidance of risk situations and so on. Alan's case study in Chapter 8 provided an example of how parents and family members were enlisted to support a young person in keeping to his plan. The case study of Graham at the end of this chapter will provide an example of a relapse prevention plan with aspects similar to the 16-stage plan above – perhaps being a little more simplified and young person-centred. Some of the techniques used in this plan are described below.

Explaining the Relapse Process

It is important for the relapse process to be fully explained to the child or young person, so that he becomes able to demonstrate a clear understanding of how it would apply to his circumstances. The manner in which this is done will depend upon the age, development and ability of the child or young person. For example, the relapse process could be drawn out as a series of illustrated cartoon captions, or a series of connecting boxes, or a connecting chain of words, such as: Thoughts → Feelings → Fantasy → Risky Thinking → Planning → Acting.

Risk Scenarios

This is really a preparatory exercise to assist a young person in understanding how the relapse process works, and to help him to begin to recognise potential 'risky' circumstances. The young person is asked to devise stories or descriptions of potential harmful sexual behaviour that could be committed in his current life:

- Who it could be against
- Where it could happen
- How it could happen
- How the young person would feel
- How the victim would feel
- What would happen if the young person was caught or the victim told

Defining High-risk Situations

Building on the previous exercise, the child or young person is asked to identify and list the high-risk situations in his life – 'I still need to avoid high-risk situations. My high-risk situations are: . . .'

Feelings Triggers

A statement reminding the young person that most people who have committed harmful sexual behaviours describe having certain feelings before they offended – for example, feeling angry, lonely or bored, or a combination of these. The young person should be asked to list the feelings that could lead to him committing a sexual offence, and how he plans to cope with them. Examples of feelings triggers could include:

- feeling angry
- feeling isolated or left out
- feeling upset because of being in trouble for something
- feeling jealous about a sibling or a friend
- feeling scared or powerless
- feeling hurt or bullied
- feeling unwanted by parents, siblings or carers
- feeling anxious about sexuality or sexual feelings.

List of Thinking Errors

A reminder for the young person about how thinking errors operate as excuses and minimisation for harmful sexual behaviours, alongside a list of the thinking errors the young person employed previously, alongside potential future 'thinking errors' in his current life. Examples of these could include:

- I thought she agreed to what I was doing
- He did not mind because I did not have to give her anything
- She agreed because she took the money
- I was only playing
- I did not mean it to happen
- It was an experiment
- It just happened
- I could not stop myself
- He came to me
- She could have told.

List of Thinking Truths

The young person can also be asked to draw up a complementary list of 'thinking truths' – statements reminding him of what the true impact and consequences of harmful sexual behaviour would be. Examples of these could include:

- I know that I hurt her
- He did not want to do it and I made him
- I knew what I was doing
- I knew it was wrong
- I threatened her and made her feel scared about telling
- He had no choice about taking part
- It was my fault not his
- I could have stopped myself from doing it.

Identifying Helpful Personal Statements

Statements that will remind the young person that there will be times when he will be reminded of the harmful sexual behaviour he committed, along-side reminders and statements that he can say to himself in response to 'risky' thoughts, etc. For example:

I know there will be times when I am reminded about the sexual abuse I have done. This does not mean that I have failed or that I will do it again. When I have these thoughts I have to remember to avoid High Risks.

When I have a thought or fantasy about sexual abuse, I have to remember to think about the bad things that could happen. I could imagine a policeman seeing what I was doing or Mum or Dad finding out, or friends at school.

I know that I cannot forget about the sexual abuse I have done. When I think about it I can say to myself – that was in the past, I know how not to do this again.

Identifying Avoidance Tactics

Helping the young person to list in advance the methods and techniques he could use to make positive choices and decisions in advance that will strengthen his resolve to always try to avoid high-risk places and circum-stances. For example, a decision never to offer to babysit or allow himself to be in a situation on his own with younger children, or a decision to only have same-age or older friendships.

Developing Programmed Responses

An already prepared statement for responding to high-risk situations, for example, a response to abusive thoughts or fantasies:

> I know this is only a thought and that acting on it will hurt others and lead me into a lot of trouble.

Planning Escape Strategies

A set of immediate strategies or responses for the young person to use in situations where he feels that his resolve to avoid high risks has been compromised, or where he feels he does not know what to do. For example, if some friends suggested going to someone's house – perhaps a friend who has a younger sibling – where younger children are present without adults. Rather than feeling any need or pressure to explain, he can suddenly look at a watch or ask the time, and in a sudden voice say, 'Oh no, I'm late, I must go home!' This requires no further explanation and allows the young person to make his exit.

Responding to Harmful Sexual Fantasies

If and when the young person has harmful or inappropriate sexual fantasies he is encouraged to switch to alternative positive sexual fantasies, the nature of which will have been discussed and planned in some detail, following the basic principles set out in Chapter 7. Added to this, if necessary, the young person is encouraged to add on bad or negative consequences to harmful sexual fantasies or thoughts – for example, attending a police interview or parents or friends discovering the behaviour in the fantasy.

Enlisting Help

The young person is asked to draw up a list of people in his current life, who have agreed to help him keep to his plan not to commit harmful or inappropriate sexual behaviours, alongside statements of how they will help.

A Final Reminder

A statement reminding the young person that a lapse or a thought is not a failure, but is an opportunity to practise what he has learnt, and prove to himself that he is able to exercise self-control.

Appropriate Sexual Behaviour

A statement reminding the young person that he is a sexual person, and that it is 'normal' to have sexual feelings, urges and fantasies. There are sexual behaviours that are appropriate and are part of loving, caring relationships. There are also sexual behaviours that are inappropriate and against the law, and which are harmful. It is important that the young person is able to demonstrate that he understands the difference.

Examples of these techniques are provided after the case study at the end of the chapter.

CONCLUSIONS

This chapter has outlined the main principles of relapse prevention with children and young people who have committed harmful or inappropriate sexual behaviours. Initially the theoretical underpinnings of the model were explained, before discussing a range of practical techniques that can be applied in helping children or young people avoid committing further harmful or inappropriate sexual behaviours. It was emphasised that it was important to establish a team of people involved with the child or young person's life who could assist with his plan, by monitoring, supervising and providing cues and reminders as necessary. The aim of a relapse prevention plan is to move the child or young person along a continuum away from supervision to self-management and self-control. The chapter emphasised the importance of these plans being unique to each individual child, tailored to the particular circumstances that led to him committing harmful or inappropriate sexual behaviours. The chapter also recognised that it was important for relapse prevention plans to be constructed in a context of recognising and building upon children and young people's strengths and competencies, so that they can have positive achievements in their lives, and meet their personal, social and sexual needs in a manner that raises their self-esteem and takes them away from the circumstances that led to them committing harmful or inappropriate sexual behaviours.

CASE STUDY – STEPHEN (9) AND GRAHAM (14)

Synopsis

Stephen is a nine-year-old white British boy who has lived in foster care with Kevin and Alison Hunter for the past two years. Graham, a 14-year-old white

British boy with moderate learning difficulties, has also lived in the placement for the past three years. Kevin and Alison have two adult children, Maria and Brian, both living away from home. Brian is married and has twin sons, Liam and Leon, aged two; he and his wife regularly visit and stay with Kevin and Alison, as does Maria.

Prior to being placed, Stephen lived with his mother Sheila, her partner Barry, and his baby brother Martin, who at Sheila's request has now been placed for adoption. Sheila and Barry have both had serious hard drug addiction problems over a number of years. Barry was often violent towards both Sheila and Stephen. When Stephen was first placed with the Hunters he had nightmares about Barry coming to take him back home. Quite often Sheila and Barry would inject heroin, in front of the children. They would often leave the children at home unattended. Prior to her relationship with Barry, Sheila had several short-term relationships with men who she had mainly met through seeking out drug supplies. Just after the children were taken into care, Sheila was convicted and sentenced to a short prison sentence for possession of a large quantity of heroin. For the past year she has been in drug rehabilitation, and she has recently begun to have contact once a month with Stephen.

Stephen's behaviour at school had for some time been very challenging and difficult to manage – he was often disruptive in lessons and quite aggressive towards other pupils, often getting himself into fights and confrontations. Recently it has been reported that on three occasions, Stephen has put his hand in between the legs of two girls in his class at school. He has also been heard asking girls to 'touch' him in the playground. Early on in the placement, Kevin and Alison had also reported that Stephen often uses inappropriate sexual language and always tries to watch adult television programmes, saying that when he was at home he was allowed to watch Sky television in his bedroom whenever he wanted to, and that he often stayed up very late.

Prior to living in foster care Graham lived with his mother; he has never met his birth father. Graham's mother now lives in another county some considerable distance away and has very little contact with him. For several years the Social Services Department had ongoing concerns about the quality of care provided by Graham's mother to the extent that Graham's name was placed on the Child Protection Register under the category of neglect. He was often undernourished and poorly clothed, often having the flu and sometimes critically untended cuts and scars from when he had been out playing. Between the ages of 5 and 10, Graham has had several bouts of respite foster care, living in four different placements. At the age of 11 he became the subject of a Care Order and was placed to live long term with Kevin and Alison Hunter. He receives additional support at school as he has reading and language difficulties.

Alison Hunter reported that one night in the foster home, Stephen went into Graham's bedroom and took his clothes off and woke Graham up asking him to show him his penis. Mrs Hunter had been disturbed from her sleep by the landing light going on and went into Graham's bedroom and found Stephen in Graham's bedroom without his pyjamas on. Stephen became distraught and blamed Graham for what had happened. Mrs Hunter was convinced by the veracity of Graham's claim, that he was fast asleep before Stephen entered his room.

Despite reassurance, Graham told his social worker that he no longer feels happy sharing his placement with Stephen, as he feels that he is going to be accused of doing something else. Stephen later admitted that Graham did not do anything to him. A multi-agency meeting was called by the Social Services Department to discuss the situation. This meeting involved the foster carers, a police child protection officer and representatives from the schools attended by Graham and Stephen. It was agreed that Stephen should receive some therapeutic work to help him with his behaviours. It was also agreed that Graham should be offered an opportunity to discuss and explore his feelings about the incident. Concerns were expressed as to why Stephen had clearly blamed Graham for what had happened, and it was agreed that a further planning meeting should be called after a social worker had made an initial investigative approach to both boys.

Kevin and Alison Hunter were strongly of the opinion that should either of the boys have to leave the placement, it should be Stephen, as Graham had lived there longer and that his attachment to them was greater. Overall the Hunters were of the opinion that Stephen had never really settled with them, his sexualised behaviours were getting worse and that he had become increasingly difficult as now he believed that he would be moving back to live with his mother – mainly because his mother had told him this during a contact visit. There were no formal plans for this to happen or at this stage for any child to leave the placement.

When Stephen was spoken to again by his social worker, he changed his explanation of what had happened and said that on several occasions over the past few weeks when he had been getting ready for bed, Graham had gone into his bedroom and played 'games' with him. Stephen said that Graham had told him that he needed to play these 'games' so that he could learn about sex and practise what to do for when he gets a girlfriend. Stephen said that both he and Graham would touch and kiss each other's penis, and that on some occasions when he had woken up at night, he had gone into Graham's bed to play the 'game'. Stephen said that Graham had told him that if ever he woke up at night, he was allowed to come into his bedroom and sleep for a while in his bed, so long as he did not tell anybody about the 'game'. Stephen said that Graham also told him that he would be taken away if anybody found out.

Following this further disclosure there was a police and Social Services strategy meeting to discuss and decide upon the next course of action. Stephen was video interviewed and repeated the explanation he had given during the therapeutic session, giving additional detail. Graham was subsequently interviewed under the Police and Criminal Evidence (PACE) procedures, and admitted that he had touched and kissed Stephen's penis on several occasions, and that Stephen had done the same to him. Graham explained that when Stephen first came to live with him, he would sometimes take down his trousers and expose his penis and ask Graham to do the same. Graham explained that at first he had told Stephen not to be rude and that for a while he stopped doing it until about four months ago when he came into his bedroom and started doing it again. Graham said that this was when he had the idea to start the 'game' that led to him exposing his penis and asking Stephen to kiss it. He also said that the reason he had asked to leave the placement is that he knew that eventually he would get caught and that he wanted to stop. Graham received a Final Warning from the police for an offence of 'sexual assault' and he agreed to undertake specialist therapeutic work to explore his sexual offending behaviour.

A further multi-agency meeting was called whereby all this information was shared and therapeutic plans for both boys were made. The designated child protection teacher from Graham's school expressed concerns at the meeting about the potential risks Graham presented to others at school, and how these could be managed. It was agreed that Graham's form teacher, the designated child protection teacher and the head teacher were the only teachers who at this stage needed to know the details of Graham's offence, but that there should be regular liaison with the Social Services Department and further multi-agency meetings to review Graham's progress.

Initial Analysis

- There are many reasons why children make statements about being sexually abused and then withdraw them (Durham, 2003). In this case Stephen initially responded to being caught out of bed at night-time, in a context of being threatened by Graham. Stephen may also have thought that his carers would believe Graham more than him – Graham was older than Stephen, he had lived with Kevin and Alison for longer, and had a better relationship with them. These beliefs were borne out initially by the carers accepting Graham's explanation over Stephen's, and later at the multi-agency meeting by consideration being voiced by the carers about Stephen having to leave the placement. From Stephen's point of view he was in trouble and at this stage there was no further opportunity in his eyes to say more about what had been happening.

- Stephen's case shows how having sexualised behaviours can make children vulnerable to sexual abuse, and how those behaviours allow the person abusing to make the victim feel responsible. On the surface, Graham was able to act as though he was responding to Stephen's 'requests'. There is evidence that initially Graham responded appropriately, and told Stephen that he was being rude. However, these behaviours were never reported to the foster carers. It appears likely that for Graham, these behaviours triggered sexual arousal and thoughts that led to him involving Stephen in sexual activity.
- There was no direct evidence in Graham's past of there being any concern about his sexual behaviour, or about him presenting sexual risks to others. However, given that in the past there was serious neglect in Graham's care, and evidence that he was often left to care for himself, he may have had experiences that will have influenced his current harmful sexual behaviour.
- This case highlights how difficult it can be to make appropriate placements in foster care, especially when carers are offering more than one placement. Graham was well established in the placement, there was no evidence to suggest that he needed to be placed on his own, or that he presented any risk to other children. Before the placement was made, there was no evidence of Stephen showing sexualised behaviours. There was little to predict any likelihood of sexual abuse occurring between Graham and Stephen. At the early stages of the placement, Stephen did show some mild sexualised behaviour, suggesting that he had seen inappropriate adult television, and had been exposed to inappropriate language. Kevin and Alison Hunter were very experienced foster carers, fully aware of the principles of 'safe caring' (see Chapter 5), and with their responses to Stephen, these behaviours subsided quickly and were not seen again at home. It was only a short time prior to the discovery of the sexual abuse that Kevin and Alison had become aware that Stephen was showing sexualised behaviours at school. The nature and timing of these school behaviours could suggest that they had surfaced as a response to Stephen being sexually abused at home by Graham. Without knowing about the sexual abuse being committed by Graham, it would have been possible to speculate that these behaviours may have been resurfacing as a representation of anxiety and uncertainty provoked by the recent recommencement of Stephen's contact with his mother.

Case Plan

All parties agreed that the two boys could no longer remain in the same placement. As Graham had committed the sexual offence, the initial thinking was that he should move out, and that Stephen should not have to move, as he was the victim. However, Stephen's relationship with Kevin and Alison began to deteriorate further, and he could not get over initially being blamed for what had happened, and began to say that he no longer wanted to stay in the foster home. Consequently, Stephen was moved to another foster home, where it was felt that he would benefit from a fresh start away from the environment in which he was sexually abused. Stephen continued to have some contact with his mother, but unfortunately she discharged herself from the drug rehabilitation clinic and failed to attend any subsequent contact meetings. At the new foster home Stephen was reported to be having nightmares and flashbacks about Graham finding him and getting back at him for telling about the abuse. Stephen also said that sometimes when he is angry about what happened to him he hears Graham's voice telling him that he should touch other children on their genitals or ask them to 'play rude dares' – taking their trousers down and running around the playing fields, or shout out 'rude' words. There were reports of further incidents of inappropriate sexual behaviour at school.

Supporting the Foster Carers

In managing Stephen and Graham in their respective foster homes, it is important that specialist placement agreements are completed, giving details of the harmful sexual behaviours that have been committed and what the professional response has been and will continue to be, alongside details of what is needed in terms of supervision and risk management (see Chapter 5 and the example of a completed placement agreement in Tony's case). It is also important for foster carers to receive ongoing support and training, and to have regular liaison with whoever is undertaking the therapeutic work. Foster carers should be considered as being important members of a team of professionals that has been formed to help the young person in his or her resolve not to commit further harmful sexual behaviours.

Therapeutic Work with Stephen

- Securing Stephen's engagement in a process of therapeutic work, providing safe opportunities for Stephen to talk through his experiences and express his feelings about being sexually abused – ensuring that Stephen fully understands that what happened to him was not his fault (see the approaches to this undertaken in Neil's case – Chapter 6).
- Providing strategies for Stephen to process his memories and feelings and to manage his flashbacks and nightmares, using cognitive behavioural

techniques – for example, adding rescue consequences on to the end of his flashbacks – Stephen turning into a 'magician' character (Stephen painted a large picture of himself in a top hat holding a magic wand, with an 'M' on his chest. This painting had the attributes of the character drawn and written alongside – Stephen can tell someone about anything that happens to him; Stephen can say, 'No, I don't want to do this'; Stephen can make bad thoughts explode and disappear); imagining his foster parents (or the police) entering the scene of his flashback and saying to Graham, 'We need to speak to you right now.'

- Helping Stephen to explain why he feels he has been sexually touching other children, exploring his thoughts and feelings before, during and after these incidents – some of this work is similar to that carried out in Mark's case (Chapter 10), but Stephen's behaviours appear to be less entrenched, and at least partially in reaction to proximate experiences of being sexually abused. It must, however, also be remembered that Stephen was showing sexualised behaviours before Graham abused him, and that therefore there may be issues to consider from his more distant past. It will nonetheless be important to explore the patterns of Stephen's behaviours, and give him techniques to divert his 'touching' thoughts, and develop alternative and positive ways to relate to his friends and peers (see Chapter 7).
- Building on the techniques used to manage flashbacks to further help Stephen manage the circumstances where he has in the past ended up sexually touching fellow pupils and friends. Helping Stephen to understand why it is wrong to engage in these behaviours and how it will affect others – drawing on Stephen's own experiences of being sexually abused to help him appreciate how others may feel about his behaviours (see Chapter 8).
- Assessing Stephen's level of sexual knowledge and providing him with some age-appropriate sex and relationships education – including basic knowledge about body changes; puberty; sexual feelings; sexual behaviour and sexual intercourse; conception and childbirth; privacy and sexual boundaries and inappropriate touching.
- Helping Stephen talk through his feelings and memories about his mother, encouraging him to explore his earlier memories and experiences, trying to establish whether or not during this time Stephen was sexually abused, or inappropriately exposed to adult sexual behaviour or information. Asking Stephen how he feels about not knowing his father. Helping Stephen come to terms with his mother's inconsistency and disappearances from his life. Teaching Stephen some relaxation techniques, to help him calm himself down at times when he is troubled by these memories, or becomes anxious about not seeing his mother again, or about what may happen to her. These included lying down and tensing and relaxing the muscles throughout his body before he goes to sleep;

some stretching exercises; encouraging Stephen to sit down, open his hands, count his pulse rate and breathe slowly and deeply when he feels himself becoming anxious or angry. Encouraging Stephen to identify places he really likes to go to or things he really likes to do, and to visualise them in his mind when he feels stressed. Encouraging Stephen to 'let go' of his stress and anger by opening his hands and relaxing, rather than tensing up and clenching his fists.

- Raising Stephen's self-esteem by helping him to build a positive future in his new foster home – encouraging Stephen to make new friends and take part in appropriate leisure activities and to develop new hobbies and interests.
- Assisting Stephen with his school difficulties, exploring the dynamics of his peer relationships and helping him to find ways to make positive friendships and avoid conflict.

Therapeutic Work with Graham

The work to be undertaken with Graham is similar to that described in the cases of Tony and Alan. The full programme for Graham will therefore only be described briefly, but special attention will be given to the relapse prevention techniques used and the issues Graham, and, indeed, most of the other case studies, present for safe management within school. It is important to note that due to Graham's learning difficulties some of these materials had to be adapted – for example, extended use of role play and graphic materials; cartooning scenarios using very simplified language; repetition of main learning points.

- Ascertaining Graham's explanation of the sexual abuse he committed and how this compares to Stephen's account – how and why he did it, challenging him over any denial or minimisation.
- Analysis of Graham's sexual history and the development of his sexual knowledge – whether or not he has had other sexual experiences, wanted or unwanted.
- Undertaking a full programme of therapeutic work similar to that undertaken in Tony's case – using the offence-specific materials described in Chapter 7, leading up to the establishment of effective relapse prevention techniques.
- A comprehensive programme of sex and relationships education – including exploring what Graham understands and feels about his own sexuality.
- Exploration of Graham's wider life experiences, most notably the long periods of unaccounted time he had to himself when he was neglected by

his mother – how he feels about this, and what experiences he may have
had that may have influenced his path into sexual offending.
- Using the therapeutic process to build Graham's confidence and self-
  esteem and help him develop positive approaches to avoiding committing sexual offences in the future.

Relapse Prevention

The theoretical principles of relapse prevention have been discussed fully
earlier in this chapter, alongside presentation of a wide range of practice
materials. Examples follow, of how some of these materials were used in
Graham's case.

The relapse process was explained to Graham and presented very
simply as a process of having feelings that lead to sexual thoughts or
fantasies that lead to 'risky' thinking leading to plans to commit sexual
abuse. After a great deal of work had been carried out, Graham was given
a seven-page A4-sized booklet that summarised in a simple format many
of the principles of the work he had undertaken, with sections and empty
boxes to complete. The content was as follows (Graham's writing is in
italics):

- Remember the stages: feeling – fantasy – risky thinking – making plans –
  abusing.
- A high risk is any thought or situation that could lead to me sexually
  abusing someone. I still need to avoid high-risk situations.
- My high-risk situations are:
  1. *Being on my own with young children.*
  2. *Thinking about younger children in a sexual way.*
  3. *Going out on purpose to places where I know younger children play.*
  4. *Thinking that if I touch little children, I can do it without getting caught.*
  5. *Having these thoughts and not telling anybody.*
- I *must not* think about little children when I am thinking about sex, even when
  I am in my room on my own doing it (masturbating). I need to think about
  people who are my age or older and can agree to do it.
- *I know I will sometimes think about the abuse I did. This does not mean that I
  will do it again. When I have these thoughts I know I have to remember to avoid
  my high risks.*
- *When I think about sexual abuse I will try to think about the bad things that
  could happen. Like a policeman seeing what I was doing or Alison finding out,
  or friends knowing about it.*
- *I know that I won't forget about the sexual abuse I did ... but ... When I think
  about it I can say to myself ... That was in the past, I don't do that any more*

. . . I know how to stop this now . . . I know that I <u>can</u> change what I think and stop myself doing it.

Some More Helpful Tips

- ***Keeping Away*** *I need to stay away from high-risk people and places.*
- ***Robot Responses*** *This is something already made up that I can say to myself if I have abusive thoughts or fantasies, e.g. 'I know this is only a thought and that doing it will hurt others and lead me into a lot of trouble.'*
- ***Emergency Escapes*** *For emergencies I need a speedy response – 'I'm late, I must go home!' No need to say anything else, or wait for what people say – just go.*
- ***Changing My Thoughts and Fantasies*** *I need to remember to add on bad endings to any bad sex* (thoughts about sexual abusing) *thoughts or fantasies I have. I now know that having these fantasies does not mean that I am weird or that I have failed.*
- *These are important people in my life, who can help me not to do it again* (commit sexual offences).
  1. *Kevin and Alison* (foster carers)
  2. *Mr Bright* (form tutor)
  3. *Andrew* (therapeutic practitioner)
  4. *Jill* (social worker)
  5. Me
- This is how will they help me
  1. *Someone I can talk to.*
  2. *Tell me things.*
  3. *Keep an eye on me.*
  4. *Remind me of things I need to know.*
  5. *Help me feel better.*
- **REMEMBER** *– Thinking about what I have done or having a bad sex thought does not mean I am a failure or I will do it again. It means that I need to think what I have learnt and practise sorting out myself. If I find this hard or if it doesn't work I know that I am going to ask for help.*

Keeping Safe in School

It is important to remember that receiving a school education is as important for Graham as it is for any other young person. Through being supported in a school environment, Graham will continue to be in situations where he has opportunities to build his social skills. When pupils like Graham are sometimes excluded from school, because of fears about risk management, they are potentially starved of important opportunities to develop the peer skills necessary to make relationships and meet their needs appropriately.

In assessing the safety of a boy like Graham in a school environment, it is important for professionals directly involved with Graham – his year head or his form teacher, and his mentor – to meet regularly through relevant multi-agency meetings such as child protection conferences, review conferences, core group meetings, looked-after reviews (when the young child or young person is 'accommodated' or on a Care Order), ad hoc meetings and day-to-day liaison as appropriate. These meetings and contacts will importantly need to work towards having common strategies of risk management and clear agreements about sharing information. There are many complex factors to be taken into account.

Assessment of Risk in School

- The immediate risks presented by Graham.
- The risks presented to Graham from others.
- Whether any other pupils have become aware of Graham's problems and how are they likely to react to him.
- The nature of the abusing or inappropriate sexual behaviour, and how likely is it to occur during the school day or on the school premises.
- Are there any legal restrictions on Graham's movements?

School Strategies

In generally managing pupils' potential harmful sexual behaviours, schools will need to consider the following:

- *Perception of risk* – to what extent do people's perceptions of risk differ from actual risk?
- *Safety of all pupils* – 'keeping safe' policies – pupils' knowledge, pupils' perception of safety, pupils' opportunities to tell.
- *Safety of staff* – feeling safe in managing risks, feeling safe from direct harm, impact of distressing information.

Managing Confidentiality

Decisions need to be made on the basis of there being a 'pressing need' for certain people to be informed of Graham's circumstances in order to manage his risk adequately and keep him and others safe.

- *Those who need to know*: designated child protection teacher; year head or form teacher; head teacher; teacher who has the best relationship with the child.
- *Those who do not need to know*: all teachers; parents; pupils.

Outcome

Graham and Stephen remained in their respective foster homes, and the therapeutic plans were carried out as described above. Graham continued receiving therapeutic help for a period of 16 months, during which time he disclosed that he himself had as a young boy around the age of five been sexually abused by a teenager in his neighbourhood, and that he thinks that he told his mother, but nothing happened as a result. Graham believes that this all came back to him when Stephen started to expose himself and that this was why he thinks he had the thoughts that led to him sexually abusing him. It was important to address this issue and explore with Graham how he may have subsequently interpreted this experience in a manner that allowed him to feel justified in abusing Stephen (see the discussion in Chapter 8). From what Graham said it became clear that at the time he had been highly traumatised by what had happened to him, and that deep down he had never forgotten about it, but had managed to accommodate it into his life. At this stage of his life he was being badly neglected all round and the difficulties this would have created for him may well have taken precedence over some of these feelings. As the work progressed, Graham again became more in touch with the impact of this sexual abuse, and this helped him to appreciate the extent of the harm he had inflicted upon Stephen. From this Graham was able to move on with the therapeutic work in terms of recognising that he presents future risks that needed to be managed. Just before his seventeenth birthday, Graham moved to live in semi-independent accommodation, maintaining a positive link with his former foster carers. He was able to secure local full-time employment and there have been no reports of him committing further offences of any kind.

At the early stages of his new foster placement Stephen's sexualised behaviours were quite persistent, especially at school. Many of the issues discussed in relation to management of Graham's risks in school applied to Stephen, although his difficult behaviours (both sexualised and more generally) were more immediate and were taking place in school. At one stage Stephen was for a short period excluded from school and returned only when additional arrangements were made to provide more supervision with a classroom support teacher. There was regular liaison with the school, particularly from Stephen's foster carers, and several multi-agency meetings. Similar behaviour management strategies were employed at home and at school, and were discussed regularly with Stephen during the therapeutic sessions. This plan worked, and Stephen was able to hold on to both his school and his foster care placement.

Eventually it was possible to set up a meeting between Stephen and his mother, whereby she stated very clearly that she loved him and wanted to keep in touch with him, but could not look after him, and therefore wanted him to remain in foster care. When Stephen was able to accept and understand that he was not going to be living with his mother, his life settled down. Stephen's foster placement became permanent and his mother was able to maintain regular but infrequent contact. Over a period of 12 months, many of the other issues relating to Stephen's sexualised behaviours and being sexually abused were worked through up to the point that therapeutic work was able to be phased out. Stephen's foster carers, having undergone specialist training, were well versed in many of the issues relating to sexual abuse, inappropriate sexual behaviours and Stephen's life in general. They were aware that further therapeutic work could be undertaken, should this become necessary, and Stephen's progress continued to be monitored through his statutory reviews.

12

EVALUATION

INTRODUCTION

In conducting programmes of therapeutic work with children and young people who have committed harmful or inappropriate sexual behaviours, it is essential to have a continuous and ongoing evaluation of the work being undertaken. The initial evaluation will be at the stage of an initial assessment report, where early important decisions about the child or young person's life will be made. These decisions will centre on the immediate needs for risk management in terms of securing and maximising the safety of all parties deemed to be at risk. They will also include decisions around the placement of the child or young person, whether or not he remains at home or in an alternative setting. The decisions may also relate to the resolution of issues raised, or information discovered during the early stages of the assessment, for example, if the child or young person has disclosed being abused, sexually or in some other way. There will also be an evaluation of the young person's response to the methodology of the initial assessment, making recommendations about the nature and direction of future work to be undertaken. As the work progresses into its interim stages, further evaluations may lead to additional assessments, changes in therapeutic direction, changes in supervision arrangements, placement changes, returns home and so on. A final evaluation will assess the overall effectiveness of a therapeutic programme, reporting positive changes or unresolved issues, and will conclude with a statement about the nature and level of ongoing risk presented by the child or young person, and the projected future role of others involved in his life, in terms of maintaining the changes made, by providing support and guidance. This chapter will consider a range of issues in carrying out these various stages of evaluation. It will initially identify the purpose of an evaluation, exploring in detail its essential content, recognising the importance of looking at risk and strength factors. The chapter will also consider statistical factors associated with a positive outcome, and will discuss some of the possible prediction errors. This will be followed by the setting out of a checklist of essential evaluation factors that can be drawn from in accordance with the age and individual circumstances of the child or young person whose progress is being evaluated. Finally the chapter will provide guidance on the nature and content of a final assessment report.

PURPOSE AND CONTENT OF EVALUATION

A holistic approach to therapeutic practice will in itself necessitate a multi-dimensional approach to evaluation with a focus beyond but not excluding offence-specific factors. The evaluation will consider the wider changes in a child or young person's life, taking in many of the diverse factors discussed throughout this book. This will include the positive changes achieved by the child or young person, new skills and strengths developed, problems solved, and the role and availability of ongoing family and social support. There will, of course, alongside this be a focus on offence-specific factors including the current level of harmful or inappropriate sexual behaviour, current patterns of arousal and sexual interests, relationships and intimacy skills, and relapse prevention – the management of identified risk factors. Interim and final evaluations will consider progress in comparison to earlier evaluations, perhaps using repeat questionnaires or interview schedules to achieve this. To make such comparisons it will be necessary to identify realistic, achievable and measurable targets throughout the process of the work. It is also important to be aware that during the later stages of a therapeutic programme, a child or young person may have become well versed in the language and approach of the work, and may have become able to provide answers and attitudes that may not be present or reported by others outside the therapeutic context. It is therefore important for evaluations to be triangulated by taking account of the views of others in different settings, most notably at home, and/or in a placement, and at school, and, if possible, reports of progress in the child or young person's peer context. Some settings will provide more information on the peer context than others, for example, reports from a peer group setting in a residential placement, although this may not accurately reflect the child or young person's performance in other less supervised peer contexts, and must therefore only be taken as an indication. School reports will also be helpful, and a good plan of therapeutic support will have already identified, for the child or young person, a key member of staff at school who will be able to provide ongoing support, and will therefore be in a position to be able to report necessary evaluative information. Additional information can also be obtained from other assessments or reviews taking place in the child or young person's life. It is also valuable to involve the child or young person in evaluating his own achievements on a regular basis. This can be done by using questionnaires about individual therapeutic sessions, or about particular aspects of the work, or about progress within a placement. These can be supplemented by discussion with the child or young person about his perception of the work he has undertaken and the achievements he feels or believes that he has made. The overall purpose of the evaluation will be to measure the impact of the therapeutic work on the life of the child or young person, taking into account his current strengths, and his willingness and ability to avoid committing further harmful or inappropriate sexual behaviours.

PREDICTION ERRORS

Evaluating the progress of therapeutic programmes and predicting risk outcomes is very complex, and will never be an exact science. The consequences of a poor assessment could result in further incidents of sexual victimisation. A poor assessment could also mean the unnecessary restriction of a child or young person's life, by failing to recognise his strengths and potential to manage, with help, his own risks. In one sense, it would be a safe option to incarcerate all children and young people who have committed harmful sexual behaviours – based on the prediction that they have done it once, and therefore could do it again – but in another sense the amount of unnecessary human suffering that this would cause is immeasurable, and by virtue of the incarceration, the true reliability of this prediction will never be known. Ethical prediction therefore recognises the possibility of both false positive predictions (type 1 errors) and false negative predictions (type 2 errors), and will seek to balance a child or young person's strengths against their risks (Moore, 1996). The assessor will also need to be aware of his or her own ethics, values and biases, about sexual behaviour and how they may potentially impact on his or her perceptions of the child or young person, and how they may influence future decisions about risk management, placements, or recommendations to police or courts about criminal justice disposals.

STATISTICAL RISK FACTORS

A range of statistical factors associated with the committal, by a child or young person, of further inappropriate or harmful sexual behaviours has been identified from existing research by Calder et al. (2001, p. 276). These are important factors and are worth listing here:

- Previous sexual offence convictions or clear evidence of previous harmful sexual behaviour.
- Diagnosis of conduct disorder or a history of aggressive behaviour.
- Poor social skills, poor peer skills, poor intimacy skills.
- The use or threat of violence during sexual offending.
- The young person reports a sexual interest in children.
- The child or young person blames the victim for the sexual offence.
- The child or young person has experienced high levels of trauma, including neglect and witnessing domestic violence.
- The child or young person's family is dysfunctional or abusive, or has harsh child-rearing regimes.
- The sexual offence committed by the child or young person involved detailed planning.
- The child or young person failed to continue to attend a planned therapeutic intervention programme.
- The child or young person has generally high levels of compulsive or impulsive behaviours.
- The child or young person has experienced a discontinuity of care, or has poor attachments.

FAMILY RISK FACTORS

The importance of conducting a family assessment was identified in Chapter 4, where a range of family-related risk factors was discussed. If these factors are not addressed, they will add to the overall level of risk of further inappropriate or harmful sexual behaviours being committed. These factors include a lack of appropriate family support and supervision for the child or young person, and poor sexual boundaries, including the presence of unresolved intergenerational sexual abuse. Familial exclusion of the child or young person from social networks, friendships and age-appropriate leisure pursuits will isolate a child or young person and will hinder his development of peer and social skills. Other family problems may include inappropriate or violent male role models, featuring a misuse of power and control, or high levels of family stress and poor patterns of communication. These factors will intersect and accumulate to create an environment that will impede the achievements a child or young person may have made in the therapeutic context. The nature, extent and impact of these family problems will have been considered during initial and ongoing family assessments that will have considered the prognosis for change, informing earlier decisions about whether or not the child or young person should remain with the family, or be placed in an alternative setting that would provide an effective complement to the therapeutic work being undertaken.

KEY INDICATIONS OF A POSITIVE OUTCOME – EVALUATION CHECKLIST

The following checklist of positive evaluative factors has been derived from a range of sources (Kahn, 1990; Ryan & Lane, 1991; Gil & Johnson, 1993; Morrison & Print, 1995; Cunningham & MacFarlane, 1996; Moore, 1996; Araji, 1997; Gilgun, 1999; Calder et al., 2001; Hackett, 2004).

Raised Self-esteem

The child or young person has a good level of self-esteem. Self-esteem was discussed at length in Chapter 10, where it was established that if a person feels good and cares about himself, he is more likely to feel good and care about others. A raised self-esteem is the foundation for improvement in almost all areas covered by the assessment, and will allow the child or young person to nurture a caring and pro-social attitude that will take him away from committing further harmful sexual behaviours.

Good Evidence of Empathy

The child or young person has demonstrated a willingness and ability to understand the plight of others, and express concern about their well-being. Chapter 8 established that the overall presence of empathy, or the capacity for empathic concern, was not a stand-alone predictor of risk. It was recognised that people with high levels of generic empathy could still commit harmful sexual behaviours. Nonetheless, the ability to experience empathy is a skill that will assist a child or young person in recognising the specific impact of his own behaviours on others.

Full Understanding of the Impact on the Victim(s); Full Acceptance of Responsibility and Genuine Remorse

The child or young person fully understands the impact of his harmful sexual behaviour on the victim(s), accepts full responsibility for his actions, does not blame the victim in any way, and has expressed genuine remorse in a variety of ways. The child or young person has an understanding and belief about how and why sexual abuse is wrong and harmful.

Resolution of Distorted Thinking ('Thinking Errors')

The child or young person has recognised and resolved the thinking errors that were involved in his committal of harmful sexual behaviours. Denial and minimisation of impact and a range of other thinking errors often feature strongly in a child or young person's pattern of harmful sexual behaviours, and allow him to ignore their true impact on the victim. 'Thinking errors' are also likely to have featured in other aspects of the child or young person's life. The extent that they have been resolved and replaced by 'thinking truths' (see Chapter 7) will relate directly to a positive outcome indicating an increased potential for successful risk management.

Sex and Relationships Education

The child or young person has good understanding of sex and relationships issues with positive non-oppressive attitudes towards gender and sexuality, and has demonstrated an ability to distinguish between appropriate and inappropriate or harmful sexual behaviour. The child or young person will need to have developed a good understanding of puberty and sexual development, and have knowledge and understanding about sex and the law, including issues around informed consent. Good progress in these areas will assist a child or young person in becoming able to meet his future sexual needs appropriately.

Age-appropriate Non-harmful Patterns of Sexual Arousal and Fantasy

The young person is able to recognise and change patterns of inappropriate or harmful sexual fantasy, and no longer has sustained patterns of inappropriate or harmful sexual arousal. At the early stages of the therapeutic programme, it is likely that a young person will continue to have memories and patterns of sexual arousal and fantasy relating to the harmful sexual behaviour he has committed. The extent of this will depend on the nature and frequency of the behaviour, and how entrenched his patterns of inappropriate sexual arousal became. One of the targets of therapeutic intervention is to teach the young person how to manage these memories and fantasies, by replacing them with age-appropriate alternatives, and changed patterns of sexual arousal that are not harmful. A significant reduction of sexually abusive or violent fantasies is essential. The achievement of this will be a very positive indication of good self-management and a movement away from harmful sexual behaviours.

Positive Management of Lapses

The young person has demonstrated that he is able to understand the relapse process, and respond appropriately in accordance with his relapse prevention plan. The setting up and management of a positive relapse prevention plan will, on a day-to-day basis, help the young person to recognise potential pathways to further offending at a very early stage. The young person will need to be able to recognise that lapses may occur, and not see them as failures, but as opportunities to practise the self-management techniques he will have learnt. Success in this area will relate to success in many other aspects of a therapeutic programme, and will therefore be another indication of a positive outcome.

Positive and Flexible Thinking Patterns; Appropriate Expression of Feelings; Improved Anger Management; Improved Problem-solving Techniques

The child or young person has become able to engage in patterns of positive thinking, and has developed appropriate ways to meet and solve the challenges in his life. He is able to understand and express his feelings. He has become more aware of how and why he gets angry, and how to manage this without targeting it against others. The young person has the ability to reflect upon his actions and look for positive solutions in his life. These factors will allow the child or young person to have a more positive lifestyle and better friendships, and will have a significant influence on his ability to meet his needs appropriately.

Availability of Good Adult Support

The child or young person has the presence of at least one confidant, but ideally several supportive adults, who are aware of his difficulties, and are available to help him, and he is prepared to ask them for help when needed. This will inevitably contribute to a reduced likelihood of the child or young person straying from his resolve not to commit further harmful or inappropriate sexual behaviours. It will also depend heavily upon the extent of the child or young person's willingness to share his concerns and ask for help when necessary. This will be particularly important if the child or young person's inappropriate or harmful sexual behaviours are impulsive, as he will need continued supervision and constant reminders and guidance, as he is likely to be less able to manage his behaviours adequately by himself (see Carl's case study at the end of this chapter).

Positive Sustained Attachments and a Consistency of Care

The child or young person has sustained positive attachments and a reasonable consistency of care. It is important to recognise that some children and young people do not have sustained and positive attachments, have disrupted lives, and may have little opportunity or ability to change this. This does not necessarily mean that they will commit further harmful sexual behaviours, but combined with some of the other factors in this checklist could become a significant indication of risk. If a child or young person has positive attachments, and a consistency of care, he will likely have people available to help him develop a positive self-esteem and assist him in maintaining the positive changes he has made through the therapeutic programme.

Good School Progress

The child or young person has a positive experience at school and has reasonable achievements within the range of his academic or intellectual abilities. Again this would be an indication of a positive life with enjoyable day-to-day experiences, and will have a positive impact on many of the other factors involved in the assessment.

Age-appropriate Friendship and Social Intimacy; Positive Social Interests

The child or young person is able to make and sustain close friendships and engage in positive social and leisure pursuits, and does not engage excessively in addictive behaviours, including alcohol substance misuse. The more socially connected a child or young person becomes, the more he will be able to develop positive social skills that will assist him and allow him to grow and develop in many aspects of his life. Many young people will drink alcohol and experiment with substances and drugs, and will not commit sexual offences. If the young person uses alcohol or drugs to block out or manage feelings, or to escape from facing up to problems, or to manage mood swings, it will potentially create a range of difficulties that are likely to interact with other risk factors.

THE FINAL ASSESSMENT REPORT

At the completion, or near completion, of a programme of therapeutic work, it is important and helpful to produce a final evaluative report. This report will ideally become a formal record of the child or young person's progress and should be shared with relevant people in the child or young person's life, and should be kept in a secure place for possible future use. The report would become particularly valuable if there were further allegations or incidents of harmful or inappropriate sexual behaviours, which may lead to a need for further work. It may also become useful, particularly if the young person has a conviction, and concerns are raised about his future parenting of his own children. The report should describe the concerning sexual behaviours and the initial referral brief, and summarise all key areas of work undertaken. It should discuss the young person's response and attitude to the work, identifying his key achievements and areas of change that will have informed the final assessment of risk. It will also need to identify and explain any ongoing concerns, or unresolved issues, and specify any necessary contingency plans or day-to-day support that will need to be in place to address or contain them. It may be necessary to identify future therapeutic needs, either immediate, or at a future stage of the child or young person's development, or at a time of specific change. For example, in the case of a younger child, it may be necessary to signpost a potential need for further therapeutic work, after he has progressed through puberty, or perhaps for when a young person moves into independence and loses some of his daily support. The report should conclude with a clear statement and explanation, based on the factors identified in this chapter, and throughout this book, about the current level of sexual risk presented by the child or young person.

CONCLUSION

This chapter has considered a range of issues relating to the evaluation of programmes of therapeutic work undertaken with children and young people who have committed harmful or inappropriate sexual behaviours. It was recognised that an evaluation would need to be multi-dimensional and reach beyond offence-specific factors, to explore the success of the work in terms of many aspects of the child or young person's life. It was also recognised that it was important to look at a child or young person's strengths and competences and balance these against his risk factors, and to involve him directly in the process of evaluation. Assessment and evaluation were seen as an ongoing process throughout the duration of a programme of therapeutic work, which would inform a range of key decisions about the continued direction of the work and factors relating to the daily life of the child or young person. The chapter considered some possible areas of assessment or prediction error, and stated the importance of assessors being aware of their own ethics and values. It listed a range of statistical factors associated with recidivism, set out and discussed a checklist of key positive evaluation factors, and provided guidance for the completion of a final assessment report. Evaluation was essentially seen as a measure of the effectiveness of the therapeutic programme in preventing further harmful or inappropriate sexual behaviours, and in bringing about positive changes in the life of the child or young person.

CASE STUDY – CARL (14)

Synopsis

Carl is a 14-year-old white British boy who lives with his mother June and stepfather David, and his brother Ian who is 17, and his brother Michael who is 19. June works part-time at a local factory and David works for a food delivery company, sometimes working away from home. Carl is of average intelligence, but has a range of physical and intellectual disabilities. He has impaired movement and coordination and he finds it difficult to write, and has some speech and language difficulties – some of his language is immature or unintelligible and he tends to talk very fast, often quite excitedly. He also has some thought-processing difficulties; he finds it hard to express himself and often misunderstands the expressions of others. His empathy is poor, and his interests are restricted and repetitive. At school he has difficulties in making and sustaining friendships, and finds it hard to understand social cues. Carl's instinctive learning is poor; he has to be taught with very specific and concrete instructions, which often have to be repeated, as he has poor memory skills. He is generally disorganised in most aspects of his life, often being very impulsive and disinhibited in his behaviours. Despite these disabilities, Carl is intellectually able in terms of general conversation; he likes to watch quite complex films, and reads quite often. He is interested in the world around him and has a strong and concrete sense of fairness and justice. Carl attends mainstream school, and receives special needs support. Whilst performing badly in a group situation, Carl has always been known to perform well in one-to-one situations with adults.

Carl is good-humoured and has a likeable personality; he has been able to form positive relationships with a succession of school support staff, who to date have mainly been female. His range of disabilities have been formally diagnosed as being dyspraxia, but the diagnosis also recognised that this may overlap with aspects of Asperger's syndrome. Dyspraxia is an impairment or immaturity of the organisation of movement. This affects the way in which the brain processes information, resulting in messages not being properly or fully transmitted. It is associated with problems of perception, language and thought. These children often have difficulty in keeping friends, or judging how to behave in company; they are slow and hesitant in most actions, unable to learn anything instinctively and need to be taught skills; they are often anxious and easily distracted. Asperger's syndrome is characterised by social isolation and eccentric behaviour in childhood. There are impairments in two-sided social interaction and non-verbal communication. Their speech is often peculiar due to abnormalities of inflection and a repetitive pattern. There is clumsiness and usually a circumscribed area of interest which usually leaves no space for more age-appropriate, common interests. Some examples are cars, trains, timetables, door knobs, hinges, football statistics, meteorology, astronomy or history. In view of Carl's disabilities, his parents have been reluctant to allow him to venture far from home, but there have been occasions when Carl has left the house without permission, to play in the local park.

Carl has for the past few years presented significant management difficulties both at home and at school; his challenging behaviour is only responsive to adult guidance in the here and now. Carl has no difficulty in owning his behaviours, but he has considerable difficulty in understanding why they cause concern. When he was younger, his repetitive interests focused onto particular games or television themes, whereby he would seek to build up collections of particular objects or toys. Throughout his primary school, Carl regularly attended appointments with psychiatrists and psychologists in relation to his diagnosis of dyspraxia. From the age of six Carl began to repeatedly fondle his genitals, both at home and in public. He would always respond immediately to gentle correction, allowing his attention to be diverted. However, this would not stop him from repeating the behaviour, which became more and more problematic, particularly as he progressed through puberty, and began to increasingly enjoy the behaviour. When Carl was 12, he began to masturbate, and would need to be reminded constantly by his parents and his brothers that this was a private activity, that should not take place in the presence or in the sight of others in the family household. At school, when he was approaching the age of 11, Carl began to expose his penis to other pupils. Initially this was in a context of changing for swimming and for other sports lessons, whereby special supervision arrangements had to be set up. However, Carl's behaviour progressed to exposures during lessons and in the playground, and attempts to get others to join in, and attempts to touch girls on their breasts and genitals, leading to a series of short-term school exclusions, up to the point when Carl moved into secondary school. With this move, it was known that Carl would need extra one-to-one support, and his school was chosen with this need in mind. There had been some discussion about placing Carl in a special needs school, but it was decided to support him in a mainstream school placement.

For the first six months at his secondary school, with the extra supervision in place, Carl's behaviours were contained, and there were no significant incidents. However, from around the age of 12, Carl's inappropriate sexual behaviours began to re-emerge, and became much more frequent than ever before. These behaviours started to become much more overtly sexual, to the point that other pupils and some staff began to feel threatened by them. These behaviours included drawing attention to himself, pointing towards his groin whenever he had an erection; repeated discussion and comments to others about masturbation and the size of his penis; rubbing himself in class; asking girls if they wanted to touch his penis, and telling them he wanted to have sex with them; repeated and blatant explicit sexual comments during lessons, directed both to staff and other pupils; drawing explicit sexual cartoons, based on pupils in the class, with suggestions as to what he would like to do with them; repeated conversations about pornography; attempting to access internet pornography sites on the school computers. These comments were often seen by other pupils as humorous and drew comments and encouragement from them. Carl was also being increasingly bullied by some of the older boys in the school, to the point that he no longer felt safe in school. Carl began to receive fixed-term exclusions from school; sometimes this was after violent incidents where Carl had been the victim. Teachers were of the view that Carl often invited the bullying. Carl's view was that this was unfair, as he was the one who had been hurt, and because he believed it was the teacher's job to protect him in school. This increased the tensions in the management of Carl in school, as his parents pursued a formal complaint that was upheld, with an immediate return to school. On other occasions Carl received exclusions because of his sexual behaviours towards others. Carl was beginning to target his behaviours towards a particular group of girls in the year below him. Carl's parents also reported that he was gravitating towards younger children in the neighbourhood. There were no specific reports of inappropriate sexual behaviours. Carl's parents believed that he chose to play with younger children to avoid being bullied and teased, but they were concerned about Carl's sexual behaviours, and therefore restricted Carl's unsupervised time in the neighbourhood. On several occasions when he was 13, Carl stayed out quite late, without informing anybody where he was, and refusing to explain his actions upon his return. On one occasion he stayed out overnight, returning home saying he was lost and had to sleep in the park. The police were involved in this incident, but Carl has never fully recounted how or why he stayed out, beyond his claim that he was lost. Carl's parents, in conjunction with his school support teacher, approached the local Social Services Department for help, and Carl, at the age of 14, was referred to a specialist service to assist in the management and control of his inappropriate sexual behaviours, and to receive further sex and relationships education, especially as his teachers had removed him from lessons at school, because of his inappropriate sexual behaviours and fears that he would disrupt the lessons.

Initial Analysis

- Carl's behaviours appear to be quite entrenched and have persisted over time, albeit with a quiet period around the age of 11. It is likely that the escalation of these behaviours is directly related to Carl's sexual development – progressing through puberty leading to an increase in sexual awareness and sexual feelings, this being an added dimension to already existing sexual preoccupations.
- Carl was already prone to having repeated interests that would often dominate his life, which was a part of his being diagnosed as having dyspraxia and borderline Asperger's syndrome. Sex or sexual behaviour appears to have become in Carl's case one of these dominating interests, which accounts for the extent of his inappropriate sexual behaviours, now escalated further by his developmental growth.
- Carl's sexualised behaviours render him vulnerable to sexual abuse. It is not clear how much sexual knowledge Carl has, or how he obtained it. It is possible that Carl may have received this from an inappropriate source, or that he may have been sexually abused during the night he stayed away, but to date he has not indicated this.
- Carl's intellectual disabilities will directly hinder and obstruct his learning, understanding and management of his sexual behaviours and relationships. They may hinder him in a variety of ways – from being aware adequately of the feelings and wishes of others; from being able to make and sustain effective close peer relationships; from being able to understand the social cues around sexual behaviour; from containing appropriately his sexual feelings and behaviours; from expressing appropriately his sexual feelings; from understanding or recognising the impact of his behaviours on others and from learning from his mistakes. Carl does appear to have learnt that his behaviours sometimes draw a level of perverse attention and 'popularity' amongst his peers, from the humour and disruption they generate.

- It appears that sex has become one of Carl's special and compulsive interests; his behaviours are therefore likely to remain persistent. He is likely to have an interest in collecting and developing information about sex, which on the positive side could lead to good cooperation with a comprehensive programme of sex and relationships education work. There is an indication that this is most likely to succeed if conducted on a one-to-one basis with an adult.

- Some of the 'mainstream' methods of working with children and young people who have harmful or inappropriate sexual behaviours may not, in view of his intellectual disabilities, work with a boy like Carl. He will have a limited capacity to maintain an understanding of the impact of his behaviours on others; he is likely to forget behavioural instructions; he will require continuous situational reminders of what he has learnt; Carl's impulsive behaviours are a key feature of his intellectual disability and he will therefore respond less well to cognitive behavioural techniques. Carl is likely himself to remain vulnerable to bullying and possible sexual abuse. His behaviours have proven themselves to be somewhat resistant to change, although he easily accepts and responds well to his behaviours being challenged in the here and now. Unfortunately, learning from these challenges is not retained, and within minutes similar behaviours often recur.

- Professionals and family members will need to be aware of the fine balance that will need to be drawn between effective and protective supervision, and oppressive over-control and containment, which will prevent Carl from having positive social experiences, and will therefore further hinder his development.

- Professionals will also need to be aware that if Carl commits sexual assaults, his disabilities will be no comfort for the victim, although they may, up to a point, influence any criminal justice response he may receive. As Carl gets older, the criminal justice system and members of the public are likely to become increasingly less tolerant towards his behaviours.

- Professionals will also need to be realistic about the changes Carl is likely to be able to achieve, and will have to accept that he is likely to need ongoing close support and supervision, into the foreseeable future. Without this acceptance, professionals are likely to experience a sense of failure and may become disillusioned or impatient in their approach and management of Carl. There is also the added danger of setting targets or expectations for Carl that he will simply be unable to achieve. This will potentially create a sense of failure for him, and put him at risk of being charged with sexual offences. Carl should have been referred for specialist help at a much earlier stage.

- Much of the long-term outcome for Carl will depend on how he is able to manage his transition into adulthood. There is an indication that Carl is able to manage adult company better than peer relationships. He may therefore find the adult world less threatening, and more helpful, than his school and neighbourhood peer groups. This creates some hope for his future prognosis.

Case Plan

Carl

Therapeutic work to support Carl and to assist him in developing a better understanding of his sexual behaviours and why they cause concern to others; providing a comprehensive programme of sex and relationships education.

- Providing an opportunity for Carl to discuss how he feels about his life, his family, and his general awareness of his disabilities, including experiences at home and school – peer experiences; being bullied; staying out overnight; being in constant trouble because of his sexual behaviours; having to be closely supervised most of the time – and assessing his motivation and desire for improvement.
- Assessment of Carl's sexual history, and current understanding of sexual behaviour (see Chapters 6 and 9), including embedded questions about unwanted sexual contact.
- Exploring Carl's awareness of the concerns about his current sexual behaviours, and his understanding of their impact on others.
- Ascertaining Carl's own description of his behaviours and the thoughts and feelings associated with them.
- In the event of Carl not volunteering information about his night away, to ask specific questions about what happened and how he spent his time, who he was with and whether or not any sexual behaviour was involved.
- Exploring Carl's feelings about the intensive supervision he receives; the extent of his acceptance and belief that it is necessary; whether he experiences it as oppressive; whether or not he has any suggestions for future supervision that he would consider more acceptable. Helping Carl to appreciate the importance and necessity of the supervision he is receiving.
- Provision of a comprehensive programme of sex and relationships education (see Chapter 9), including informed consent, mutuality in sexual relationships, sex and the law, appropriate and inappropriate sexual behaviours, meeting sexual needs appropriately, etc.
- Establishing Carl's views about pursuing opportunities in his life for him to be able to enjoy age-appropriate peer experiences – supported

youth clubs, local school holiday and after-school schemes, other youth opportunities.
- Helping Carl to understand the best ways to keep himself safe.

June, David and Ian

A range of tasks, providing support and guidance, mainly to be carried out by the family social worker, with the involvement of Carl's specialist worker as necessary.

- Provision of opportunities in parallel to the work with Carl for June and David to discuss their concerns about Carl and to receive professional support and guidance as required, including a full discussion of the therapeutic programme planned for Carl.
- To ask June and David to provide additional information about Carl's history and the past management of his disabilities.
- To provide an opportunity for Carl's brothers Ian and Michael to discuss anything they wish about living with Carl.
- To provide advice about making adjustments to allow the supervision of Carl to become more subtle, and less intrusive as Carl gets older. Ensuring that Carl has opportunities for privacy, and more age-appropriate social opportunities – accessing supported youth schemes, community schemes, etc.
- To assist June and David in their liaison with Carl's school and in exploring the possibility of other schooling options for Carl.

School

- Liaison with Carl's special needs support teacher, providing suggestions and advice about the management of his behaviours in school.
- To explore the possibility of less intrusive supervision and monitoring of Carl's behaviours.
- To attend and advise at Carl's school review meetings.

Outcome

Carl responded very well to his individual therapeutic plan, saying that it had been what he had wanted for ages – 'someone outside of everything to talk to'. Carl received therapeutic support over a period of 18 months. For the first three months the sessions were weekly, then they became fortnightly, and eventually monthly. As predicted, Carl was very willing to talk about his life and was motivated to receive an extensive programme of sex and relationships education. The work with Carl was delivered using a variation of methods to repeat and develop key messages – reading materials; films; websites; CD ROM; making video diaries; discussing and cartooning life scenarios, identifying thoughts and feelings in each frame (including both fictitious and real examples of situations from Carl's life). As the work progressed there was some evidence of a reduction in the frequency and intensity of Carl's inappropriate sexual behaviours. As Carl approached the age of 15, he demonstrated an improved understanding of appropriate sexual relationships, and spoke in terms of wanting to have a 'serious' relationship with a girl the same age as him. This did not lead to a complete cessation of Carl's inappropriate sexual behaviours, but they were very much reduced and no longer involved any specific targeting of others. Throughout this period Carl continued to have close supervision, and he used the therapeutic sessions to report and discuss his current experiences.

When asked about the time he did not return home, Carl stated that he stayed at the house of a 17-year-old friend from his neighbourhood, whose parents were away from home. He did admit that there was some sexual behaviour – talking about sex and girls and masturbating – but he did not wish to say who this person was, and stated that at the time he wanted to spend time with him, as he was always in trouble at home. Carl also mentioned that this boy had a pornographic video film that he had watched on two occasions. Carl was able to accept the view that the other boy was much older than him, and may have taken advantage of him, but did not want to say anything more about it. He was persuaded and able to agree that it would be better for his parents to be told, but did not want to be present when this happened. He was persuaded on the basis that they needed to be told, as they were fearful that something much worse had happened on the night in question.

Carl remained very matter of fact and disinhibited in talking openly and explicitly about sex, which continued to unnerve those around him. For example, he could not understand the need to cover himself up when he had an erection, saying it was natural and he could not help how he was feeling, or why not to state how he feels about girls, and what he would like to do with them. By this stage, Carl's inappropriate contact behaviours had stopped. He stated that the main reason he stopped was because of the trouble he would be in, and that he knew it made him unpopular, and that he would therefore never be able to get a girlfriend. Carl was also very afraid of getting into any trouble with the police; there was a notable reduction in his contact behaviours after this had been talked about in the programme. The intention was not to scare Carl, but this outcome helped to prevent him from getting into serious trouble. However, his sexualised language and explicit sexual comments continued, and Carl's school eventually issued him with a final ultimatum that one further incident of inappropriate sexual behaviour would result in his permanent exclusion.

Carl himself had become increasingly despondent with his school situation, stating that he believes that he is watched all the time, and when other pupils make sexual comments to him, they are written down and he is blamed. On one occasion he was verbally victimised by another pupil, and as a result was sent home. Carl's reputation at school deteriorated to the extent that it became very difficult for him to rise above the negative expectations of both staff and pupils, and the school were unable to protect him from being bullied. Carl stated that he was scared every day he walks into the school. Carl was offered a weekly boarding place at a residential school that offered small group teaching and had specialist services for children and young people with dyspraxia and Asperger's syndrome. Carl's move to this school was very successful, and he very quickly received a series of positive and encouraging reports. He thrived in a small group-teaching environment, and really began to enjoy his schooling, even though he often missed being at home during the week. Carl's inappropriate sexual behaviours were less difficult to manage in a small group environment, and became less of an issue. At his request, he attended occasional further therapeutic sessions during the first two sets of school holidays, before the work with him came to a final close. Carl continued to receive subtle supervision at home and school; there have been no reports of him committing sexual offences.

13

CONCLUSIONS

This book has presented an analytical practice framework for holistic approaches to therapeutic intervention with children and young people who have committed inappropriate or harmful sexual behaviours. This framework locates children and young people's experiences in their wider social and political context, taking account of social oppression, based upon restrictive constructions of childhood and gender, compulsory heterosexuality and homophobia, and racism. In particular, it was recognised that an understanding of constructions of 'hegemonic masculinity' is fundamental to understanding why the majority of sexual abuse in our society is committed by men or boys. It was argued that the framework was able to accommodate many of the existing theoretical approaches, whilst at the same time highlighting the importance and relevance of the social context of children and young people's experiences as being pivotal to understanding how and why these inappropriate or harmful sexual behaviours take place.

The practice framework allows the practitioner to address his or her power relationship with the child or young person and emphasises the importance of a transparent approach, which explains clearly the process of the work from the outset, and maintains a high level of respect for the child or young person, whilst acknowledging that some of his behaviours are problematic. The framework allows us to examine how young people may have internalised oppressive stereotypes, beliefs and misunderstandings, through which they may have in some ways become able to justify their actions to themselves, or may have generated powerful motivations for committing harmful or inappropriate sexual behaviours.

The book has provided guidance for assessing children and young people's sexual behaviours, highlighting their rapidly changing social context and the consequent difficulty in establishing a common baseline of appropriate and acceptable sexual behaviour. It was recognised that through changes in technology, children and young people are potentially gaining more access to explicit sexual material, and that quite often some of this is exploitative and harmful. Guidance was also provided for assessing and supporting the families of these children and young people, emphasising the importance of recognising existing parental strengths alongside identifying gaps and learning needs. Similar guidance was provided for the provision of support to foster carers, recognising the complex and challenging nature of their task. It was recognised that particularly at the early stages of a therapeutic intervention, there are likely to be significant potential risks to other children and young people, and that it is important for there to be a clear and explicit exchange of information between key family members and relevant professionals.

In providing guidance for completing a comprehensive initial assessment of children and young people who have committed inappropriate or harmful sexual behaviours, the uniqueness of the child or young person's life, circumstances, history and personality was emphasised. Practitioners were also reminded not to be expecting to find single causes for young people's harmful or inappropriate sexual behaviours. Causes often amount to an intersection of many events and circumstances in a child or young person's life, creating a unique pathway to the behaviours in question. The assessment is about uncovering that pathway by exposing the connections between the different experiences, and explaining how they acted together to precipitate the sexual behaviours. Following this the book explored a range of relevant cognitive behavioural interventions, presenting a range of useful practice materials, that allowed patterns of behaviour to be broken down into their component parts, providing opportunities and ideas for assisting children and young people to engage in behavioural change. The book also explored the significance of inappropriate sexual fantasies and 'thinking errors' and discussed ways of enhancing the child or young person's understanding of the impact of their behaviours on the victim. It was noted that victim empathy work needed to be a carefully timed component of a wider intervention programme. There was an exploration of how victim empathy work may lead a child or young person who has sexually harmed towards disclosing and/or coming to terms with his own victim experiences, and how this should be managed.

This book has explored a range of issues relating to sex and relationships education, which builds upon other aspects of the therapeutic programme to provide the young person with the knowledge and understanding to develop the necessary skills to become more able to meet his sexual needs appropriately. There was an exploration of sexual values with an emphasis on their variation between different cultures and religions, and a discussion of sexual oppression, with reference to homophobia and oppressive forms of masculinity. Building on this the book explored issues relating to enhancing the child or young person's self-esteem. It was recognised that building self-esteem permeates the whole intervention programme and is an essential ingredient to engagement and positive change. In considering the latter stages of an intervention, the main principles of 'relapse prevention' were discussed, outlining a range of additional practical techniques to move the child or young person along a continuum away from supervision by others to self-management and self-control. It was emphasised that it was important to involve a team of people involved with the child or young person's life who could assist him with his plan, by monitoring, supervising and providing cues and reminders as necessary. It was noted that it was important for relapse prevention plans to be constructed in a context of recognising and building upon children and young people's strengths and competencies, so that they can have positive achievements in their lives, and meet their personal, social and sexual needs in a manner that raises their self-esteem and takes them away from the circumstances that led to them committing harmful or inappropriate sexual behaviours. Finally, the book considered a range of issues relating to evaluating the outcome of the work undertaken, again recognising that this needed to be multi-dimensional and reach beyond offence-specific factors, to explore the success of the work in terms of many aspects of the child or young person's life. In conducting an evaluation, it was recognised that it was important to look at a child or young person's strengths and competencies and balance these against his risk factors, and to involve him directly in the process of evaluation. Evaluation was essentially seen as a measure of the effectiveness of the therapeutic programme in preventing further harmful or inappropriate sexual behaviours, and in bringing about positive changes in the life of the child or young person.

Alongside exploring the components of an intervention programme, the book has analysed seven detailed case studies, exploring in detail the inappropriate or harmful sexual behaviours of nine young men – Neil (15), Tony (14), Alan (15), Luke (15) and Jon (15), Mark (9), Stephen (9) and Graham (14), and Carl (14). These were composite studies developed from practice experiences, drawn from a large number of cases over a number of years. All the names used were pseudonyms, and the circumstances described had no direct resemblance to people in real life. Each of these case studies provided a detailed synopsis and initial analysis of the young man's behaviours, followed by detailed case plans that identified the therapeutic needs of all parties involved. In each case, the plan for the young man was discussed in detail, followed by a detailed discussion of the outcome – the young man's response to the therapeutic plan, and the subsequent changes that took place in his life, and whether or not there were any further reports of inappropriate or harmful sexual behaviours. Additionally, each case study had an extended focus on a particular aspect of the work that was undertaken.

Neil's case study explored the complexities of providing post-abuse counselling that incorporated therapeutic work to address inappropriate sexual behaviours. There were also issues about Neil feeling responsible for being

abused because he was gay. Tony's case study provided detail of a specialist written agreement that was set up for his foster placement. It also
described how Tony's patterns of harmful sexual behaviour were analysed,
and how his 'thinking errors' were challenged and changed. Alan's case
study provided details of a 'family safety plan' that was set up for his return
to live at home, following a period of living with relatives, as a consequence
of sexually abusing the sons of his father's partner. Luke and Jon's case study
considered ostensibly consenting sexual behaviours between twin siblings,
and considered issues of power and appropriate consent, homophobia and
racism. Mark's case study considered many aspects of his disrupted life and
the splintered attachments that had contributed to his committal of a range
of harmful sexual behaviours at home and at school. Stephen and Graham's
case study explored a situation of harmful sexual behaviours occurring
between children in a foster home, and provided specific details of a relapse
prevention plan that was set up for Graham. Carl's case study looked at
issues of intellectual disability. Autism and dyspraxia had contributed to
Carl committing a range of inappropriate sexual behaviours that were very
impulsive and persistent.

These case studies highlighted how the therapeutic programme discussed
throughout the book was applied uniquely to the circumstances of each
young man. Clearly there were common elements to each young man's plan
– mainly around offence-specific work and the sex and relationships education. There were particularly common aspects between some of the young
men in relation to their concerns about their sexuality and sexual identity,
and the role of pornography and other aspects of the media, not only as an
influence on the extent and nature of some of their sexual behaviours, but
also on how they perceived and lived out their masculine identities. Again,
in this respect the practice framework was particularly helpful in analysing
and contextualising the young men's experiences. Between the case studies,
there was a huge variation in the content, emphasis and delivery of this
work, in accordance with the assessed wider individual needs and circumstances of each young man. The case studies demonstrated how the anti-
oppressive principles expounded by the practice framework allowed a
positive engagement of each young man, in discussing very sensitive personal issues, without losing sight of the harm their sexual behaviours had
caused to others. In particular, taking a strengths-based approach allowed
case plans to be focused on building upon each young man's existing
strengths and competencies, filling the gaps as necessary and being very
clear about the need to manage any potential risk to others. The focus was
always on a belief that the young man had the ability to move away from
committing harmful or inappropriate sexual behaviours, to being recognised
as being able to make valuable contributions to the lives of others, by
meeting his needs appropriately.

It is important to acknowledge that therapeutic work undertaken with children and young people is often challenging and difficult. Children and young people can be resistant to fully accepting or acknowledging aspects of their inappropriate or harmful sexual behaviours. Sometimes they will deny it outright and refuse to engage in any work, or will require substantial persuasion and motivation. Sometimes parents will find it easier to deny or disbelieve the reports of their child's behaviour, supporting his denial at face value, and expressing reluctance to allow the involvement of professionals. Parents are at times resistant to schools being informed about their child's behaviours, particularly if they have occurred in the home and not in school. Sometimes, in these circumstances, child protection procedures and police involvement will be instrumental in underlining the seriousness of the behaviours in question. Sometimes it will be necessary and appropriate to secure a criminal conviction in order to create a legal mandate for the work. 'Family safety plans' can often be very disruptive to the flow of normal family life, tempting family members to compromise issues of safety and protection. There may be resentment expressed towards the repeated involvement of social workers or other professionals who are seeking to monitor or enforce the plan. This may involve placing the names of particular children on the Child Protection Register, and informing a wide range of professionals in other agencies about the nature of the risks involved. In these circumstances considerable focus and persistence are required.

The work with the young people in the case studies was conducted in a framework of carefully thought out and planned inter-agency child protection policies that are compatible with recommendations set out in *Working Together to Safeguard Children* (Department of Health et al., 1999). These are detailed in the Appendixes and formed an essential context for the work. The case studies signify the importance of such policies and the need for supportive legislation and government direction that acknowledges the scale of the problem and the complex difficulties in meeting the needs of these children and young people. They also signify the need for government support and policy for meeting the needs of children and young people who have been sexually abused. The case studies have demonstrated the value of practice research, and will hopefully encourage other professionals to research and present their professional experiences. This is a growing field of practice that will always be helped by the development of additional knowledge. Practitioners will continue to need to seek out specialist and regular training, and effective and frequent consultation and professional support.

Appendix A

DETAILS OF THE SEXUALISED INAPPROPRIATE BEHAVIOURS SERVICE (SIBS) IN WARWICKSHIRE

SIBS

The Sexualised Inappropriate Behaviours Service (SIBS) is a countywide Social Services provision in Warwickshire. It provides direct services, resources, research, consultation and training for therapeutic work with children and young people who have sexual behaviour difficulties, or who have difficulties arising from the sexual behaviour of others. The overarching aim is the protection of known and potential victims from the harms caused by sexual (and other forms of) abuse.

- Reduce the risks presented by children and young people with sexual behaviour difficulties.
- Improve the well-being of children and young people with sexual behaviour difficulties, so that they can meet their needs appropriately.
- Improve the well-being of children and young people who have difficulties because of the sexual behaviour of others.
- Enhance the ability of teams to be able to fully meet the needs of these children and young people.

OBJECTIVES

- SIBS has established within the county a set of policies and procedures for undertaking this work. The service emphasises a person-centred approach, in a framework of children and young people's rights.

- It has produced written guidelines and agreements, covering many aspects of its work. SIBS has established links with other agencies, and maintains a reference library of research publications and practice resources. Guidelines have also been produced for helping workers to assist families in establishing safe routines, which ensure the protection of family members from the inappropriate sexual behaviours of others.
- SIBS offers a consultation service to Children's Services social work practitioners across the county, and when necessary will provide a direct therapeutic service to children and young people. The consultation service often involves in-depth case discussions and the provision of therapeutic guidance for direct work. It also involves attendance at meetings, reviews and child protection case conferences. The service is also offered to health practitioners.
- SIBS provides comprehensive training courses for practitioners and related professionals, such as foster carers, and professionals from Health and Education. As SIBS operates in a multi-agency context, some of these services are extended to other agencies.

Dr Andrew Durham
Consultant Practitioner
Sexualised Inappropriate Behaviours Service (SIBS)

Appendix B

EXCERPT FROM WARWICKSHIRE SAFEGUARDING CHILDREN BOARD (WSCB) INTER-AGENCY CHILD PROTECTION PROCEDURES

(To be read with reference to the flow chart in Figure B1)

5.10 YOUNG PEOPLE WHO DISPLAY ABUSIVE BEHAVIOUR

Introduction

- Work with children and young people who abuse others – including those who sexually abuse/offend – should recognise that such children are likely to have considerable needs themselves, and also that they may pose a significant risk of harm to other children.
- Evidence suggests that children who abuse others may have suffered considerable disruption in their lives, been exposed to violence within the family, may have witnessed or been subject to physical or sexual abuse, have problems in their educational development, and may have committed other offences.

Reproduced by permission of Chris Hallet, Chair, Warwickshire Local Children's Safeguarding Board.

- Such children and young people are likely to be children in need, and some will in addition be suffering or be at risk of significant harm, and may themselves be in need of protection.
- Children and young people who abuse others should be held responsible for their abusive behaviour, whilst being identified and responded to in a way which meets their needs as well as protecting others.

Intervention Principles

- There should be a coordinated multi-agency approach, with consideration for involving Social Services, Youth Offending Team (YOT), Education, Health and Probation as appropriate.
- The needs of children and young people who abuse others should be considered separately from the needs of their victims.
- An assessment should be carried out in each case, appreciating that these children may have considerable unmet developmental needs, as well as specific needs arising from their behaviour.
- A parallel assessment of the child or young person's family should be conducted.

In responding to cases involving children or young people who have committed sexually abusive behaviours, *all teams should initially refer to the county's Sexualised Inappropriate Behaviours Service (SIBS) for advice, consultation or a direct service.* A wide range of practice guidance, knowledge and therapeutic materials has been developed by SIBS, to inform interventions relating to children and young people with sexual behaviour difficulties.

Sexual Offences

Interventions for young people who have committed sexual offences will need to balance criminal justice issues against the need for the young person to receive a therapeutic intervention at the earliest possible stage.

When a young person is being interviewed under the Police and Criminal Evidence Act (PACE) for a sexual offence, the police must inform both the local Children's Team and YOT. Here the police may request a YOT practitioner to attend the PACE interview as an appropriate adult, and may subsequently request a YOT Asset assessment, to help them to decide on their disposal.

Child Protection/Child in Need Assessment

At this stage, the local Children's Team will consider whether there is a need to invoke child protection procedures (Children Act 1989 Section 47), because the young person is at risk of significant harm, or whether to set up the provision of services for a child in need (Children Act 1989 Section 17).

These circumstances will be potentially more complicated where a young person denies an offence, and criminal justice issues and child protection and safety issues will still have to be considered.

In most circumstances, when there is to be a prosecution, the long-term intervention will be undertaken or supervised by YOT. There will still be a need for the Children's Team to consider the wider needs of the young person, and the protection and safety of others.

Apart from when there is to be a prosecution, *it is the responsibility of the Children's Team to set up a SIBS intervention for the child or young person as a matter of urgency.*

Multi-agency Meeting

If child protection procedures are invoked, then a multi-agency meeting will take place in the form of the Child Protection Conference. If child protection procedures are not invoked, services will need to be provided under Section 17 Children in Need. To fully consider the needs of a child or young person who has abused, *a multi-agency Child in Need meeting* will need to be set up.

When the child is over 10 and a sexual offence has been committed, the meeting should include representatives from the police and YOT. For all children and young people, the meeting should seek to include representatives from SIBS, Health and Education. Sometimes it may be necessary to include Probation.

The purpose of the meeting is to:

- share all relevant known information about the child or young person and their family;
- inform all agencies of the risks presented to and by the young person;
- consider all possible courses of action necessary to meet the child or young person's needs;
- specify an intervention plan;
- agree and clarify respective roles for each agency;
- assess the need for further multi-agency meetings.

One possible outcome of a multi-agency meeting may be that in the light of new information or further discussion, Child Protection procedures should be invoked. Alternatively, the outcome of a Child Protection Conference may be that the needs of the child or young person can be met under Section 17 provision for a Child in Need.

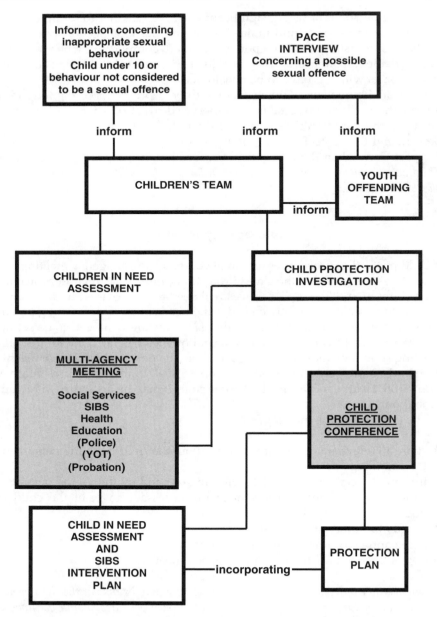

Figure B.1 Protocol for interventions with children and young people who abuse

Appendix C

PROTOCOL FOR REFERRAL BETWEEN YOT, CHILDREN'S TEAMS AND SIBS IN CIRCUMSTANCES WHEN YOUNG PEOPLE HAVE COMMITTED SEXUAL OFFENCES

(To be read with reference to the flow chart in Figure C1)

INTRODUCTION

This protocol has been written to indicate when Children's Teams and YOT will be required to undertake therapeutic intervention with young people (aged 10–17 in most circumstances) who have committed sexual offences, and to clarify the role of SIBS in providing support and consultation and sometimes a direct intervention for both teams.

The protocol seeks to balance criminal justice issues against the need for a young person who has committed a sexual offence to receive a therapeutic intervention at the earliest possible stage.

As a first principle, where young people have committed sexual offences, all direct interventions will be carried out by either YOT or the respective local Children's Team. With this task in hand, each team can refer for assistance from SIBS. *In all circumstances, each team is required to independently inform SIBS that a young person in their area has committed a sexual offence.*

FIRST NOTIFICATION

Teams will be usually first notified that a young person has committed a sexual offence at the stage of the PACE interview. If an appropriate adult is for whatever reason not available, this role *must* be fulfilled by a YOT practitioner. At this stage, the police will inform YOT and the local Children's Team that a young person has been interviewed about the committal of a sexual offence.

CHILD PROTECTION/CHILD IN NEED ASSESSMENT

At this stage, the local Children's Team will need to consider whether there is a need to invoke Child Protection procedures (Children Act 1989 Section 47), or whether or not to set up provision of services for a Child in Need (Children Act 1989 Section 17). These circumstances will be potentially more complicated where a young person denies an offence, and criminal justice issues and child protection and safety issues will still have to be considered.

POLICE DECISION

When a young person has admitted committing a sexual offence, the police decision-making unit will consider options of No Further Action, a Reprimand, a Final Warning, Prosecution, or a referral for a YOT assessment.

YOT ASSESSMENT

If the police are considering a Final Warning, they may request an assessment from YOT, which must be completed within the next 10 working days. This will be done using the ASSET form, but will additionally involve assessing the young person and family's acceptance of the problem and commitment to a longer-term therapeutic programme of SIBS work.

It is recommended that at this stage YOT refers to SIBS for consultation. If the option of consultation is not required, YOT must in any case inform SIBS with basic details, that a young person in or from the county has committed a sexual offence. YOT could recommend: No Further Action, a Reprimand, a Final Warning, or Prosecution.

Reprimand

In most circumstances following the issue of a Reprimand, there will be no further action. YOT will be informed, and at this stage must then inform the local Children's Team and SIBS.

Final Warning

YOT interventions under a Final Warning are limited to a maximum of six hours. In most circumstances, following the committal of a sexual offence, a young person will require substantially more intervention than this, so following the initial assessment, it will be necessary for YOT to refer the case on to the local Children's Team for a full assessment and intervention. There may or may not already be an involvement from the Children's Team under Child Protection or Child in Need procedures.

At this stage, the Children's Team must inform SIBS with basic details of any planned intervention, or make a referral to SIBS for consultation and/or a direct involvement. The first option will be to always make an attempt to seek the availability of a Children's Team social worker to undertake the assessment and intervention using SIBS consultation, before requesting a direct intervention from SIBS.

Prosecution

If the decision is to prosecute, then the file will be referred to the Crown Prosecution Service, who will decide whether or not there will be court proceedings or no further action. If there is no further action, YOT must inform both the local Children's Team and SIBS with basic details of the case. If the case goes to court, the case will continue to be managed primarily by YOT, who at this stage must inform both the local Children's Team and SIBS with basic details of the case.

If the young person has admitted the offence, it would be beneficial at this stage for YOT to refer to SIBS for an intervention (consultation or direct) which could be used in conjunction with options offered in the pre-sentence report. It would be additionally advantageous for all for therapeutic work to commence at the earliest stage possible. Again, at this stage it is important for YOT to inform the local Children's Team (and SIBS) with basic details of the case.

There may be an additional involvement from the local Children's Team, if there are issues which need to be dealt with through Child Protection and/or Child in Need procedures, following on from the initial involvement at the time the information was passed on following the PACE interview.

In all cases, it remains important for YOT to inform the local Children's Team with basic details of the case. In circumstances where YOT become involved in a case already known to the Children's Team, and vice versa, the allocation of roles and responsibilities will be considered through existing joint protocol arrangements.

Both YOT and the Children's Teams have the right to refer to SIBS for advice, consultation or a direct service, at any stage of their involvement with a young person known to have committed a sexual offence.

Dr Andrew Durham
Consultant Practitioner
Sexualised Inappropriate Behaviours Service (SIBS)

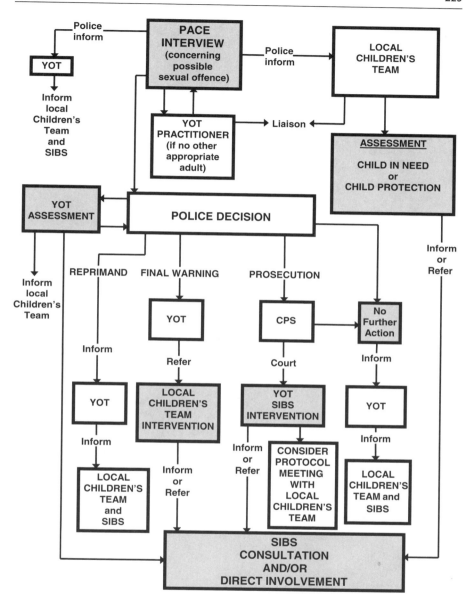

Figure C.1 SIBS/YOT/Children's Team referral flow chart
Reproduced by permission of Chris Hallet, Chair, Warwickshire Local Children's Safeguarding Board.

Appendix D

YOUNG PEOPLE WHO DISPLAY INAPPROPRIATE SEXUAL BEHAVIOURS – ISSUES FOR SCHOOLS

ASSESSMENT OF RISK

- What are the immediate risks presented by the young person?
- What are the immediate risks to the young person?
- Risk factors:
  - predisposing
  - precipitating
  - perpetuating

What was the nature of the abusing or inappropriate sexual behaviour, and how likely is it to occur during the school day or on the school premises?

PERCEPTION OF RISK

- To what extent do people's perception of risk differ from actual risk?

SAFETY OF <u>ALL</u> PUPILS

- 'Keeping safe' policies:
  - pupils' knowledge
  - pupils' perception of safety
  - pupils' opportunities to tell

SAFETY OF STAFF

- Feeling safe in managing risks
- Feeling safe from direct harm
- Impact of distressing information

MANAGING CONFIDENTIALITY

- Who needs to know?
  - Teachers
  - Designated child protection teacher
  - Year head or form teacher
  - Head teacher
  - Teacher who has the best relationship with the child
- Who does not need to know?
  - All teachers
  - Parents
  - Pupils
  'Pressing need' – risk management
  To what extent can the young person's liberty be legally restricted?

SHARING INFORMATION

Multi-agency meetings and Child Protection conferences, review conferences, core group meetings and day-to-day liaison.

OTHER ISSUES

- Other pupils finding out – vigilantes
- The importance of school for the young person with sexual behaviour difficulties
- Sex and relationships education

Dr Andrew Durham
Consultant Practitioner
Sexualised Inappropriate Behaviours Service (SIBS)

BIBLIOGRAPHY

Ahmad B (1990) *Black Perspectives in Social Work.* Birmingham, Venture Press.
Alaggia R & Michalski JH (1999) The Use of Peer Support for Parents and Youth Living with the Trauma of Child Sexual Abuse: an Innovative Approach. *Journal of Child Sexual Abuse* 8(2), 57–73.
Araji SK (1997) *Sexually Aggressive Children – Coming to Understand Them.* Thousand Oaks, Calif., Sage.
Araji S & Finkelhor D (1986) Abusers: a Review of the Research. In Finkelhor D, Araji S, Baron L, Browne A, Peters SD & Wyatt GE (eds) *A Sourcebook on Child Sexual Abuse.* Newbury Park, Calif., Sage.
Archard D (1993) *Children: Rights and Childhood.* London, Routledge.
Babiker G & Herbert M (1996) The Role of Psychological Instruments in the Assessment of Child Sexual Abuse. *Child Abuse Review* 5, 239–51.
Bain O & Sanders M (1990) *Out in the Open. A Guide for Young People Who Have Been Sexually Abused.* London, Virago Press.
Barbaree HE, Marshall WL & Hudson SM (eds) (1993) *The Juvenile Sex Offender.* New York, Guilford Press.
Barrett M & Phillips A (1992) *Destabilizing Theory.* Cambridge, Polity Press.
Becker JV, Kaplan MS, Tenke CE & Tartaglini A (1991) The Incidence of Depressive Symptomatology in Juvenile Sex Offenders with a History of Abuse. *Child Abuse and Neglect* 15, 531–6.
Benoit JL & Kennedy WA (1992) The Abuse History of Male Adolescent Sex Offenders. *Journal of Interpersonal Violence* 7(4), 543–8.
Bentovim A, Vizard E & Hollows A (eds) (1991) *Children and Young People as Abusers.* London, NCB.
Bolton FG Jr, Morris LA & MacEachron AE (1989) *Males at Risk.* Beverly Hills, Calif., Sage.
Bremner J & Hillin A (1993) *Sexuality, Young People and Care.* London, CCETSW.
Briggs F (1995) *From Victim to Offender.* St Leonards, NSW, Allen and Unwin.
Brown HC (1998) *Social Work and Sexuality.* London, Macmillan.
Buckley K & Head P (eds) (2000) *Myths, Risks and Sexuality.* Lyme Regis, Dorset, Russell House Publishing.
Butler I & Shaw I (1996) *A Case of Neglect?* Aldershot, Avebury.
Butler I & Williamson H (1994) *Children Speak.* Harlow, Longman.
Calder MC (ed.) (1999) *Working with Young People Who Sexually Abuse – New Pieces of the Jigsaw Puzzle.* Lyme Regis, Dorset, Russell House Publishing.
Calder MC (ed.) (2002) *Young People Who Sexually Abuse – Building the Evidence Base for Your Practice.* Lyme Regis, Dorset, Russell House Publishing.

Calder M, Goulding S, Hanks H, Rose K, Skinner J & Wynne J (2000) *The Complete Guide to Sexual Abuse Assessments*. Lyme Regis, Dorset, Russell House Publishing.

Calder M, Hanks H & Epps KJ (1997) *Juveniles and Children Who Sexually Abuse: a Guide to Risk Assessment*. Lyme Regis, Dorset, Russell House Publishing.

Calder M, Hanks H, Epps KJ, Print B, Morrison T & Henniker J (2001) *Juveniles and Children Who Sexually Abuse: Frameworks for Assessment*, second edition. Lyme Regis, Dorset, Russell House Publishing.

Campbell D (1994) Breaching the Shame Shield: Thoughts on the Assessment of Adolescent Child Sex Abusers. *Journal of Child Psychotherapy* **20**(3), 309–26.

Carr J (2003) *Child Abuse, Child Pornography and the Internet*. London, NCH.

Carrigan T, Connell B & Lee J (1987) Hard and Heavy: Toward a New Sociology of Masculinity. In Kaufman M (ed.) *Beyond Patriarchy*. Don Mills, Ontario, Oxford University Press.

Cawson P, Wattam C, Brooker S & Kelly G (2000) *Child Maltreatment in the United Kingdom: a Study of Child Abuse and Neglect*. London, NSPCC.

Connell RW (1987) Theorising Gender. *Sociology* **19**(2), 260–72.

Connell RW (1989) *Gender and Power, Society, the Person and Sexual Politics*. Cambridge, Polity Press.

Cook S & Taylor J (1991) *Working with Young Sex Offenders*. Liverpool, SSD/Barnardo's North West.

Cooper D (1995) *Power in Struggle*. Buckingham, Open University Press.

Cornwall A & Lindisfarne N (eds) (1994) *Dislocating Masculinity*. London, Routledge.

Craig S (ed.) (1992) *Men, Masculinity and the Media*. London, Sage.

Cunningham C & MacFarlane K (1996) *When Children Abuse*. Brandon, Vt, Safer Society Press.

Davies D & Neal C (eds) (1996) *Pink Therapy – a Guide for Counsellors and Therapists Working with Lesbian, Gay and Bi-sexual Clients*. Buckingham, Open University Press.

Davis GE & Leitenberg H (1987) Adolescent Sex Offenders. *Psychological Bulletin* **101**(3), 417–27.

Department of Health, Department for Education and Employment and Home Office (1999) *Working Together to Safeguard Children – a Guide to Inter-agency Working to Safeguard and Promote the Welfare of Children*. London, The Stationery Office.

Department of Health, Department for Education and Employment and Home Office (2000) *Framework for the Assessment of Children in Need and their Families*. London, The Stationery Office.

Doyle C (1996) Sexual Abuse by Siblings: the Victims' Perspectives. *Journal of Sexual Aggression* **2**(1), 17–32.

Durham AW (1997) The Groupwork Support of Sexually Abused boys. In Bates J, Pugh R & Thompson N (eds) *Protecting Children: Challenges and Change*. Aldershot, Arena.

Durham AW (1999) Young Men Living through and with Child Sexual Abuse – a Practitioner Research Study. Ph.D. thesis, University of Warwick.

Durham AW (2000) From Victim to Survivor: the Groupwork Support of Sexually Abused Boys. In Baldwin N (ed.) *Protecting Children Promoting Their Rights*. London, Whiting and Birch.

Durham AW (2002) Developing a Sensitive Practitioner Research Methodology for Studying the Impact of Child Sexual Abuse. *British Journal of Social Work* **32**, 429–42.

Durham AW (2003) *Young Men Surviving Child Sexual Abuse – Research Stories and Lessons for Therapeutic Practice*. Chichester, Wiley.

Durham AW (2004a) Children and Young People with Sexual Behavioural Difficulties: a Practice Framework for Holistic Interventions. In White V & Harris J (eds) *Developing Good Practice in Children's Services*. London, Jessica Kingsley.

Durham AW (2004b) Analysis of a Sample of 248 Referrals to SIBS of Children and Young People Reported to Have Initiated Inappropriate Sexual Behaviours during the Five Year Period 1997 to 2001. Appendix Two in White V & Harris J (eds) *Developing Good Practice in Children's Services*. London, Jessica Kingsley.

Elliot M (ed.) (1993) *Female Sexual Abuse of Children*. Harlow, Longman.

Ennis J & Williams BK (1993) *Practice Issues in Work with Perpetrators of Child Sexual Abuse*. Dundee, Department of Social Work, University of Dundee.

Fegan L, Rauch A & McCarthy WB (1993) *Sexuality and People with Intellectual Disability*. Artarmon, NSW, MacLennan and Petty.

Fenwick E & Walker R (1994) *How Sex Works – a Clear and Comprehensive Guide to Growing Up Physically, Emotionally and Sexually*. London, Dorling Kindersley.

Finkelhor D (1984) *Child Sexual Abuse – New Theory and Research*. New York, Free Press.

Finkelhor D, Araji S, Baron L, Browne A, Peters SD & Wyatt GE (1986) *A Sourcebook on Child Sexual Abuse*. Newbury Park, Calif., Sage.

Fisher D (1994) Adult Sex Offenders. In Morrison T, Erooga M & Beckett C (eds) *Sexual Offending against Children*. London, Routledge.

Fisher N (1991) *Boys about Boys – the Facts, Fears and Fantasies*. London, Macmillan.

Fisher N (1994) *Living with a Willy – the Inside Story*. London, Macmillan.

Friedrich WN (1995) *Psychotherapy with Sexually Abused Boys*. Thousand Oaks, Calif., Sage.

Fromuth ME, Burkhart BR & Jones CW (1991) Hidden Child Molestation. An Investigation of Adolescent Perpetrators in a Nonclinical Sample. *Journal of Interpersonal Violence* 6(3), 376–84.

Frosh S (1993) The Seeds of Masculine Sexuality. In Ussher JM & Baker CD (eds) *Psychological Perspectives on Sexual Problems*. London, Routledge.

Frosh S, Phoenix A & Pattman R (2002) *Young Masculinities*. Basingstoke, Hants, Palgrave.

Gil E (1996) *Treating Abused Adolescents*. New York, Guilford Press.

Gil E & Johnson TC (1993) *Sexualised Children Assessment and Treatment of Sexualised Children and Children Who Molest*. Rockville, Md, Launch Press.

Gilgun JF (1999) CASPARS Clinical Assessment Instruments that Measure Strengths and Risks in Children and Families. In Calder MC (ed.) *Working with Young People Who Sexually Abuse – New Pieces of the Jigsaw Puzzle*. Lyme Regis, Dorset, Russell House Publishing.

Gilgun JF & Reiser E (1990) The Development of Sexual Identity among Men Sexually Abused as Children. *Families in Society* Nov., 515–23.

Gill M & Tutty L (1997) Sexual Identity Issues for Male Survivors of Childhood Sexual Abuse: a Qualitative Study. *Journal of Child Sexual Abuse* 6(3), 31–47.

Glaser BG & Strauss AL (1967) *The Discovery of Grounded Theory*. Chicago, Aldine.

Glasgow D, Horne L, Calam R & Cox A (1994) Evidence, Incidence, Gender and Age in Sexual Abuse of Children Perpetrated by Children. Towards a Developmental Analysis of Child Sexual Abuse. *Child Abuse Review* 3, 196–210.

Gonsiorek JC (1995) Gay Male Identities: Concepts and Issues. In D'Augelli AR & Patterson CJ (eds) *Lesbian, Gay and Bisexual Identities over the Lifespan*. New York, Oxford University Press.

Gonsiorek JC, Bera WH & LeTourneau D (1994) *Male Sexual Abuse*. Thousand Oaks, Calif., Sage.

Gramsci A (1971) *Selections from the Prison Notebooks of Antonio Gramsci*. London, Lawrence and Wishart.

Gray AS & Pithers WD (1993) Lapse Prevention with Sexually Aggressive Adolescents and Children: Expanding Treatment and Supervision. In Barbaree HE, Marshall WL & Hudson SM (eds) *The Juvenile Sex Offender*. New York, Guilford Press.

Grubin D (1998) Sex Offending against Children: Understanding the Risk. Police Research Series Paper 99. London, Crown Copyright.

Hackett S (2001) *Facing the Future – a Guide for Parents of Young People Who Have Sexually Abused*. Lyme Regis, Dorset, Russell House Publishing.

Hackett S (2004) *What Works for Children and Young People with Harmful Sexual Behaviours*. Ilford, Essex, Barnardo's.

Hall DK, Matthews F & Pearce J (2002) Sexual Behaviour Problems in Sexually Abused Children: a Preliminary Typology. *Child Abuse and Neglect* **26**, 289–312.

Harris RH & Emberley M (1994) *Let's Talk about Sex – Growing Up, Changing Bodies, Sex and Sexual Health*. London, Walker Books.

Hearn J (1996) Is masculinity dead? A critique of the concept of masculinity/masculinities. In Mac-an-Ghaill M (ed.) *Understanding Masculinities*. Buckingham, Open University Press.

Hearn J (1998) *The Violences of Men*. London, Sage.

Hendry J (1989) Sexual Abuse of Boys, the 'Sexual Assault Cycle' and the Implications for Social Work Practice. *Child Abuse Review* **3**(1), 13–16.

Herman JL (1990) Sex Offenders. A Feminist Perspective. In Marshall WL, Laws DR & Barbaree HE (eds) *Handbook of Sexual Assault*. New York, Plenum.

Hoghughi MS, Bhate SR & Graham F (eds) (1997) *Working with Sexually Abusive Adolescents*. London, Sage.

Home Office (1997) *Criminal Statistics for England and Wales 1996*. London, Government Statistical Service.

Hunter JH (1995) Victim to Victimizer: Identification of Critical Victimization Variables Predictive of Later Sexual Perpetration in Juvenile Males. Final Report. Grant No. 90-CA-1454.

Hunter M (ed.) (1990a) *The Sexually Abused Male – Prevalence Impact and Treatment*. Volume 1. New York, Lexington Books.

Hunter M (ed.) (1990b) *The Sexually Abused Male – Application of Treatment Strategies*. Volume 2. New York, Lexington Books.

Hunter M (1995) *Child Survivors and Perpetrators of Sexual Abuse – Treatment Innovations*. Thousand Oaks, Calif., Sage.

Jackson S (1992) The Amazing Deconstructing Woman. *Trouble and Strife* 25, Winter, 25–31.

Jackson V (1996) *Racism and Child Protection – the Black Experience of Child Sexual Abuse*. London, Cassell.

Jenkins A (1990) *Invitations to Responsibility*. Adelaide, Dulwich Centre.

Johnson TC (1999) *Understanding Your Child's Sexual Behaviour – What's Natural and Healthy*. Oakland, Calif., New Harbinger Pubs.

Johnson, TC & Feldmeth, JR (1993) Sexual Behaviours a Continuum. In Gil E & Johnson TC (eds) *Sexualised Children Assessment and Treatment of Sexualised Children and Children Who Molest*. Rockville, Md, Launch Press.

Joll J (1977) *Gramsci*. Glasgow, Fontana.

Jubber K (1991) The Socialization of Human Sexuality. *SA Sociological Review* **4**(1), 27–49.

Kahn TJ (1990) *Pathways*. Brandon, Vt, Safer Society Press.

Kaufman M (1987) The Construction of Masculinity and the Triad of Men's Violence. In Kaufman M (ed.) *Beyond Patriarchy*. Don Mills, Ontario, Oxford University Press.

Kelly L (1988) *Surviving Sexual Violence*. Cambridge, Polity Press.

Kelly L, Regan L & Burton S (1991) An Exploratory Study of the Prevalence of Sexual Abuse in a Sample of 16–21 Year Olds. London, Child Abuse Studies Unit, Polytechnic of North London.

Lane S & Zamora P (1984) A Method for Treating the Adolescent Sex Offender. In Mathias R, Demuro P & Allinson R (eds) *Violent Juvenile Offenders*. San Francisco, National Council on Crime and Delinquency.

Loss P & Ross JE (1988) *Risk Assessment/Interviewing Protocol for Adolescent Sex Offenders*. New London, Conn., and Mt Pleasant, SC, Ross and Loss Publications.

Loss P, Ross JE & Richardson J (1988) *Psychoeducational Curriculum for Adolescent Sex Offenders*. New London, Conn., Mt Pleasant, SC, and Warwick, RI, Ross, Loss and Richardson Publications.

Mac an Ghaill M (ed.) (1996) *Understanding Masculinities*. Buckingham, Open University Press.

MacLeod M & Saraga E (1991) Clearing a Path through the Undergrowth: a Feminist Reading of Recent Literature on Child Sexual Abuse. In Carter P, Jeffs T & Smith M (eds) *Social Work and Social Welfare Yearbook 3*. Buckingham, Opening University Press.

Maltz W & Holman B (1987) *Incest and Sexuality. A Guide to Understanding and Healing*. Lexington, Mass, Lexington Books.

Marshall WL, Laws DR & Barbaree HE (1990) *Handbook of Sexual Assault*. New York, Plenum.

Martinson FM (1994) *The Sexual Life of Children*. Westport, Conn., Bergin and Garvey.

Masson H & Morrison T (1999) Young Sexual Abusers: Conceptual Frameworks, Issues and Imperatives. *Children and Society* **13**, 203–15.

Mayle P (1973) *'Where Did I Come From?' – the Facts of Life without any Nonsense and with Illustrations*. London, Pan Macmillan.

Mendel MP (1995) *The Male Survivor*. Thousand Oaks, Calif., Sage.

Meredith S (1985) *Growing Up – Adolescence, Body Changes and Sex*. London, Usborne.

Meredith S & Gee R (1985) *Understanding the Facts of Life*. London, Usborne.

Mezey GC & King MB (eds) (1992) *Male Victims of Sexual Assault*. Oxford, Oxford University Press.

Miller W & Rollnick S (1991) *Motivational Interviewing: Preparing People to Change Addictive Behaviour*. New York, Guilford Press.

Monat-Haller RK (1992) *Understanding and Expressing Sexuality – Responsible Choices for Individuals with Developmental Disabilities*. Baltimore, Md, Paul H. Brookes Publishing Co.

Monck E & New M (1996) *Report of a Study of Sexually Abused Children and Adolescents, and of Young Perpetrators of Sexual Abuse Who Were Treated in Voluntary Agency Community Facilities*. London, HMSO.

Moore B (1996) *Risk Assessment: a Practitioner's Guide to Predicting Harmful Behaviour*. London, Whiting & Birch Ltd.

Moore S & Rosenthal D (1993) *Sexuality in Adolescence*. London, Routledge.

Morris LA (1997) *The Male Heterosexual*. Thousand Oaks, Calif., Sage.

Morrison T, Erooga M & Beckett C (eds) (1994) *Sexual Offending against Children*. London, Routledge.

Morrison T & Print B (1995) *Adolescent Sexual Abusers*. Hull, NOTA.

Nayak A & Kehily MJ (1997) Maculinities and Schooling – Why Are Young Men So Homophobic? In Steinberg L, Epstein D & Johnson R (eds) *Border Patrols*. London, Cassell.

NCH (1992) *The Report of the Committee of Enquiry into Children* and *Young People who Sexually Abuse Other Children*. London, NCH.

O'Callaghan D & Print B (1994) Adolescent Sexual Abusers. In Morrison T, Erooga M & Beckett RC (eds) *Sexual Offending against Children, Assessment and Treatment of Male Abusers*. London, Routledge.

Openshaw DK, Graves RB, Ericksen SL, Lowry M, Durso DD, Laurel A et al. (1993) Youthful Sexual Offenders: a Comprehensive Bibliography of Scholarly References 1970–1992. *Family Relations* **42**, 222–6.

Pavanel J (2003) *The Sex Book – a No Nonsense Guide for Teenagers*. Cambridge, Wizard Books.

Perry G & Orchard J (1992) *Assessment and Treatment of Adolescent Sex Offenders*. Sarasota, Fla, Professional Resource Press.

Phillips A (1992) *Destabilizing Theory*. Oxford, Polity Press.

Pithers WD (1990) Relapse Prevention with Sexual Aggressors: a Method for Maintaining Therapeutic Gain and Enhancing External Supervision. In Marshall WL, Laws DR & Barbaree HE (eds) *Handbook of Sexual Assault*. New York, Plenum.

Pithers WD, Gray AS, Cunningham C & Lane S (1993) *From Trauma to Understanding: a Guide for Parents of Children with Sexual Behaviour Problems*. Safer Society Series Number Ten. Brandon, Vt, Safer Society Press.

Ponton L (2000) *The Sex Lives of Teenagers – Revealing the Secret World of Adolescent Boys and Girls*. New York, Plume.

Postlethwaite J (1998) A Critical Approach to Working with Young Abusers. *Nota News* No. 28, 30–8.

Pringle K (1995) *Men, Masculinities and Social Welfare*. London, UCL Press.

Ryan G (1989) Victim to Victimiser. *Journal of Interpersonal Violence* **4**(3), 325–41.

Ryan GD & Lane SL (1991) *Juvenile Sexual Offending*. Lexington, Mass., Lexington Books.

Salter AC (1988) *Treating Child Sex Offenders and Victims*. Newbury Park, Calif., Sage.

Santry S & McCarthy G (1999) Attachment and Intimacy in Young People Who Sexually Abuse. In Calder MC (ed.) *Working with Young People Who Sexually Abuse – New Pieces of the Jigsaw Puzzle*. Lyme Regis, Dorset, Russell House Publishing.

Saradjian J (1998) *Women Who Sexually Abuse*. Chichester, Wiley.

Sedgwick EK (1990) *Epistemology of the Closet*. Berkeley and Los Angeles, Columbia University Press.

Steinberg L, Epstein D & Johnson R (1997) *Border Patrols*. London, Cassell.

Sullivan J (2002) The Spiral of Sexual Abuse: a Conceptual Framework for Understanding and Illustrating the Evolution of Sexually Abusive Behaviour. *NOTA News* **41**, 17–21.

Tallmadge A & Forster G (1998) *Tell It Like It Is – a Resource for Youth in Treatment*. Brandon, Vt, Safer Society Press.

Walby S (1992) Post-Post Modernism? Theorizing Social Complexity. In Barrett M & Phillips A (eds) *Destabilizing Theory*. Oxford, Polity Press.

Warner M (1993) *Fear of a Queer Planet*. Minneapolis, University of Minnesota Press.

Warwickshire County Council (2003a) *Sex and Relationships Education Policy Guidelines – For Staff and Carers Working with Looked After Children and Children in Need in Warwickshire*. Warwick, WCC.

Warwickshire County Council (2003b) *Sex and Relationships Education Policy – For Looked After Children and Children in Need in Warwickshire*. Warwick, WCC.

Watkins B & Bentovim A (1992) The Sexual Abuse of Male Children and Adolescents: a Review of Current Research. *Journal of Child Psychology and Psychiatry* **33**(1), 197–248.

Wellings K, Field J, Johnson AM & Wadsworth J (1994) *Sexual Behaviour in Britain – the National Survey of Sexual Attitudes and Lifestyles*. London, Penguin.

Wolfe DA, Wekerle C & Scott K (1997) *Alternatives to Violence*. Thousand Oaks, Calif., Sage.

INDEX